CHILD PHONOLOGY

Volume 2
Perception

This is a volume in

PERSPECTIVES IN

NEUROLINGUISTICS, NEUROPSYCHOLOGY, AND PSYCHOLINGUISTICS

A Series of Monographs and Treatises

A complete list of titles in this series appears at the end of this volume.

CHILD PHONOLOGY
Volume 2
Perception

Edited by

GRACE H. YENI-KOMSHIAN

Department of Speech and Hearing Sciences
University of Maryland
College Park, Maryland

JAMES F. KAVANAGH

Center for Research for Mothers and Children
National Institute of Child Health and Human Development
National Institutes of Health
Bethesda, Maryland

CHARLES A. FERGUSON

Department of Linguistics
Stanford University
Stanford, California

ACADEMIC PRESS   1980
A Subsidiary of Harcourt Brace Jovanovich, Publishers
New York   London   Toronto   Sydney   San Francisco

Proceedings of a conference in a series entitled *Communicating by Language,* sponsored by the National Institute of Child Health and Human Development.

ACADEMIC PRESS, INC.
111 Fifth Avenue, New York, New York 10003

United Kingdom Edition published by
ACADEMIC PRESS, INC. (LONDON) LTD.
24/28 Oval Road, London NW1 7DX

Library of Congress Cataloging in Publication Data
Main entry under title:

Child phonology.

(Perspectives in neurolinguistics, neuropsychology
and psycholinguistics: A series of monographs and
treatises)
Proceedings of a conference convened by the National
Institute of Child Health and Human Development, May 28–
31, 1978, at the National Institutes of Health, Bethesda, Md.
Vol. 2 has subtitle: Perception and production.
Includes bibliographies and indexes.
CONTENTS: v. 1. Production.––v. 2. Perception.
1. Language acquisition––Congresses. 2. Grammar,
Comparative and general––Phonology––Congresses.
3. Speech perception––Congresses. I. Yeni–Komshian,
Grace H. II. Kavanagh, James F. III. Ferguson, Charles
Albert. IV. United States, National Institute of Child
Health and Human Development.
[DNLM: 1. Language development––Congresses. 2.
Phonetics––Congresses. 3. Speech––In infancy and
childhood––Congresses. WS 105.5.C8 C537 1978 (P)]
P118.C46   401'.9   80–981
ISBN 0–12–770602–X (v. 2)

PRINTED IN THE UNITED STATES OF AMERICA

80 81 82 83   9 8 7 6 5 4 3 2 1

CONTENTS

Chapter 8

Speech Perception of Language-Delayed Children   155

PAULA TALLAL AND RACHEL E. STARK

Chapter 9

Two Hypotheses for Phonetic Clarification in the Speech of Mothers to Children   173

BATHSHEBA J. MALSHEEN

Chapter 10

Phonetic Variation as a Function of Second-Language Learning   185

LEE WILLIAMS

LIST OF CONTRIBUTORS

Numbers in parentheses indicate the pages on which authors' contributions begin.

RICHARD N. ASLIN (67), Department of Psychology, Indiana University, Bloomington, Indiana 47405

KAY ATKINSON-KING (229), McLean, Virginia

DAVID BARTON (97), Department of Linguistics, Stanford University, Stanford, California 94305

SHEILA E. BLUMSTEIN (9), Department of Linguistics, Brown University, Providence, Rhode Island 02912

PATRICIA A. BROEN (117), Department of Communication Disorders, University of Minnesota, Minneapolis, Minnesota 55455

REBECCA E. EILERS (23), Mailman Center for Child Development, University of Miami, Miami, Florida 33124

CHARLES A. FERGUSON (1), Department of Linguistics, Stanford University, Stanford, California 94305

JAMES J. JENKINS (217), Center for Research in Human Learning, University of Minnesota, Minneapolis, Minnesota 55455

JAMES F. KAVANAGH, Center for Research for Mothers and Children, National Institute of Child Health and Human Development, National Institutes of Health, Bethesda, Maryland 20205

PATRICIA K. KUHL (41), Child Development and Mental Retardation Center, University of Washington, Seattle, Washington 98105

BATHSHEBA J. MALSHEEN (173),* Passaic, New Jersey

DAVID B. PISONI (67), Department of Psychology, Indiana University, Bloomington, Indiana 47405

RACHEL E. STARK (155), The John F. Kennedy Institute and Johns Hopkins University School of Medicine, Baltimore, Maryland 21205

WINIFRED STRANGE (117), Center for Research in Human Learning, University of Minnesota, Minneapolis, Minnesota 55455

PAULA TALLAL (155), Department of Psychiatry, University of California at San Diego, La Jolla, California 92093

LEE WILLIAMS (185),† Research Laboratory of Electronics, Massachusetts Institute of Technology, Cambridge, Massachusetts 02139

GRACE H. YENI-KOMSHIAN (1), Department of Hearing and Speech Sciences, University of Maryland, College Park, Maryland 20742

* The author formerly wrote under the name of Barbara J. Moslin.
† Present address: 35 West St., Cambridge, Mass. 02139.

PREFACE

The importance of the study of child phonology for the sciences dealing with speech sounds is only slowly being recognized, and the field is a relatively new area of systematic investigation. Typical of a new field, this one clearly shows its multidisciplinary origins. Researchers in this field come from different disciplines, and their professional identities and research methods differ correspondingly. During the past 10 years there has been active research in child phonology, and the findings are penetrating established areas in linguistics, psychology, and speech science. Acknowledging the need for an interdisciplinary conference, the National Institute of Child Health and Human Development (NICHD) convened a conference on child phonology at the National Institutes of Health in Bethesda, Maryland, May 28–31, 1978, the seventh in the NICHD series on "Communicating by Language." The series has led to such publications as *The Genesis of Language* and *Language by Ear and by Eye*.

All the participants in the conference have a strong interest in phonology—the study of human speech sounds. Except for a few, all have conducted research on some aspect of child phonology. Some participants, better known for their work in adult phonology, were invited to explore how certain aspects of phonology in adults relate to child phonology. Each participant was invited to prepare a paper addressing a specific topic in one of the following areas: speech production, speech perception, and the relationship between perception and production. The papers were prepared prior to the meeting and following the conference the participants were provided with time to revise their papers. This two-volume work is based on the revised papers, however a few of the original papers were omitted and one was added.

The main focus of Volume 1 is on production and in Volume 2 it is on perception. Both volumes contain chapters on aspects of the relationship between perception and production. The two volumes may be viewed as a unitary publication on child phonology in which theoretical and methodological issues are discussed, including a fairly detailed presentation of recent research findings. Since a variety of disciplines are represented, the publication provides different perspectives on how children acquire the phonology of their language(s). Normal acquisition is emphasized, although some aspects of deviation are also addressed. Each volume contains a glossary of terms that also contains a table of phonetic symbols.

We would like to thank Victoria Fromkin, Jerry Punch, and Suzanne Bennett for their advice on technical problems in phonology, and we gratefully acknowledge the help of Daphene Cave, Linda Hale, and Janet Thomson for preparing the manuscript for publication.

CONTENTS OF VOLUME 1

Chapter 1

AN INTRODUCTION TO SPEECH PERCEPTION IN THE CHILD

GRACE H. YENI-KOMSHIAN AND CHARLES A. FERGUSON

Until fairly recently, the study of the speech sounds perceived and produced by infants and children was a rather limited field of research. Interest in child phonology came from several sources, such as general interest in child development, professional concern with language or speech problems requiring special education or therapy, or linguistic speculations about the relation between phonological development in the child and sound change in language. In all these cases, the interest in child phonology was marginal to other interests, and the research commitment was correspondingly limited. Furthermore, the study of child phonology presented methodological problems more severe than the study of adult phonology. Children are harder subjects to deal with. In production, established techniques of transcription and measurement are hard to adapt to the requirements of child speech, and the sounds of children are variable and unstable. In perception, researchers had to solve the difficult problem of obtaining reliable and valid responses from infants and children. Anyone who has tried to work in this area will attest to the ingenuity, skill, and patience required in conducting rigorous experiments with infants and immature responders. It is very exciting to see the rapid growth of research in speech perception, in particular the extensive work on infant speech discrimination since the publication of the frequently quoted article by Eimas *et al.* (1971). It is our hope that this volume and the accompanying volume on *Production* will lead to clarification of major issues and the identification of promising lines of research, whether in continuation of present efforts or in new directions.

Just over 10 years ago, data and theory on speech perception in adults had advanced to a level of sophistication that permitted researchers to ask precise questions concerning its developmental aspects. Progress in the technology of synthesizing speech sounds was directly related to progress in the search for critical acoustic cues that best differentiated among various classes of speech sounds. The pioneering work in this field was done at Haskins Laboratories, and since the early 1950s, research results and theory formulated by them has inspired the work of many researchers (for reviews see Liberman *et al.*, 1967; Liberman and Studdert-Kennedy, 1978). For example, Liberman *et al.* (1954) reported that the acoustic cue for place of closure is in the transition of the second formant. Systematic variations in the second formant correspond to perceptions of /ba/, /da/, and /ga/. Moffitt (1971) was the first to make use of this kind of information from adult speech-perception studies to investigate speech perception in infants. He reported that 4- and 5-month-old infants could discriminate between synthesized tokens of /ba/ and /ga/. These were very exciting results, because they demonstrated for the first time that infants, who were unable to produce these stops, were able to discriminate between them. As the stimuli were synthesized, all differences except for the second formant transition were controlled.

Soon after, a more startling finding was reported by Eimas *et al.* (1971). In this case, the infants were as young as 1 month of age. These infants appeared to be able to discriminate between voice onset time (VOT) differences that reflected a sensitivity to adult phoneme categories. Thus, not only were infants discriminating between speech sounds they could not produce, but this discrimination appeared to be categorical. That is, the discrimination was limited to stimuli that crossed phonetic categories, and differences of equal magnitude within phonetic categories were not discriminated.

Categorical perception with adult listeners is determined by two sets of data: identification and discrimination of stimuli that differ in equal steps to form a continuum. The identification function typically reveals the phonetic categories in question. When discrimination is near perfect between phonetic categories and at chance level within phonetic categories, the result is called *categorical perception*. When discrimination between categories is as good as within categories, it is called *continuous perception*. Initial interpretation of this phenomenon suggested that categorical perception is the mode of processing speech sounds, whereas continuous perception is the mode of processing nonspeech sounds, that is, sounds that cannot be produced by the human vocal tract.

The distinction between speech and nonspeech sounds is very important to one model of speech perception (Liberman and Studdert-Kennedy, 1978).

Perception of speech sounds is said to be special because it entails both *auditory* and *phonetic* levels of analyses. Auditory analysis is at the level of the acoustic properties of the stimulus. Whereas, phonetic analysis is at a level beyond auditory analysis, and it requires the extraction of information that is not part of the acoustic properties of the stimulus. Categorical perception is said to be at a phonetic level and continuous perception at an auditory level.[1] This model of speech perception is not universally accepted. Some of its main premises have not been supported by recent research. In fact, the field is without an accepted general theory.

More recent studies on infant speech perception have shown that they perceive the contrasts /ba/ versus /da/, and /ra/ versus /la/ categorically (Eimas, 1974, 1975; Miller and Morse, 1976). These studies have included a nonspeech control condition by presenting stimuli that contain the isolated acoustic cue for the phonetic contrasts listed above. The nonspeech control stimuli were second formant transitions for the stops and third formant transitions for the liquids. The results from these control conditions indicated that infants were able to discriminate, equally well, the between and the within category stimuli. That is, the infants' discrimination of these nonspeech stimuli was continuous. These findings support the view that perception of speech is special and different from perception of nonspeech stimuli.

The results of another set of studies, however, do not support the notion that the perception of speech is special and different from the perception of nonspeech stimuli. Cutting and Rosner (1974) generated a nonspeech continuum of stimuli that varied in rise time; these stimuli are better known as "plucks" and "bows," as of a stringed instrument. Adult listeners were asked to identify and discriminate these stimuli, and the results revealed that the stimuli from this nonspeech continuum were perceived categorically. Infants tested with these stimuli also showed that they perceived them categorically (Jusczyk *et al.*, 1977). Other types of nonspeech continua also have been reported to have been perceived categorically by adult listeners (Miller *et al.*, 1976; Pisoni, 1977). Until the publication of these studies, the phenomenon of categorical perception seemed to be limited to a selected class of speech sounds; now a selected class of clearly nonspeech sounds also appear to be perceived in a categorical manner. This is an example of

---

[1] The terms "auditory" and "phonetic" in this connection are somewhat confusing for phonologists in that the difference corresponds in some respects to the latters' distinction between "phonetic" and "phonological." The linguist's use of phonetic typically includes phenomena that are accounted for by the physiology of articulation and audition as opposed to phonological, which includes phenomena accounted for by the functional organization or rule structure of speech sounds in particular languages. But since phonetic in this sense also may include nondistinctive but nonphysiologically determined phenomena, and both phonetic and phonological in the linguist's usage may refer to universals, this whole issue represents a point where the perceptionists' and the phonologists' models of speech processing are incompatible. This issue is, therefore, a good point at which to promote further discussion.

how findings from adult and infant listeners combine to provide a strong motivation to reformulate and refine existing models and theories of speech perception.

At present, the catalog of phoneme contrasts that infants have been shown to be able to discriminate is quite impressive. To cite a few examples, Trehub (1973) has demonstrated that infants discriminate differences in vowel contrasts, and Eilers and Minifie (1975) have demonstrated that certain fricative contrasts are discriminable. Most of these studies utilized real speech stimuli and, therefore, did not directly address the question of categorical and continuous perception. These studies did, however, demonstrate that the human infant is able to detect differences between stimuli that are representative of phonemes in adult speech. To account for the infant's impressive speech-discrimination capabilities at such an early age, Eimas and other investigators have proposed a mechanism of *phonetic feature detectors*, which are thought to be innate and to operate after minimal exposure to speech sounds (Eimas *et al.*, 1971; Cutting and Eimas, 1975; Eimas, 1975; Eimas and Miller, 1978).

Some of the current investigations are concerned with the question of the innateness of feature detectors and how they are related to phonetic categories found in languages other than English, such as voicing distinctions relevant to French, Spanish, and Arabic, but not to English. This line of inquiry also has stimulated questions that have to do with the effects of exposure to different linguistic environments during the first 6 months of life on the perception of phonetic categories of different languages. There are two published studies on the perception of voicing by infants raised in linguistic environments where voicing-lead constitutes a phonetic category (Lasky *et al.*, 1975; Streeter, 1976). In both studies, it was found that the infants were able to discriminate across the voicing-lead and short-lag categories, a distinction that infants raised in English-speaking environments appear to be unable to do. However, the infants raised in non-English-speaking environments were also able to discriminate voicing contrasts that are relevant to English but not to their own linguistic environment. The results of these studies do not support the notion of innate feature detectors in a simple and direct way.

Whereas the early infant studies were based on data obtained from adults, the proposed mechanisms of feature detectors in infants provided the basis for numerous experiments with adults to examine possible characteristics of such detectors (for a review see Eimas and Miller, 1978). The research on feature detectors has, in turn, stimulated modifications in existing theories or formulations of new theories attempting to state the mechanisms involved in speech perception more concretely than has been done previously. At present, the question of whether feature detectors operate at a phonetic or at an auditory level is being investigated by various researchers. In addition, the validity of feature detectors in speech perception is being questioned (Remez, 1979).

Information obtained from nonhuman listeners has contributed to the discussion of some of the problems concerning the mechanisms involved in human speech perception. Recently, Kuhl and Miller (1978) reported a study in which the response of chinchillas to three synthesized continua along the VOT dimension could be interpreted to reflect identification functions that were very similar to that of adult English-speaking listeners. In addition, Sinnott (1974) and Morse and Snowden (1975) tested rhesus monkeys with stimuli that varied on place of closure. Although their procedures were different, both studies reported that the monkeys were able to discriminate between-category and within-category stimuli. However, Morse and Snowden also reported that the between-category discrimination was more pronounced than the within-category discrimination.

Another area of fruitful exchange has to do with the apparent lack of correspondence between infant and child speech perception. For example, it has been reported that 2- and 3-year-old children are not consistent in identifying voicing differences in stop consonants (Garnica, 1973; Zlatin and Koenigsknecht, 1975), whereas infants are able to discriminate similar distinctions. The obvious differences in the demands of the two tasks, identification for children and discrimination for infants, could have produced these results. However, this has led researchers to focus on the design of paradigms that are similar to an identification task for infants. In addition, the problem of comparing the performance of infants and children is beginning to be solved by attempts to devise paradigms that can be used to test a wide age range. A related problem is the nature of phonemic perception in children. That is, does the child respond differently to a given phonetic contrast when the contrast is tested by the use of known words in comparison to the use of non-words? At present, a clear-cut answer to this question is not available.

The relation between perception and production is another topic of concern in the study of child phonology. Cross-linguistic research is one way of investigating the effects of exposure to a given phonological system on the perception and the production of phones from another phonological system. Another fruitful avenue of research in this area is the systematic comparison of children's productions to their perceptions of the same phonetic contrasts. Such an approach is useful for investigating the phonology of normally developing children and language delayed children.

The chapters in this volume address theoretical and methodological issues relevant to speech perception research in infants and children. Many of the chapters contain extensive empirical findings. Most of the issues mentioned above are discussed in some detail. It is clearly evident that this field has had a tremendous gain in sophistication and rigor within a very short time. We hope that researchers in the next decade will be able to answer most of the questions raised in these chapters.

The following four chapters are primarily concerned with perception in infants. Blumstein's chapter presents a model of speech perception based on adult performance. She discusses how this model may contribute to the development of a model for perception in infants and children. Eilers reviews the methodologies and research findings regarding the prolific repertoire of the infant in speech perception. Kuhl focuses on a relatively recent issue, namely the study of perceptual constancy for speech sound categories in early infancy. Aslin and Pisoni stress the need for new theories or revisions of existing theories in speech perception. They present a conceptual framework to evaluate the current theories of infant speech perception and to explain the published empirical findings.

The next three chapters focus on the study of English-speaking children who have at least acquired their first words. This entails phonemic perception, that is, perception of contrasts which signify meaning differences to the listener. Barton presents a review of the literature on studies which utilize natural speech and a discussion of problems in methodology and interpretation of results. Strange and Broen focus on the problem of the relation between perception and production. They present a critical and detailed evaluation of current theories and research results on developmental aspects of phonemic perception and production. Their chapter concludes with a presentation of their own research on the perception and production of selected words by 3-year-old children. The chapter by Tallal and Stark is concerned with speech perception in language delayed children as compared to normally developing children. They present a review of the literature on perception of nonspeech and speech stimuli. They also present a summary of their recent research findings.

The chapter by Williams is on the perception and production of stops by Spanish-English bilingual children between the ages of 8 and 16 years. The results are presented in relation to variables such as the response of Spanish and English speaking adults, the extent of exposure to English, and the age at which the children began to learn English.

The results presented in Malsheen's (Moslin) paper are obtained from adults. However, the point of interest is to examine how mothers speak to their children. This paper presents an acoustic analysis of stops produced in mother–child interactions and in adult–adult conversations.

In the concluding chapter, Jenkins offers his comments, criticisms, and advice to researchers concerned with the study of child phonology. His chapter contains a discussion of issues raised in this volume and in the accompanying volume on *Production*.

The technical terms and phonetic notations used in this volume and the accompanying volume on *Production* are defined in the Glossary and the table of phonetic symbols prepared by Atkinson-King.

References

Cutting, J.E., and Eimas, P. (1975) "Phonetic Feature Analyzers and the Processing of Speech in Infants, in J.F. Kavanagh and J.E. Cutting, eds., *The Role of Speech in Language*, MIT Press, Cambridge, Mass. pp. 127–148.

Cutting, J.E., and Rosner, B.S. (1974) "Categories and Boundaries in Speech and Music," *Perception & Psychophysics*, 16, 564–570.

Eilers, R., and Minifie, F. (1975) "Fricative Discrimination in Early Infancy," *Journal of Speech and Hearing Research*, 18, 158–167.

Eimas, P. (1974) "Linguistic Processing of Speech by Young Infants," in R. Schiefelbusch and L. Lloyd, eds., *Language Perspectives: Acquisition, Retardation, and Intervention*, University Park Press, Baltimore, pp. 55–73.

Eimas, P. (1975) "Auditory and Phonetic Coding of the Cues for Speech: Discrimination of the (r–l) Distinction by Young Infants," *Perception & Psychophysics*, 18, 341–347.

Eimas, P., and Miller, J. (1978) "Effects of Selective Adaptation on the Perception of Speech and Visual Patterns: Evidence for Feature Detectors," in R.D. Walk and H.L. Pick, Jr., eds., *Perception and Experience*, Plenum, New York, pp. 307–345.

Eimas, P.D., Siqueland, E.R., Jusczyk, P., and Vigorito, J. (1971) "Speech Perception in Infants," *Science*, 171, 303–306.

Garnica, O.K. (1973) "The Development of Phonemic Speech Perception," in T. Moore, ed., *Cognitive Development and the Acquisition of Language*, Academic Press, New York, pp. 214–222.

Jusczyk, P.W., Rosner, B.S., Cutting, J.E., Foard, C.F., and Smith, L.B. (1977) "Categorical Perception of Non-Speech Sounds by Two-month-old Infants," *Perception & Psychophysics*, 21, 50–54.

Kuhl, P.K., and Miller, J.D. (1978) "Speech Perception by the Chinchilla: Identification Functions for Synthetic VOT Stimuli," *Journal of the Acoustical Society of America*, 63, 905–917.

Lasky, R.E., Syrdal-Lasky, A., and Klein, R.E. (1975) "VOT Discrimination by Four to Six and a Half Month Old Infants from Spanish Environments," *Journal of Experimental Child Psychology*, 20, 215–225.

Liberman, A.M., Delattre, P.C., Cooper, F.S., and Gerstman, L.J. (1954) "The Role of Consonant–Vowel Transitions in the Perception of Stop and Nasal Consonants," *Psychological Monographs*, 68, No. 379.

Liberman, A.M., Cooper, F.S., Shankweiler, D.P., and Studdert-Kennedy, M. (1967) "Perception of the Speech Code," *Psychological Review*, 74, 431–461.

Liberman, A.M., and Studdert-Kennedy, M. (1978) "Phonetic Perception," in R. Held, H.W. Leibowitz, and H.L. Teuber (eds.), *Handbook of Sensory Physiology*, New York: Springer-Verlag. Also, Haskins Laboratories: *Status Report on Speech Research* SR–50, 21–76.

Miller, C., and Morse, P. (1976) "The Heart of Categorical Speech Discrimination in Young Infants," *Journal of Speech & Hearing Research*, 19, 578–589.

Miller, J.D., Wier, C.C., Pastore, R., Kelley, W.J., and Dooling, R.J. (1976) "Discrimination and Labeling of Noise–Buzz Sequences with Varying Noise–Lead Times: An Example of Categorical Perception," *Journal of the Acoustical Society of America*, 60, 410–417.

Moffitt, A. (1971) "Consonant Cue Perception by Twenty- to Twenty-four-week-old Infants," *Child Development*, 42, 717–731.

Morse, P.A., and Snowdon, C.T. (1975) "An Investigation of Categorical Speech Discrimination by Rhesus Monkeys," *Perception & Psychophysics*, 17, 9–16.

Pisoni, D.B. (1977) "Identification and Discrimination of the Relative Onset of Two Component Tones: Implications for the Perception of Voicing in Stops," *Journal of the Acoustical Society of America*, 61, 1352–1361.

Remez, R.E. (1979) "Adaptation of the Category Boundary Between Speech and Non-Speech: A Case against Feature Detectors," *Cognitive Psychology*, 11, 38–57.

Sinnott, J.M. (1974) "A Comparison of Speech Sound Discrimination in Humans and Monkeys," Doctoral Dissertation, University of Michigan.

Streeter, L.A. (1976) "Language Perception of 2-Month-old Infants Shows Effects of Both Innate Mechanisms and Experience," *Nature*, 259, 39–41.

Trehub, S. (1973) "Infants' Sensitivity to Vowel and Tonal Contrasts," *Developmental Psychology*, 9, 81–96.

Zlatin, M.A., and Koenigsknecht, R.A. (1975) "Development of the Voicing Contrast: Perception of Stop Consonants," *Journal of Speech and Hearing Research*, 18, 541–553.

Chapter 2

SPEECH PERCEPTION: AN OVERVIEW

SHEILA E. BLUMSTEIN

The speech-perception abilities of young children seem to be quite re-markable. As early as several days of age, an infant can discriminate speech sounds in a manner very nearly like that of an adult. Several chapters in this volume address this issue. I would like to discuss how theories of speech perception developed from research with normal adults can contribute to the development of a model of speech for young infants and children. Such a model may specify the nature of the perceptual mechanism of the child and, in particular, characterize his innate perceptual abilities, the contri-bution of experience in the further shaping of these abilities, and the inter-action between nature and nurture in the evolving speech-perception mech-anism.

One of the aims of research in speech perception has been to understand how the listener perceives a continuous sound stream in terms of discrete phonetic units. Early speech research pioneered by the Haskins Labora-tories investigated this question by looking for invariant acoustic cues in the speech signal that would uniquely characterize a particular phonetic dimen-sion. Their methodology consisted primarily of assessing the perceptual role of individual components seen on the sound spectrogram by means of syn-thetic speech experiments or manipulation of natural speech stimuli. For example, in investigations of place-of-articulation perception, researchers

CHILD PHONOLOGY
VOLUME 2: PERCEPTION

examined the role of such attributes as the frequency and spectrum of the burst release (Cole and Scott, 1974; Cooper *et al.*, 1952; Dorman and Studdert-Kennedy, 1977; Fischer-Jorgensen, 1972; Schatz, 1954; Winitz *et al.*, 1972), the absolute onset or locus of the second and third formants (Delattre *et al.*, 1955; Liberman *et al.*, 1954), and the direction and extent of the formant motions (Stevens, 1975; Stevens and Blumstein, 1975) as invariant acoustic cues. The findings of this research showed a lack of a one-to-one correspondence between acoustic cue and phonetic percept. Perceptual shifts occurred for a particular consonantal cue when it was paired with different vowels or when it was in different syllabic positions (Liberman *et al.*, 1967). As the schematic stimuli shown in Figure 2.1 indicate, the burst frequency, the onset frequencies of Formants 2 and 3 (F_2; F_3), and the direction of the formant motions for a particular place of articulation are affected by the vowel context that follows. Similarly, comparing the formant motions for a particular place of articulation in initial and final position shows that the formant motions are almost mirror images of each other.

On the basis of these findings, a model of speech perception was hypothesized in which the acoustic signal is restructured or encoded, as a function of context, by the perceptual system in reference to the articulatory or phonetic characteristics of the signal (Liberman *et al.*, 1967). The particular details of the theory (i.e., whether or not the characteristics reflect

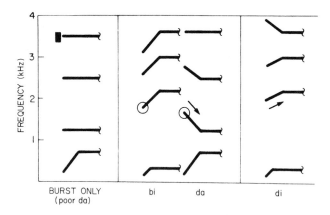

FIGURE 2.1 *Schematic stimuli for CV syllables indicating the lack of acoustic invariance for place of articulation when individual components of the stimulus are analyzed. The far left panel shows a synthetic [da] stimulus with steady formants (except for F_1) and a burst of energy exciting F_4. The burst alone fails to provide an invariant cue for place of articulation. The middle panel shows that the onset frequencies of F_2 are the same for both [bi] and [da], and thus fails to provide an invariant cue. The direction of formant transitions also fails to provide invariance, as F_2 is falling (indicated by the arrow) in the [da] stimulus, but is rising in the case of [di] shown in the right panel.*

invariant motor patterns tied to articulatory muscles, neuromuscular com-
mands, or to an abstract phonetic dimension similar to linguistic features,
is not crucial to this discussion). The major point here is that, as a consequence of the failure to find acoustic invariance in the signal, a model of
speech was hypothesized that required a specialized processing mechanism
actively operating by means of complex computational techniques to derive
linguistic sense from the acoustic signal (Halle and Stevens, 1964; Liberman
et al., 1967; Neisser, 1967). Such a theory suggests a fairly extreme disso-
ciation between the perceiver and his environment, and, furthermore, implies that the acoustic signal is only minimally structured to derive linguistic
meaning. Thus, there is no "direct" perception for speech in the sense that
the acoustic attributes of the signal are related in a simple or direct way to
the phonetic percept. With regard to a model of speech perception in infants,
it is necessary to hypothesize a complex biologically innate mechanism,
specialized for constructing phonetic invariance.

Nevertheless, as indicated, the search for invariant acoustic cues carried
out by these researchers focused on those acoustic attributes of the speech
signal that were separately observable from a spectrographic representation,
and was further predicated on the assumption that speech perception involves the extraction of those attributes independently and their combination
at a later stage of the perception process. However, it has been hypothesized
(Cole and Scott, 1974; Fant, 1960; Stevens, 1972, 1975) that the perceptual
system responds to more global properties reflecting the integration of those
attributes as a single property. The attributes may be based on the spectral
characteristics of the signal sampled over a particular time domain. For
example, in the case of place of articulation for stop consonants, global
integrated properties may be extracted, reflecting the configuration of acoustic events occurring at the release of the stop consonant (Fant, 1960, 1969;
Stevens, 1975; Stevens and Blumstein, 1978). Such a configuration is based
upon the spectral characteristics of the speech sound at the moment of consonantal release, and thus is a consequence of a particular place of articulation. For example, Figure 2.2 shows examples of onset spectra for the
natural production of the consonants [b], [d], [g] followed by the vowel
[a]. These are linear prediction spectra obtained by preemphasizing the
higher frequencies and using a 26 msec time window beginning at the consonantal release. Note that three distinct patterns emerge for each place of
articulation based on the gross shape of the spectrum. The labial and alveolar
consonants can be described in terms of a diffuse spread of energy, with the
shape of the spectrum either flat or tilted toward lower frequencies for the
labial consonant, and tilted toward higher frequencies in the case of the
alveolar consonant. For the velar consonant, spectral energy is concentrated
in a prominent midfrequency peak.

According to the acoustic theory of speech production, these patterns
should remain the same across vowel environment, syllable position, and

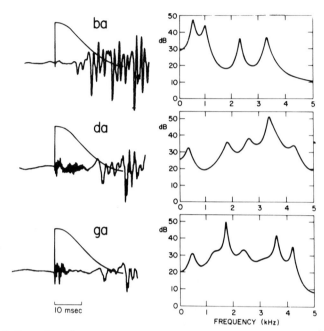

FIGURE 2.2 *Examples of waveforms and obtained spectra sampled at consonantal release for the three syllables [ba], [da], and [ga]. Superimposed on each waveform is the time window (width 26 msec) that is used for sampling the spectrum.*

speaker (Fant, 1956, 1960; Stevens and Blumstein, 1978). Because the short-time spectrum reflects the articulatory configuration at the moment of release, it should remain invariant, independent of the following vowel. Furthermore, although the absolute positions of the formants may vary within limits. owing to vowel context effects or vocal-tract size differences, the gross shape of the spectrum should remain unaffected. Finally, because at consonantal release, the formant frequencies approach target values appropriate to the consonantal place of articulation, the spectrum shape for the various places of articulation should be similar to those derived for the onset spectra.

The possibility that the short-time spectra at consonantal release provide distinctive shapes for place of articulation in stop consonants has been noted in several investigations of natural speech. Halle *et al.* (1957) and Zue (1976) have shown that spectral analyses of the burst in isolation give rise to three classes of patterns associated with the three places of articulation—labial, alveolar, and velar. The work of Fant (1969) and Jakobson *et al.* (1963), in particular, has attempted to characterize the distinct patterns derived from the short-time spectra of stop–vowel utterances. As discussed earlier, labial and alveolar consonants can be described in terms of a diffuse spread of spectral energy, with the shape of the spectrum either flat or tilted toward lower frequencies in the case of labials and tilted toward higher frequencies for alveolars. For the velar consonants, spectral energy is concentrated in a prominent midfrequency peak, giving rise to a compact pattern. Figures 2.3, 2.4, and 2.5 show onset spectra for a number of CV utterances containing labial, alveolar, and velar stop consonants produced in different vowel contexts and spoken by different speakers. Inspection of these spectra indicates that, with the exception of the lower right-hand panel in each figure, the gross shape of the spectrum can be characterized as diffuse–falling or flat corresponding to the labials (Figure 2.3), diffuse–rising corresponding to the alveolars (Figure 2.4), and compact corresponding to the velars (Figure 2.5).

The work of Blumstein and Stevens (1979) attempted to provide a more quantitative measure for assessing the extent to which these properties are intrinsic to the place-of-articulation dimension. To this end, we developed a set of templates corresponding to each place of articulation that were to reflect the acoustic properties: diffuse–rising, diffuse–falling or flat, and compact. The following discussion will focus on the properties and measurement procedures for the diffuse–rising template. For a detailed discussion of the other two templates, see Blumstein and Stevens (1979). Figure 2.6 schematizes the diffuse–rising template and several spectra that were fitted

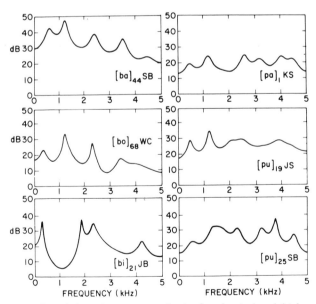

FIGURE 2.3 *Examples of short-time spectra of voiced and voiceless labial stop consonants followed by different vowels and spoken by different speakers. Except for the bottom right panel, the spectra show either the diffuse–falling or diffuse–flat property characteristic of labial consonants.*

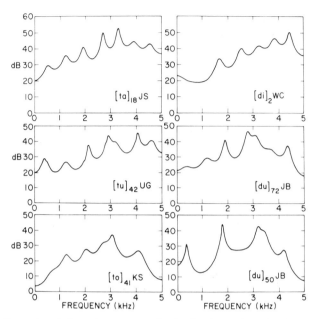

FIGURE 2.4 *Examples of short-time spectra of voiced and voiceless alveolar stop consonants followed by different vowels and spoken by different speakers. Except for the bottom right panel, these spectra show the diffuse–rising property characteristic of alveolar consonants.*

to it. To meet the requirements of this template, a spectrum must contain at least two energy peaks within the template boundaries with one of those peaks occurring above 2200 Hz. Furthermore, the higher peak also must be higher in amplitude than a lower-energy peak. The top of the figure shows a spectrum that fits the conditions of this template. Note its overall shape is diffuse–rising (i.e., the peaks are spread along the frequency domain, and the shape of the spectrum is tilted toward the higher frequencies). The bottom of the figure shows two spectra that do not fit the diffuse–rising template. Note that the onset spectrum for [ba] contains only one peak within the template boundaries, has an F_2 peak jutting above the template boundary, and is higher in amplitude relative to the higher-frequency peaks. For the [gi] onset spectrum, there is only one peak of energy, that dominates the spectrum, and thus it does not have the diffuse–rising shape required.

Similar procedures were used to fit a large number of spectra derived from a sample of natural CV and VC utterances to the three templates devised. In all, 1800 utterances were analyzed, 900 CV syllables and 900 VC syllables representing five repetitions of the six stop consonants with five different vowels produced by six speakers (four male and two female). Short-time spectra of these utterances were then determined for the first difference of the waveform (sampled at 10 kHz) and were smoothed using linear prediction algorithms. These spectra were preemphasized at the higher frequencies. For syllable-initial consonants, the spectra were sampled at the point of consonantal release. For syllable-final stops, they were sampled at two points: at the point of consonantal closure, and at the release burst of the consonant (if the final consonant was indeed released). In principle, the spectrum sampled at both of these points should contain the characteristics observed in the onset spectra.

Results of these analyses for initial consonants can be seen in Table 2.1. Overall, about 85% of the utterances were correctly accepted by these templates, and about the same percentage of utterances were correctly rejected. In other words, a given template (such as the diffuse–rising template) accepted the voiced and voiceless stop consonants containing the same place of articulation (i.e., alveolar consonants) and correctly rejected consonants having a different place of articulation (i.e., labial and velar consonants).

The results of the template-matching procedures applied to the final consonants is shown in Table 2.2. It is quite clear that the closure fails to provide a reliable index for correctly accepting or rejecting a given place of articulation based on the gross shape of the short-time spectrum. In con-

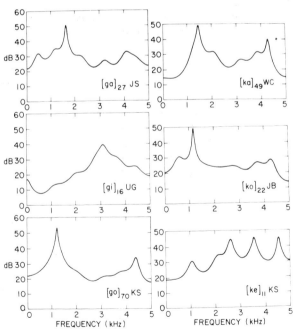

FIGURE 2.5 *Examples of short-time spectra of voiced and voiceless velar stop consonants followed by different vowels and spoken by different speakers. Except for the bottom right panel, the spectra show the compact midfrequency prominence characteristic of velar consonants.*

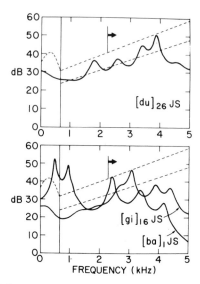

FIGURE 2.6 *Examples of short-time spectra that have been fitted to the diffuse–rising template. The top panel shows the onset spectrum of an alveolar consonant that meets the requirements of the template. The spectrum is adjusted vertically so that a spectral peak falling at about 2200 Hz (indicated by the arrow) touches the top reference line (see text for details). The bottom panel shows onset spectra for a velar and a labial consonant, neither of which meets the requirements of the diffuse–rising template.*

trast, the release burst correctly accepts the appropriate place of articulation approximately 76% of the time and correctly rejects the two other places of articulation approximately 84% of the time.

Overall, the results of the template-matching procedures indicate that there are indeed unifying acoustic properties for place of articulation across phonetic contexts (i.e., different vowels) and syllable positions (i.e., initial and final) and among different speech sounds (i.e., voiced and voiceless stop consonants). These properties can be derived from the short-time spectrum at consonantal release and can provide higher-order invariant acoustic cues for place of articulation directly derivable from the acoustic signal. These cues represent higher-order invariance, in the sense that they reflect the relative shape of the spectrum for a particular consonantal configuration, rather than an absolute measure of a particular attribute such as specific frequency locations and amplitudes of spectral peaks.

These results have important implications for a model of speech perception. The fact that the acoustic signal provides unique patterns characteristic of the phonetic dimensions of speech suggests a speech-processing mechanism selectively tuned to detect the invariant properties residing in the short-time spectrum at onset or offset. This view is predicated on the assumption that the perceptual system is not dissociated from its environment, but is adaptive in the sense that it has evolved to be maximally sen-

TABLE 2.1
Percentage of Correct Acceptance and Rejection of Template-matching Procedures for Initial Stop Consonants

Labial template		
Correct acceptance	Correct rejection	
[b] 82.5	[d] 80.7	[g] 90.0
[p] 80.0	[t] 95.3	[k] 94.7
Alveolar template		
Correct acceptance	Correct rejection	
[d] 83.3	[b] 86.0	[g] 88.5
[t] 88.0	[p] 80.0	[k] 85.3
Velar template		
Correct acceptance	Correct rejection	
[g] 86.7	[b] 91.3	[d] 82.7
[k] 83.3	[p] 86.7	[t] 88.0

sitive to the invariances provided by the signal itself (cf. Gibson, 1966; Neisser, 1976). Such a system requires that it be sensitive to abrupt changes in intensity at onset or offset of stimuli, and that it can assign certain simple properties to the spectrum sampled at those points in time. There is some preliminary evidence from auditory psychophysics and auditory physiology to suggest that the auditory system processes abrupt discontinuities at onset in a special manner (Kiang *et al.*, 1965; Leshowitz and Cudahy, 1975; Watanabe *et al.*, 1965; Zhukov *et al.*, 1974). Not only have complexes of neurons been found to respond selectively to abrupt discontinuities at onset, but a briefly presented gated masker is always more effective than a continuous steady-state masker. Thus, the auditory system seems to show a particular sensitivity to abrupt discontinuities in the acoustic signal. Presumably the extraction of these properties is dependent upon the interaction of sets of individual neurons that together can extract particular features or attributes from a complex auditory pattern. In addition, there is some evidence from perceptual experiments that normal subjects can accurately identify place of articulation in short synthetic stimuli of about 25 msec duration containing only onset spectra information (Blumstein and Stevens, 1980). These results indicate that a subject can perceive place of articulation across vowel contexts even when the stimulus is stripped of context-dependent information such as formant motions and vowel environment. Presumably, the subject is responding to the gross shape of the onset spectrum to make his phonetic decision.

Nevertheless, as earlier research has shown, there are contextually dependent cues that can also serve to signal the phonetic dimensions of speech. These cues, however, always covary in natural speech with the invariant context-independent acoustic properties. There is little doubt that

TABLE 2.2

Percentage of Correct Acceptance and Rejection of Template-matching Procedures for Final Stop Consonants Measured at Consonantal Closure and Release Burst

Labial template			
Correct acceptance		Correct rejection	
Closure	Burst	Closure	Burst
[b] 77.3	78.7	[d] 42.5	82.0
[p] 76.5	75.0	[t] 40.0	91.2
		[g] 42.7	82.0
		[k] 40.0	83.2

Alveolar template			
Correct acceptance		Correct rejection	
Closure	Burst	Closure	Burst
[d] 31.2	74.7	[b] 90.0	85.2
[t] 31.7	78.4	[p] 88.7	83.2
		[g] 85.8	79.7
		[k] 81.0	84.0

Velar template			
Correct acceptance		Correct rejection	
Closure	Burst	Closure	Burst
[g] 57.8	70.0	[b] 71.3	86.8
[k] 46.0	80.8	[p] 75.2	89.6
		[d] 67.8	78.0
		[t] 73.2	87.2

listeners can and do make use of these contextually determined cues in the experimental situation as well as in the normal communication process. First, it has been shown that adult listeners can identify place of articulation for two-formant synthetic stimuli (Cooper *et al.*, 1952; Delattre *et al.*, 1955) that apparently do not possess the general properties already discussed. Presumably, the listener invokes the context-dependent cues such as formant motions and the formant frequencies of the following vowel to make his phonetic decision. Second, the normal communication process is such that the perceptual system may need to rely on both contextually independent and dependent cues. On the one hand, normally articulated speech is often rapid and imprecise, providing the listener with a minimally optimal acoustic signal from which to derive meaning. On the other hand, speech occurs in the context of a noisy channel where extraneous noise may mask some of the acoustic information within the signal itself. A perceptual system that could not make use of the context-dependent information provided in the speech stream would most certainly be maladaptive.

If the model of speech perception presented here is correct, an explanation would be provided for the ability of infants to discriminate phonetic dimensions, such as place of articulation in a manner similar to adults. In this view, these abilities reflect the operation of innate biological mechanisms selectively tuned to the invariant acoustic properties. It is these context-independent acoustic properties that provide the first set of cues used by the infant in perceiving the phonetic dimensions of speech. The context-dependent cues that provide further information about the phonetic structure of speech are presumably learned by the infant and are ultimately integrated as part of the speech-processing mechanism.

On the basis of the results just presented, it would be expected that infants would be able to discriminate place-of-articulation distinctions for initial- and final-released stops. However, because of the failure to find acoustic invariance for unreleased stops, these sounds should theoretically present discrimination difficulties for the infant. (It is also the case that adults have greater difficulty identifying unreleased stops in comparison to released stops. Nevertheless, they can generally perform such tasks with varying degrees of success; Halle *et al.*, 1957; Malécot, 1958; Wang, 1959.) Reliable discriminations for unreleased stops would presumably occur only after the child has been exposed to enough linguistic stimulation to learn to make use of context-sensitive information provided in the acoustic signal. Put in a larger theoretical framework, any phonetic dimension that is not signaled by acoustic invariance would theoretically be discriminated by the infant only after sufficient linguistic exposure. It remains for further speech research to determine which contrasts, in fact, are signaled by invariant versus context-dependent cues. However, likely candidates that may not show acoustic invariance are those defined by linguists as marked (cf. Jakobson, 1968). Examples of some of these would be the distinction between alveolar and retroflex consonants found in Hindi (Stevens and Blumstein, 1975) or alveolar and dental consonants found in Malayalam (Ladefoged, 1971).

In summary, it is hypothesized that the normally processing speech system depends upon both the *primary* invariant acoustic cues and the *secondary* context-dependent cues for effective communication. The invariant cues are considered primary because they comprise the finite set of properties to which the innate property-detecting mechanisms are tuned, and the context-dependent cues are considered secondary because they are learned through interaction with the linguistic environment. Despite the important role of these secondary context-dependent cues, the speech-perception process depends crucially on acoustic invariance. Because of this invariance, there is a fairly direct relation between the acoustic signal itself and its phonetic percept. The context-dependent cues, however, are derived and require a more complex relation between acoustic signal and phonetic percept. This relation is determined as a direct consequence of the cooccurrence of these cues with the invariant acoustic properties.

Acknowledgments

This work was supported in part by the John Simon Guggenheim Foundation, the Radcliffe Institute, and Grant NS–04332 from the National Institute of Neurological Communication Diseases and Strokes.

References

Blumstein, S.E., and Stevens, K.N. (1979) "Acoustic Invariance in Speech Production: Evidence from Measurements of the Spectral Characteristics of Stop Consonants," *Journal of the Acoustical Society of America*, 66, 1001–1017.

Blumstein, S.E., and Stevens, K.N. (1980) "Perceptual Invariance and Onset Spectra for Stop Consonants," *Journal of the Acoustical Society of America*, 67, 648–662.

Cole, R.A., and Scott, B. (1974) "Towards a Theory of Speech Perception," *Psychological Review*, 81, 348–74.

Cooper, F.S., Delattre, P.C., Liberman, A.M., Borst, J.M., and Gerstman, L.J. (1952) "Some Experiments on the Perception of Synthetic Speech Sounds," *Journal of the Acoustical Society of America*, 24, 597–606.

Delattre, P.C., Liberman, A.M., and Cooper, F.S. (1955) "Acoustic Loci and Transitional Cues for Consonants," *Journal of the Acoustical Society of America*, 27, 769–773.

Dorman, M.F., Studdert-Kennedy, M., and Raphael, L. (1977) "The Invariance Problem in Initial Voiced Stop Consonants: Release Bursts and Formant Transitions as Functionally Equivalent Context-dependent Cues," *Perception & Psychophysics*, 22, 109–122.

Fant, G. (1956) "On the Predictability of Formant Levels and Spectrum Envelope from Formant Frequencies," in M. Halle, ed., *For Roman Jakobson*, Mouton; The Hague. pp. 109–120.

Fant, G. (1960) *The Acoustic Theory of Speech Production*, Mouton, The Hague.

Fant, G. (1969) "Stops in CV syllables," *Speech Transmission Laboratory QPSR*, Royal Institute of Technology, Stockholm, 4, 1–25.

Fischer-Jorgensen, E. (1972) "Perceptual Studies of Danish Stop Consonants," *Annual Report of the Institute of Phonetics*, University of Copenhagen, 6, 75–168.

Gibson, J.J. (1966) *The Senses Considered as Perceptual Systems*, Houghton Mifflin, Boston.

Halle, M., Hughes, G.W., and Radley, J.-P.A. (1957) "Acoustic Properties of Stop Consonants," *Journal of the Acoustical Society of America*, 29, 107–116.

Halle, M., and Stevens, K.N. (1964) "Speech Recognition: A Model and a Program for Research," in J.A. Fodor and J.J. Katz, eds., *The Structure of Language*, Prentice-Hall, Englewood Cliffs, N.J., pp. 604–612.

Jakobson, R. (1968) *Child Language, Aphasia, and Phonological Universals*, Mouton, The Hague.

Jakobson, R., Fant, G., and Halle, M. (1963) *Preliminaries to Speech Analysis*, MIT Press. Cambridge.

Kiang, N.Y.-S., Watanabe, T., Thomas, E.C., and Clark L.F. (1965) *Discharge Patterns of Single Fibers in the Cat's Auditory Nerve*, MIT Press, Cambridge.

Ladefoged, P. (1971) *Preliminaries to Linguistic Phonetics*, University of Chicago Press, Chicago.

Leshowitz, B., and Cudahy, E. (1975) "Masking Patterns for Continuous and Gated Sinusoids," *Journal of the Acoustical Society of America*, 58, 235–242.

Liberman, A.M., Cooper, F.S., Delattre, P.C., and Gerstman, L.J. (1954) "The Role of Consonant–vowel Transitions in the Perception of Stop and Nasal Consonants," *Psychological Monographs*, 68, 379.

Liberman, A.M., Cooper, F.S., Shankweiler, D.P., and Studdert-Kennedy, M. (1967) "Perception of the Speech Code," *Psychological Review*, 74, 431–461.

Malécot, A. (1958) "The Role of Releases in the Identification of Released Final Stops," *Language*, 34, 370–380.

Neisser, U. (1967) *Cognitive Psychology*, Prentice-Hall, Englewood Cliffs, N.J.

Neisser, U. (1976) *Cognition and Reality*, W. H. Freeman, San Francisco, Calif.

Schatz, C.D. (1954) "The Role of Context in the Perception of Stops," *Language*, 30, 47–56.

Stevens, K.N. (1972) "The Quantal Nature of Speech: Evidence from Articulatory–Acoustic Data," in P.B. Denes and E.E. Davids, eds., *Human Communication, A Unified View*, McGraw-Hill, New York, pp. 51–66.

Stevens, K.N. (1975) "The Potential Role of Property Detectors in the Perception of Consonants," in G. Fant and M.A.A. Tatham, eds., *Auditory Analysis and Perception of Speech*, Academic Press, London pp. 303–330.

Stevens, K.N., and Blumstein, S.E. (1975) "Quantal Aspects of Consonant Production and Perception: A Study of Retroflex Consonants," *Journal of Phonetics*, 3, 215–234.

Stevens, K.N., and Blumstein, S.E. (1978) "Invariant Cues for Place of Articulation in Stop Consonants," *Journal of the Acoustical Society of America*, 64, 1358–1368.

Wang, W.S.-Y. (1959) "Transition and Release as Perceptual Cues for Final Plosives," *Journal of Speech and Hearing Research*, 3, 66–73.

Winitz, H., Scheib, M. E., and Reeds, J. A. (1972) "Identification of Stops and Vowels for the Burst Portion of /p,t,k/ Isolated from Conversational Speech," *Journal of the Acoustical Society of America*, 51, 1309–1317.

Zhukov, S.Ya., Zhukova, M.G., and Chistovich, L.A. (1974) "Some New Concepts in the Auditory Analysis of Acoustic Flow," *Soviet Physics & Acoustics*, 20, 237–240.

Zue, V.W. (1976) "Acoustic Characteristics of Stop Consonants: A Controlled Study," Unpublished ScD Thesis, MIT.

Chapter 3
INFANT SPEECH PERCEPTION: HISTORY AND MYSTERY

REBECCA E. EILERS

Over the past 10 years, the study of infant speech perception has grown rapidly. Research has been inspired by findings in related areas such as speech perception in adults, children, nonhuman primates, and other mammalian species. Continuing interest in infant speech perception has led to the modification of old paradigms and the development of new ones for posing a series of new questions about the infant's language capacity. Researchers are now interested in the process of developmental change in speech perception, the role of linguistic experience on subsequent development, the origins of infant abilities, the phylogenetic significance of these abilities, and the relationship between speech perception in infancy and in later childhood. Researchers have begun to explore more complex speech and speechlike stimuli and to ask the infant to perform more complex speech-processing tasks. This chapter is intended to organize the existing data relating to infant speech perception so that the area may be viewed within the broader context of a growing body of research on human communication.

Methodologies for Studying Infant Speech Perception

To date, three general procedures have been developed to assess the speech perception ability of infants between birth and 18 months of age. These are the high-amplitude sucking paradigm (HAS), the heart-rate par-

CHILD PHONOLOGY
VOLUME 2: PERCEPTION

adigm (HR), and the visually reinforced infant speech discrimination paradigm (VRISD). A description of each follows:

High-Amplitude Sucking Paradigm (HAS)

In this paradigm (first successfully employed by Eimas *et al.*, 1971), infants are presented with a repeating speech stimulus contingent on high-amplitude sucking. Thus, the infant controls stimulus presentation; the more sucks emitted, the greater the number of presentations of the stimulus to the infant. The HAS paradigm is divided into three stages: acquisition, habituation, and dishabituation. During acquisition, the infant increases the number of high-amplitude sucks over baseline, presumably, to receive contingent reinforcement. After several minutes, the infant's sucking typically asymptotes and begins to fall off until the rate equals some previously set arbitrary criterion. Once this criterion rate is met (e.g., 80% of the maximum pre-habituation sucking rate), the infant is considered to have habituated to the stimulus, and one of two conditions is then applied. Half of the babies in a particular study are given a new stimulus (experimental group), and half are maintained on the old stimulus (control group). Dishabituation, or a significant increase in sucking in the experimental group relative to the control group, is accepted as evidence that infants can discriminate between the two stimuli.

The HAS paradigm was recently modified by Spring (1975) in an effort to lessen memory load for participating infants. In the alternating high-amplitude sucking (AHAS) version, the infant is presented with a new stimulus (S_2) alternating with the old stimulus (S_1) during the experimental dishabituation phase. The rationale for the AHAS version of the paradigm is based on the possibility that, if the infant can discriminate S_1 from S_2, the alternating pattern may be more salient and require less memory than the single shift from S_1 to S_2 employed in the HAS paradigm. As predicted, Spring and Dale (1977) showed greater recovery from habituation using the AHAS procedure than was observed with the traditional paradigm.

Both HAS and AHAS paradigms are applicable to groups of subjects between birth and 3–4 months of age.

Heart-Rate Paradigm (HR)

The HR paradigm (first successfully introduced by Moffitt, 1971) differs from HAS in that the infant does not control stimulus presentation. Speech stimuli are presented in fixed-blocked trials during which time the infant's heart rate decelerates from some baseline rate. (This heart-rate deceleration is thought to be an index of the orienting response in young infants.) Each block of trials is followed by a relatively long inter-trial-interval (ITI) in which the infant's heart rate returns to normal. After several blocks of a single stimulus are presented, a new stimulus is introduced. If recovery of the orienting response (renewed deceleration) is found, discrimination is inferred.

The heart-rate procedure has also undergone modification to allow for more sensitive measurement of discrimination. To minimize memory constraints imposed by the relatively long ITI in the traditional HR paradigm, Leavitt *et al.* (1976) used a 20–20 procedure in which 20 syllables of Stimulus 1 (S_1) were presented, followed by an ITI equal in length to the inter-stimulus-interval (ISI) between any two tokens of S_1. Twenty syllables of Stimulus 2 (S_2) were then presented. Using the modified 20–20 paradigm, these researchers were able to demonstrate discrimination of place of articulation in 6-week-old infants. Evidence of discrimination was not obtained using the blocked-trial paradigm.

HR procedures may be used on groups of infants ranging in age from 1 month to about 6–8 months. In theory, this procedure can be used with older infants; but, in fact, it is difficult to maintain older infants in states suitable for testing. Whereas the HR procedure is most often used with groups, it can be adapted for within-subject designs.

Visually Reinforced Infant Speech Discrimination (VRISD)

Visually reinforced head-turn paradigms (first successfully introduced by Eilers *et al.*, 1976) typically involve the presentation of a repeating background stimulus (S_1) that is changed to some new stimulus (S_2) for a fixed interval (usually 4 sec) and then returned to the original background (S_1). During this change interval, a head turn toward the sound source is reinforced by the activation of a lighted animated toy placed at the source. Evidence of discrimination is obtained when infants turn appropriately during change intervals but do not turn during equivalent control intervals in which the repeating background stimulus is not changed. The VRISD paradigm has been successfully modified by Kuhl (1976) so that multiple tokens of stimuli may be used rather than a single token of each stimulus-pair member. (See Kuhl, Chapter 4, this volume, for details of perceptual constancy research.)

The VRISD paradigm is applicable to infants between 6 and 18 months of age and can yield within-subject data on a number of speech contrasts.

Given these tools, researchers have begun to study the infant's capacity to discriminate features of the speech code. The following sections review and organize the available data into subsections on the perception of consonants, vowels, and suprasegmental features.

Discrimination of Stop Consonants Cued by Voice Onset Time

A number of studies of infant perception have focused on the voice onset time (VOT) continuum. Discrimination studies of the VOT continuum have been undertaken with infants for a variety of reasons: (*a*) VOT is claimed to be sufficient to cue differences in the abstract feature of voicing of stop consonants across many language communities (Abramson and Lisker, 1968); (*b*) different language groups partition the VOT continuum into distinct phonemic areas, the boundary values of which are restricted in similar ways across languages; (*c*) adult data on the perception of VOT have been available for comparison with infant findings; and (*d*) available methods for synthesizing stop consonants differing in VOT have made experimental manipulation of these stimuli relatively simple.

Given these facts, it is not surprising that the first major study in infant speech perception, conducted by Eimas *et al.* (1971), was undertaken using stimuli that varied in VOT. Using the HAS procedure, Eimas *et al.* demonstrated that 1- and 4-month-old infants could discriminate /ba/ versus /pa/ categorically in a manner similar to discrimination by English-speaking adults. In adult English, the VOT continuum is divided into two categories: phonemic /ba/, phonetically [pa], and phonemic /pa/, phonetically [pʰa]. Other languages, for example, Spanish, use different categories corresponding to phonetic [ba] and [pa]. Although they may sometimes prove to be discriminable, [ba] and [pa] both sound like /ba/ to the English ear. Eimas *et al.* (1971) found that infants discriminated across category stimuli (in this case, stimuli with VOT values on either side of the lag or "English" boundary) but did not provide evidence of discriminating stimuli taken from within the English [pa] category, despite the fact that the absolute VOT difference between the members of the two stimulus pairs was identical. These researchers concluded that infant speech perception was innate as infants perceived the speech stimuli categorically and in a manner approximating adult perception.

Many aspects of the Eimas *et al.* study have been replicated, though the interpretation of the data remains open.[1] Trehub and Rabinovitch (1972) tested infants with HAS using naturally produced [pa] and [pʰa] (English boundary) stimuli and found evidence of discrimination for these natural tokens. Later, Eilers *et al.* (in press), using the VRISD procedure, demonstrated that English-learning infants could discriminate synthetic [pa] and [pʰa] stimuli falling on either side of the English boundary but could not provide evidence of discrimination of eight other bilabial pairs differing in

---

[1] It is not clear whether categorical perception can be assumed to be linguistic in nature, as many nonlinguistic continua are perceived categorically by both adults and infants. Furthermore, the stimulus pair chosen as a within-category pair may in fact have been a between-Spanish-category stimulus pair.

VOT when both members of the pairs were within either the English [pʰa] category or within the English [pa] category. Thus all of the data collected with both natural and synthetically produced stimuli suggest that the English boundary is discriminable by babies between 1 and 8 months of age whether the HAS or VRISD paradigm is used to assess discrimination.

Another perspective on infants' abilities is gained by examining the discrimination data collected from infants whose native language includes [ba] category stops. Streeter (1976) tested Kikuyu infants, and Lasky *et al.* (1975) tested Guatemalan infants using HAS and HR procedures, respectively. These researchers found that, when the native language included prevoiced stops ([ba]s), infants were able to discriminate between these stops and [pa]s. English-learning infants, however, with the exception of a single study,[2] do not provide evidence of discriminating [ba] from [pa]. For example, Eilers *et al.* (in press), using VRISD, presented English-learning infants with stimuli nearly identical to those presented to the Kikuyu and Guatemalan infants just mentioned. No evidence of discrimination was obtained. In a later single study, Eilers *et al.* (in press) presented a native Spanish contrast [ba] versus [pa] and a native English contrast [pa] versus [pʰa] to both Spanish- and English-learning infants. Spanish infants were able to discriminate across both the English boundary and the Spanish boundary. English infants only provided evidence of discriminating the English contrast.

Given the differing perceptual abilities of Spanish- and English-learning infants, a strong innateness hypothesis does not seem to be tenable. It should be kept in mind, however, that whereas discrimination across the Spanish boundary is, to some extent, influenced by linguistic environment, discrimination of the English boundary is relatively unaffected by linguistic history. Part of the explanation for this phenomenon may be found in the suggestion that the English boundary is an especially salient boundary in a purely acoustic sense (Butterfield and Cairns, 1974; Eilers and Minifie, 1975; Stevens and Klatt, 1974). Stevens and Klatt (1974) argued that this boundary included an additional cue beyond VOT per se (namely, the presence or absence of transition information for the first formant). Formant cutback is not available as a cue in the lead region of the VOT continuum.

The speculation that the lag boundary is particularly salient is supported by the results of several studies:

1. All infants tested for discrimination at the English boundary provide

---

[2] Eimas (1975) reported evidence of discrimination with the pair +10 versus −70 msec VOT. This finding is difficult to interpret because an 80 msec difference is involved rather than a 20–40 msec difference as has been used in other research. The large VOT difference necessary to obtain evidence of discrimination in Eimas' (1975) study suggests that marginally relevant factors (such as perceived loudness of the two stimuli) might be responsible for the discriminations.

evidence of discrimination (Eilers *et al.*, 1976; Eimas *et al.*, 1971; Lasky *et al.*, 1975; Trehub and Rabinovitch, 1972), even if their native language did not contain an English-like contrast (Lasky *et al.*, 1975; Streeter, 1976)

2. Adults whose native language did not contain an English-like contrast were able to discriminate this contrast (Lasky *et al.*, 1975; Streeter, 1976)

3. The South American chinchilla, a member of the rodent family, uses a boundary value comparable to the one used by speakers of English to differentiate stop consonants (Kuhl and Miller, 1975).

All of these results suggest that the English boundary has special acoustic properties to which mammalian ears are particularly sensitive.

Although it is reasonable to suggest that experience plays a central role in infant speech perception on the basis of these available results, and that the specific form of experience influences the specific form of perceptual capacities, just how the child makes use of this experience is unclear. At the very least, the child must be engaged in an active analysis of the frequency of occurrence of speech sounds at various points along phonetic continua long before these sounds are associated with arbitrary linguistic meanings. That the child should or could engage in such an analysis is surprising, as there seems to be no immediate instrumental payoff for the effort.

To date, only stimuli differing in VOT have shown specific linguistic experience effects. In a recent study, Eilers *et al.* (1978) presented 16 6–8-month-old Spanish-learning ($N = 8$) and English-learning ($N = 8$) infants with four pairs of stimuli, two of which were phonemic in English and two of which were phonemic in Spanish. The English stimuli were [bit] versus [bIt] and [awá] versus [ará]. The Spanish stimuli were [be] versus [bej] and [alá] versus [ará] (where ſ = flap). All of the infants discriminated the English pairs ([bit]–[bIt], [awá]–[ará]) and one of the two Spanish pairs ([ala]–[ará]). Both groups of infants found the remaining Spanish pair, [be]–[bej], fairly difficult, with only 11 infants presenting evidence of discrimination. Six of these 11 were English-learners, the remaining 5 were Spanish-learners.

In this study, no obvious differences were seen between the discriminative performance of the English- and Spanish-learning children. Although it is likely that other phonemic contrasts showing the effects of linguistic experience will be identified in future research, the task of finding out why VOT stimuli show these strong effects, whereas other stimuli examined to date do not, remains. One possibility is that the synthetic form of the prevoiced VOT stimuli does not incorporate crucial natural language cues that may be crucial for infants, though not necessary for adults.

Appealing as this explanation might be on intuitive grounds, it is not entirely consistent with other data collected for naturally produced fricative consonants differing in voicing. Eilers and Minifie (1975) tested 2–4-month-old infants using the HAS procedure for discrimination of three fricative pairs. Whereas evidence of discrimination was found for [va] versus [sa] and [sa] versus [ʃa], no evidence of discrimination was found for [sa] versus [za], a pair differing primarily in voicing of the initial consonant. This result was replicated by Eilers (1977). The [sa] versus [za] voicing contrast, then, like prevoiced stops, appears to be difficult for infants to process.

Through repeated experimentation, other peculiar qualities of VOT stimuli as presently used have been discovered. Although the HAS procedure has been a successful method for demonstrating discrimination of the English and Spanish VOT boundaries in stops by infants learning Kikuyu, studies of the same stimuli using HR procedures with English-learning infants have generally not shown evidence of discrimination. For instance, Roth and Morse (1975) were unable to find evidence of discrimination in 3–4-month-old infants in a within-subject study using the HR procedure, despite the fact that the stimuli used were identical to those employed by Eimas et al. (1971). Later Miller and Ruzicka (in press), in a series of HR studies that used both natural and synthetic VOT stimuli, were unable to demonstrate discrimination. Lest the HR procedure seem at fault, suffice it to say that place-of-articulation contrasts do not suffer the same fate using HR. As we will see later, HR and HAS collective results have proved to be extremely replicable when voicing contrasts in stops are *not* involved.

Multisyllabic real speech stimuli with consonants differing in VOT designed to show phonetic context effects also seem to have different properties from synthetic stimulus pairs differing in place of articulation. Trehub and Jakubovicz (in press) studied infant discrimination of VCV, CVCV, and VCVCV stimuli where the consonants and vowel in question were stops and [a], respectively. Using HAS, these investigators found that 1–3-month-old infants were able to discriminate [aba] from [apa] and [kaba] from [kapa] as long as syllable duration was maintained at 500 msec. An attempt to find evidence of discrimination in [ataba] versus [atapa], where syllable duration was reduced to 300 msec, failed to yield statistically significant results. The authors reasoned that either the infants were not able to process three-syllable stimuli, or that the shorter syllable duration of the three-syllable stimuli made it difficult for infants to perceive differences in the final syllable. To distinguish between these alternatives, another [kaba] versus [kapa] stimulus set was constructed with 300-msec syllables. Performance was consistent with the expectation that short vowel duration would impede discrimination of the adjoining consonant, with infants providing no evidence of discrimination.

The Trehub and Jakubovicz results are consistent with data on voicing discrimination collected by Eilers et al. (1977) using the VRISD procedure. Eilers et al. found no evidence of discrimination of [a:t] versus [a:d] (the colon indicates a long vowel), a contrast differing mainly in voicing of the final consonant with 6-month-old infants, but did find evidence of discrimination when vowel duration differed in the two syllables, [at] versus [a:d]. By 12 months, half of the infants provided evidence of discrimination for the [a:t]–[a:d] pair. Evidence of discrimination was not obtained for the pair [at]–[a:t], a contrast differing only in vowel duration, indicating that discriminability of the pair [at]–[a:d] was probably a function of the presence of both voicing and vowel-duration cues. Another reason for the failure of the infants on the [a:t]–[a:d] contrast might have been that the syllables to be discriminated were too short (i.e., under 500 msec).

In contrast to the data on perception of voicing reported by Trehub and Jakubovicz (in press) and Eilers *et al.* (1977), Jusczyk and Thompson (1978), using the HAS procedure, reported evidence of discrimination for place of articulation of [da], [ba], and [ga] in both initial- and final-syllable position in two-syllable stimuli despite the fact that the average syllable duration was only 286 msec. In another HAS study, Williams and Bush (1978) found that intervocalic stops differing in place of articulation (e.g., [ada] versus [aga] were discriminable with 270-msec syllables.[3]

On the surface, it may appear that some studies show the effects of short syllables and others do not, but the data are consistent if the type of segmental contrast is considered. Durational differences seem to affect discriminability only when stimuli are contrastive for voicing. Thus, Trehub and Jakubovicz (in press) and Eilers *et al.* (1977), who showed duration effects, studied [b] versus [p] and [t] versus [d], respectively, which are voicing contrasts. Jusczyk and Thompson (in press) and Williams (1977), who did not obtain duration-dependent effects, examined place-of-articulation contrasts [b] versus [d] versus [g].

A final bit of interesting evidence concerning infant perception of VOT was gathered using electrophysiological measures of hemispheric cortical activity. Molfese and Molfese (1978), employing a factor-analytic method for analyzing auditory evoked response data, found that, in adults, 2–3-month-olds, and newborns, the left hemisphere responded to differences in place of articulation. The right hemisphere, however, responded differently to voiceless–unaspirated versus voiceless–aspirated stops in adults, preschoolers, and 2–5-month-olds. No evidence of this effect was found in neonates. This finding is surprising in light of the results of dichotic listening studies with both adults (Shankweiler and Studdert-Kennedy, 1967) and infants (Entus, 1975). The evidence of a right-ear advantage in dichotic tasks led researchers in the area to conclude, until recently, that the left hemisphere was responsible for processing speech information. Molfese and Molfese (1978) seem to have found evidence that the left hemisphere may handle place of articulation for speech but that the right may be primarily

---

[3] Williams (1977) and Williams and Bush (1978) found that single-syllable 300-msec stimuli differing in place, [ad] versus [ag], were not discriminable when synthesized without release bursts and that discrimination of medial consonants was dependent on an interruption in voicing during closure.

involved in categorical responding to VOT. Further research is needed to help clarify these results.

In summary, although infants have been shown to discriminate among certain VOT stimuli, researchers have obtained results indicating that VOT may not be a typical kind of acoustic dimension (if a typical dimension exists). At present, studies of voicing in stop consonants have yielded evidence of context-sensitive perception (including effects attributable to vowel duration), linguistic experience effects, and paradigm-sensitivity effects. As we shall see in subsequent sections, such effects have not been widely documented for other speech-sound categories.

Place of Articulation

Data documenting the infant's capacity to discriminate among minimally paired place contrasts show a somewhat different pattern of results than the data presented for voicing contrasts. Moffitt (1971), using the standard HR paradigm, was the first to discover that infants (4–5 months old) could discriminate between [ba] and [ga]. Morse (1972) extended ths finding to the 6–9-week age range using the HAS procedure. Although a subsequent attempt to replicate the Morse (1972) findings by Leavitt *et al.* (1976) using the HR paradigm failed to disclose evidence of discrimination, Leavitt *et al.* did demonstrate discrimination in same-aged infants when the modified 20–20 HR procedure was used. This procedure allowed young infants to demonstrate their discrimination skills by reducing memory constraints imposed by the long ITI in the traditional paradigm. Similar results were reported by Miller *et al.* (1977) using both the traditional and modified HR paradigm with 3–4-month-old infants. Evidence of discrimination was obtained for the pair [bu] versus [gu] with the modified procedure but not with the standard HR paradigm. The [bu] and [gu] stimuli in this study differed only in the initial release-burst cue. Williams and Bush (1978) using a HAS procedure, provided evidence that 6–12-week-old infants could discriminate [da] from [ga] on the basis of formant-transition information with or without burst cures present. There was some evidence, however, in the Williams and Bush (1978) study that burst-cue information further improved performance. The results suggested that the presence of burst cues alone, formant-transition information alone, or some combination of these cues is sufficient to produce discrimination of initial-position place contrasts in infants as young as 6 weeks of age.

Categorical discrimination of place contrasts was first demonstrated using the HAS procedure by Eimas (1974) in 2–3-month-old infants. Infants discriminated between category pairs across the [bæ]–[dæ]–[gæ] continuum but did not discriminate within categories. Eimas also reported that infants did not show categorical discrimination of isolated nonspeech cues modeled from the place continuum. Eimas's (1974) results were later replicated by Miller and Morse (1976) using the modified 20-20 HR procedure to show categorical discrimination of [dæ] versus [gæ], and by Till (1976) using new synthetic stimuli and the 20-20 procedure with 4-5-month-olds.

Recently, the research on place contrasts has undergone a shift in emphasis from single-syllable stimuli to multisyllabic stimuli. Jusczyk (1977) demonstrated that 2-month-olds in the HAS paradigm could discriminate [d] versus [g] in initial- and final-syllable position. In addition, Jusczyk and Thompson (1978), using HAS, compared discriminability of contrasts in initial and in medial position and found both to be discriminable by 2-month-olds.

Using the HAS procedure, Williams (1977) also investigated young infants' (6-12 weeks) ability to discriminate place contrasts in initial, medial, and final positions. Evidence of discrimination was obtained for CV syllables but not for phonetically identical unreleased VC syllables. Infants did provide evidence of discrimination for all intervocalic contrasts as long as the consonant was marked by a period of silence during articulatory closure. Williams argued that the characteristics of place contrasts that seem to enhance discrimination by infants (release bursts and silence in intervocalic position), appear to be the same characteristics that are exaggerated in "childese," or speech to children.

Fricatives

Research with fricative consonants where pairs were discriminable on the basis of voicing differences, place differences, or along both dimensions has provided the first evidence that some speech-perception skills improve across the first year of life. Eilers and Minifie (1975), using the HAS procedure with 1-4-month-olds, demonstrated infant discrimination for [va] versus [sa] and [sa] versus [ʃa] but not for [sa] versus [za], a pair differentiated by the voicing status of the initial consonant. These results for the [sa]-[za] pair were replicated by Eilers (1977) using the modified HAS procedure (AHAS). In this same study, infants succeeded in discriminating [s] versus [z] in postvocalic position when differential vowel duration covaried naturally with the voicing status of the consonant (e.g., [a:s] versus [a:z] was not discriminated, although [as] versus [a:z] was). Eilers (1977a) also failed to obtain evidence of discrimination for [fa] versus [Өa] and [fi] versus [Өi] in 1-4-month-olds. Eilers et al. (1977) later tested 6-8- and 12-14-month-old infants with the VRISD paradigm on these same fricative stimuli. The 6-8-month-olds provided evidence of discriminating [sa] versus [va], [sa] versus [ʃa], [sa] versus [za], [as] versus [a:z], and [a:s] versus [a:z], but only one of eight infants successfully discriminated [fi] versus [Өi]. Furthermore, all eight infants failed to provide evidence of discrimination of

[fa] versus [ʃa]. At 12–14 months of age, in addition to discriminating all contrasts discriminable by 6–8-month-olds, infants successfully discriminated [fi] versus [Өi]. No evidence of discrimination for [fa] versus [Өa] was obtained. The HAS data and VRISD data taken collectively suggest that discrimination of some fricative consonants improves across the first year.

Further support for this position is provided in an independent study conducted by Holmberg et al. (1977), who used a modified VRISD procedure to test perceptual constancy for fricative consonants. These researchers found that discrimination of [f] and [Ө] was far more difficult than discrimination of [s] versus [ʃ] (i.e., in a training task, it took infants more than twice as many training trials to reach an arbitrary criterion with the [f] versus [Ө] pair as opposed to the [s] versus [ʃ] pair). In fact, the difficulty of the [f] versus [Ө] pair has been well documented for both 24-month-olds (Eilers and Oller, 1976) and for 4–5-year-olds (Abbs and Minifie, 1969).

The investigation of perception of foreign (non-English) fricatives by English-learning infants has been limited to date. Trehub (1976) observed that 5–17-week-olds could discriminate the Czech contrast /řa/[4] versus /ža/ . Adult English speakers in the Trehub study had difficulty discriminating these stimuli, although their scores were above chance. Work on this Czech contrast with the VRISD procedure (Eilers et al., 1980) with 6–8-month-old Spanish-learning and English-learning infants has also shown discrimination. However, in the Eilers et al. work, adults presented with an analog of the VRISD task also discriminated the Czeck contrast with near-perfect accuracy. Because of differences in the adult and infant paradigms and differences in adult and infant task competencies, it remains uncertain at this writing whether infants or adults are superior in this foreign-language discrimination.

Vowels

The literature on infant speech perception suggests that the infant has the capacity to discriminate among many vowel sounds. Trehub (1973) found that 4–17-week-old infants were able to discriminate [u] versus [i] and [i] versus [a], as well as the embedded vowel contrasts [pʰa] versus [pʰi] and [tʰa] versus [tʰi]. Swoboda et al. (1976), using HAS with at-risk and normal 8-week-old in fants, showed discrimination of both within-category and between-category pairs along the [I]–[i] continuum. Eilers et al. (1978), using the VRISD procedure with 6–8-month-old Spanish-learning and 6–8-month-old English-learning infants, demonstrated that the natural stimulus pair [bIt] versus [bit] was discriminable by both groups of infants despite the fact that the [I] vowel does not occur in Spanish. These same infants provided group

---

[4] These stimuli are phonetically fricatives. English listeners often perceive both as [ža].

evidence of discrimination for the natural Spanish pair [bej] versus [be] although individual Spanish-learning (three of eight) and English-learning (two of eight) infants failed to reach the 9 out of 10 criterion used to index successful discrimination. In a similar vein, Trehub (1976), using HAS, demonstrated that 5–17-week-old English-learning infants discriminated a French nasal–oral vowel distinction [pa] versus [pā].

Perhaps the most impressive documentation of the infants' ability to process vocalic information is derived from studies of perceptual constancy (see Kuhl Chapter 4, this volume). Kuhl and Miller (1975) used the HAS procedure with 4–16-week-old infants and demonstrated that infants could detect vowel changes from [a] to [i] despite the fact that random intonation variations were presented as distractors. Later, Kuhl (1976, 1977) demonstrated that 6-month-old infants tested with a modified VRISD paradigm responded to changes in [a] versus [i] and [a] versus [ɔ] despite distractors in the form of variations in speakers and intonation contours.

In summary, then, infant perception of vowels is documented for a number of stimulus pairs. Although little research directly assesses the impact of linguistic experience on perception of these phonetic elements, linguistic experience effects, if present, seem fairly subtle. Demonstration of developmental effects awaits further investigation with additional stimuli across a wider age range.

Semivowels

Recently, there has been increased research attention to the perception of semivowels by infants. Eimas (1975), using the HAS procedure, found that [ra] and [la] were discriminated categorically by 2–3-month-old infants. Japanese adults, however, seemed to discriminate [r] and [l] continuously, whereas English-speaking adults appeared more like the English-learning infants (Miyawaki, et al., 1975). Full interpretation of these results awaits the testing of Japanese-learning infants with the [r] and [l] stimuli. If Japanese infants appear more like Japanese adults than English adults, the evidence will suggest that specific linguistic experience affects the perception of semivowels in infants.

In a study of perception of Spanish and English liquid and glide contrasts, Eilers et al. (1978) tested 6–8-month-old infants with the VRISD procedure. Spanish-learning and English-learning infants were presented with the English phonemic pair [awá] versus [ará] ([w] is often found to be substituted for [r] in early child speech) and the Spanish pair [ará] versus [alá]. Infants from both linguistic environments were able to discriminate all pairs despite differences in past linguistic experience.

Jusczyk et al. (1977), using the HAS procedure, have recently provided evidence that 2-month-olds discriminate [w] and [j] (orthographic "y") in both initial and final position of two-syllable stimuli. Hillenbrand *et al.* (1977), using the VRISD procedure, demonstrated that 6–8-month-old infants perceived differences in rate of change of formant transitions. Liberman *et al.* (1956) demonstrated that lengthened transitions influenced adults to perceive [be] as [we]. When these transitions were lengthened still further, [be] was perceived as [ue]. Infants in the Hillenbrand *et al.* study were able to discriminate among [be], [we], and [ue] when natural tokens were used but could not make successful discriminations when two-formant synthetic stimuli were used.

Summarizing; in a relatively small number of studies infants provide evidence of discriminating glides and liquids. Future research, including the use of more subtle measures of the role of linguistic experience, is necessary in this area.

Discrimination of Suprasegmental Features

The infant literature has often expressed a belief that discrimination of suprasegmental features precedes discrimination of segmental features. Given that infants as young as 1 month successfully discriminate subtle, minimal segmental contrasts (Eimas *et al.*, (1971), it is hard to imagine how suprasegmental discrimination could empirically be shown to "precede" segmental discrimination. A rapidly emerging literature suggests that infants are also sensitive to intonation and stress cues (Kaplan, 1969; Morse, 1972; Spring and Dale, 1977) in the first months. Instead of asking which comes first, it now seems more reasonable to detail the relationship between segmental and suprasegmental information in infant speech processing. Relatively few studies have addressed this latter question.

Kuhl (1976), using HAS, found that, although 1–4-month-old infants discriminated between a rising–falling and monotone pitch contour when these contours were superimposed on a single vowel, when vowel quality was added as a distractor ([a] versus [i]), infants failed to attend to the discriminable changes in pitch. Kuhl interpreted these results as suggesting that infants do not exhibit perceptual constancy for pitch. Put in a slightly different manner, it would seem that the segmental aspects of the stimuli were more potent for the infants than the suprasegmental aspects. This seems to be *one* case in which, given both segmental and suprasegmental cues simultaneously, infants seem to focus on the segmental information.

Both Jusczyk and Thompson (in press), and Williams and Bush (1978) found that placing linguistic stress on a single syllable within a multisyllabic utterance had no demonstrable effect on the infant's ability to discriminate place contrasts. This was true even if the stressed syllable was essentially a distractor (i.e., it did not contain the phoneme that differentiated the stimulus items, e.g., [áda] versus [ága]). Since stop-consonant place contrasts do not seem difficult for infants, failure to obtain an interaction between stress and segmental units is not surprising and may indicate that a ceiling effect was obtained. The problem, then, becomes one of finding a sufficiently difficult segmental contrast, placing it under stress, and observing if the addition of the suprasegmental force enhances performance levels for the difficult contrast. Trehub and Jakubovicz (in press) found that infants did not provide evidence of discrimination for the stimuli [kaba] and [kapa] when syllable duration was 300 msec. In a second experiment, these stimuli were altered so that stress (operationalized as a 4 dB difference between Syllables 1 and 2) was placed on the second syllable of both stimulus-pair members. Infants again failed to provide evidence of discrimination with the stressed stimuli. It is possible that stress cues based on intensity alone do not provide sufficient information to signal "stress" to the infant.

In summary, infants seem able to discriminate some suprasegmental information at least as early as the second month of life. It is not clear, however, how and when suprasegmental information is used by the infants to aid in subtle segmental discriminations. It must be emphasized that the empirical separation of segmental from suprasegmental phonology for the infant (as well as for the adult) is fraught with practical difficulties because in natural speech, prosodic programming has a direct influence on segmental phonology. At the same time, it is clear that, during the process of language acquisition, the perceptual mechanisms of infants and young children must recognize segmental variations that are dictated by nonsegmental productive programming.

Summary and Future Directions

At this time, we are experiencing a rapid growth in both interest and expertise in the area of infant speech perception.

Whereas, just a few years ago, research centered almost entirely around the issue of categorical perception of speechlike sounds, today many new and exciting areas have been opened to investigation. These areas include developmental change, individual differences, the role of linguistic experience, the effect of linguistic context on perception, and the relationship between segmental and suprasegmental cues in perception. In this chapter, an attempt has been made to review and organize the research findings regarding discrimination of speech contrasts by infants. It is clear that future research will continue to address these questions from different perspectives and with new tools. One of the most important challenges in future years will be to build accurate neurocognitive models of the developing perceptual system. These models, to be successful, will have to account for relationships between speech perception in infancy and speech perception in later childhood and adulthood. In addition, these models must reflect a variety of context-sensitive variations in perception and a role for linguistic experience. It would seem that a critical mass of data is available with which to begin the model-building task, though some important areas have been little investigated. For instance, almost all data relate to single distinctive-feature contrast, comparisons. Few data are available that address multiple distinctive-feature comparisons or the kinds of substitutions employed by children at the onset of meaningful speech. Few data address perceptual salience, as opposed to discrimination per se, and at present no studies are available assessing discrimination in running speech or other rich linguistic environments.

Beyond these untapped sources, other available sources of information can be used to shed light on the nature and origins of the infant's speech-discrimination capacity. For instance, research on perceptual constancy, animal speech perception, perception of nonspeech stimuli, and speech perception by adults (see Kuhl, Chapter 4, Aslin and Pisoni, Chapter 5, this volume) all help to provide an interpretive base for the infant data. The continuing interest in the development and modification of paradigms for studying infant speech perception, coupled with broadening interest in the relationship between infant perception and later productive development, promises a fertile era of research.

Acknowledgments

This chapter was partially supported by NICHD grant HD 09906–03 by NIMH grant MH 30634 and by funds from the Mailman Foundation. The author wishes to thank Diane Coleman and Terril Tharp for their valuable assistance.

References

Abbs, M., and Minifie, F.D. (1969) "Effect of Acoustic Cues in Fricatives on Perceptual Confusions in Preschool Children," *Journal of the Acoustical Society of America*, 44, 1535–1542.

Abramson, A.S., and Lisker, L. (1968) "Voice Timing: Cross-Language Experiments in Identification and Discrimination," Paper presented at the seventy-fifth meeting of the Acoustical Society of America, Ottowa, Canada.

Butterfield, E., and Cairns, G. (1974) "Whether Infants Perceive Linguistically is Uncertain, and if They Did, its Practical Importance Would Be Equivocal," in R. Schiefelbusch and L. Lloyd, eds., *Language Perspectives: Acquisition, Retardation and Intervention*, University Park Press, Baltimore, Md.

Eilers, R.E. (1977) "Context-Sensitive Perception of Naturally Produced Stop and Fricative Consonants by Infants," *Journal of the Acoustical Society of America*, 61, 1321–1336.

Eilers, R.E. (1977) "On Tracing the Development of Speech Perception," Paper presented at the Society for Research in Child Development, New Orleans, Louisiana. (a)

Eilers, R.E., and Minifie, F.D. (1975) "Fricative Discrimination in Early Infancy," *Journal of Speech and Hearing Research*, 18, 158–167.

Eilers, R.E., and Oller, D.K. (1976) "The Role of Speech Discrimination in Developmental Sound Substitutions," *Journal of Child Language*, 3, 319–329.

Eilers, R.E., Gavin, W.J., and Oller, D.K. (1980) "Cross-Linguistic Perception in Infancy— Beyond VOT." Paper presented at the International conference on Infant Studies, New Haven, Conn.

Eilers, R.E., Gavin, W., and Wilson, W.R. (in press) "Linguistic Experience and Phonemic Perception in Infancy: A Cross-Linguistic Study," *Child Development*.

Eilers, R.E., Oller, D.K., and Gavin, W.J. (1978) "A Cross-linguistic Study of Infant Speech Perception," Paper presented at the Southeastern Conference on Human Development, Atlanta, Georgia.

Eilers, R.E., Wilson, W.R., and Moore, J.M. (1976) "Discrimination of Synthetic Prevoiced Labial Stops by Infants and Adults," *Journal of the Acoustical Society of America*, 60, Supplement 1, S91. (Abstract)

Eilers, R.E., Wilson, W.R., and Moore, J.M. (in press) "Speech Discrimination in the Language-Innocent and the Language-Wise: A Study in the Perception of Voice-onset-time," *Journal of Child Language*.

Eilers, R.E., Wilson, W.R., and Moore, J.M. (1977) "Developmental Changes in Speech Discrimination in Infants," *Journal of Speech and Hearing Research*, 20, 766–780.

Eimas, P.D. (1974) "Auditory and Linguistic Processing of Cues for Place of Articulation by Infants," *Perception & Psychophysics*, 16, 513–521.

Eimas, P.D. (1975) "Auditory and Phonetic Coding of the Cues of Speech: Discrimination of the [r–l] Distinction by Young Infants," *Perception & Psychophysics*, 18, 341–347.

Eimas, P.D., Siqueland, E., Jusczyk, P., and Vigorito, J. (1971) "Speech Perception in Infants," *Science*, 171, 303–306.

Entus, A.K. (1975) "Hemispheric Asymmetry in Processing of Dichotically Presented Speech and Nonspeech Stimuli by Infants," Paper presented at the Biennial Meeting of the Society for Research in Child Development, Denver, Colorado.

Hillenbrand, J., Minifie, F.D., and Edwards, T.J. (1977) "Tempo of Frequency Change as a Cue in Speech-Sound Discrimination by Infants," Paper presented at the Biennial Meeting of the Society for Research in Child Development, New Orleans, Louisiana.

Holmberg, T.L., Morgan, K.A., and Kuhl, P.A. (1977) "Speech Perception in Early Infancy: Discrimination of Fricative Consonants," *Journal of the Acoustical Society of America*, 62, Supplement 1, S99. (Abstract)

Jusczyk, P.W. (1977) "Perception of Syllable-Final Stop Consonants by Two month old Infants," *Perception & Psychophysics*, 21, 450–454.

Jusczyk, P.W., Copan, H.C., and Thompson, E.J. (1977) "Perception of Glides in Multisyllabic Utterances by Infants," Paper presented at the ninety-fourth meeting of the Acoustical Society of America, Miami, Florida.

Jusczyk, P., and Thompson, E. (1978) "Perception of a Phonetic Contrast in Multisyllabic Utterances by 2-month-old Infants," *Perception & Psychophysics*, 23, 105–109.

Kaplan, E. (1969) "The Role of Intonation in the Acquisition of Language," Unpublished Doctoral Dissertation, Cornell University, Ithaca, N.Y.

Kuhl, P. (1976) "Speech Perception in Early Infancy: Perceptual Constancy for Vowel Categories," *Journal of the Acoustical Society of America*, 60, Supplement 1, S90. (Abstract)

Kuhl, P. (1977) "Speech Perception in Early Infancy: Perceptual Constancy for the Vowel Categories /a/ and /ɲ/," *Journal of the Acoustical Society of America*, 61, Supplement 1, S39 (Abstract)

Kuhl, P.K., and Miller, J.D. (1975) "Speech Perception by the Chinchilla: Voiced–Voiceless Distinction in Alveolar Plosive Consonants," *Science*, 190, 69–72.

Lasky, R.E., Syrdal-Lasky, A., and Klein, R.E. (1975) "VOT Discrimination by Four to Six and a Half Month Old Infants from Spanish Environments," *Journal of Experimental Child Psychology*, 20, 215–225.

Leavitt, L.A., Brown, J.W., Morse, P.A., and Graham, F.K. (1976) "Cardiac Orienting and

Auditory Discrimination in 6-week-old Infants," *Developmental Psychology*, 12, 514–523.

Liberman, A.M., Delattre, P., Gerstman, L.J. and Cooper, F.S. (1956) "Tempo of Frequency Change as a Cue for Distinguishing Classes of Speech Sounds," *Journal of Educational Psychology*, 52, 127–137.

Miller, C., and Morse, P. (1976) "The Heart of Categorical Speech Discrimination in Young Infants," *Journal of Speech and Hearing Research*, 19, 578–589.

Miller, J., Morse, P., and Dorman, M. (1977) "Cardiac Indices of Infant Speech Perception: Orienting and Burst Discrimination," *Quarterly Journal of Experimental Psychology*, 29, 533–545.

Miller, C., and Ruzicka, E. (1978) "A Parametric Investigation of the Cardiac No-delay Discrimination Paradigms and Voice-onset-time Discrimination in Infants," *Research Status Report II, Infant Development Laboratory*, University of Wisconsin.

Miyawaki, K., Strange, W., Verbrugge, R., Liberman, A., Jenkins, J., and Fijimura, O. (1975) "An Effect of Linguistic Experience: The Discrimination of /r/ and /l/ by Native Speakers of Japanese and English," *Perception & Psychophysics*, 18, 331–340.

Moffitt, A.R. (1971) "Consonant Cue Perception by Twenty- to Twenty-four-week-old Infants," *Child Development*, 42, 717–731.

Molfese, D., and Molfese, V. (1978) "VOT Discriminations—Developmental Changes," Paper presented at the Southeastern Conference on Human Development, Atlanta, Georgia.

Morse, P.A. (1972) "The Discrimination of Speech and Non-Speech Stimuli in Early Infancy," *Journal of Experimental Child Psychology*, 14, 477–492.

Roth, D., and Morse, P. (1975) "An Investigation of VOT Discrimination Using the Cardiac OR," *Research Status Report I, Infant Development Laboratory*, University of Wisconsin, 207–218.

Shankweiler, D., and Studdert-Kennedy, M. (1967) "Identification of Consonants and Vowels Presented to the Left and Right Ears," *Quarterly Journal of Experimental Psychology*, 19, 59–63.

Spring, D.R. (1975) "Discrimination of Linguistic Stress Location in One-to-four-month-old Infants," Doctoral Dissertation, University of Washington, Seattle, Washington.

Spring, D.R., and Dale, P.S. (1977) "Discrimination of Linguistic Stress in Early Infancy," *Journal of Speech and Hearing Research*, 20, 224–231.

Stevens, K., and Klatt, D. (1974) "Role of Formant Transitions in the Voiced–voiceless Distinction for Stops," *Journal of the Acoustical Society of America*, 55, 643–659.

Streeter, L.A. (1976) "Language Perception of Two-month-old Infants Shows Effects of Both Innate Mechanisms and Experience," *Nature*, 259, 39–41.

Swoboda, P.J., Morse, P.A., and Leavitt, L.A. (1976) "Continuous Vowel Discrimination in Normal and at-Risk Infants," *Child Development*, 47, 459–465.

Till, J. (1976) "Infants' Discrimination of Speech and Nonspeech Stimuli," Unpublished Doctoral Dissertation, University of Iowa, Iowa City, Iowa.

Trehub, S.E. (1973) "Infants' Sensitivity to Vowel and Tonal Contrasts," *Developmental Psychology*, 9, 91–96.

Trehub, S.E. (1976) "The Discrimination of Foreign Speech Contrasts by Infants and Adults," *Child Development*, 47, 466–472.

Trehub, S.E., and Jakubovicz, N.P. (in press) "Infants' Discrimination of Multisyllabic Stimuli: The Role of Temporal Factors.

Trehub, S.E., and Rabinovitch, M.S. (1972) "Auditory–Linguistic Sensitivity in Early Infancy," *Developmental Psychology*, 6, 74–77.

Williams, L. (1977) "The Effects of Phonetic Environment and Stress Placement on Infant Discrimination of the Place of Stop Consonant Articulation," Paper presented at the second annual Boston University Conference on Language Development.

Williams, L. and Bush, M. (1978) "The Discrimination by Young Infants of Voiced Stop Consonants With and Without Release Bursts," *Journal of the Acoustical Society of America*, 63, 1223–1225.

Chapter 4

PERCEPTUAL CONSTANCY FOR SPEECH-SOUND CATEGORIES IN EARLY INFANCY

PATRICIA K. KUHL

Introduction

The perception of an invariant characteristic, some relation that remains constant over many transformations, is a behavior normally associated with visual perception. Object perception, for example, depends upon the recognition of certain relations that remain constant despite the fact that the object, or the perceiver, moves about in space. Although the parallel has not always been drawn (Kuhl, 1976a, 1977, 1978; Shankweiler *et al.*, 1975), the lack of invariant perceptual cues for speech sounds is very similar. In both cases, the perceiver must recognize the stimulus relations that remain constant amidst transformations. This phenomenon in visual perception is often referred to as "perceptual constancy."

The term "constancy," as applied in the field of vision, has carried the connotation that the underlying relations perceived by the observer are not simple, directly measurable variables, but more abstract characteristics that remain constant over transformations. The term has typically been applied when a complex relationship between perceptual attributes and the underlying physical representation exists. In the case of speech-sound perception, we are very familiar with the problem of specifying the invariant relations for speech-sound categories (Liberman *et al.*, 1967). For example, although we know that vowel identity depends upon the locations of the formant

CHILD PHONOLOGY
VOLUME 2: PERCEPTION

frequencies and resulting spectral peaks, we cannot specify the precise relationship between formants that allows the adult listener to recognize the similarity between the same vowel produced by vocal tracts of different sizes (Fant, 1973).

In certain instances, the acoustic cues appear particularly disjunctive; the voicing distinction is cued by a set of different acoustic dimensions depending on its position in a syllable, and the acoustic cues in each instance are not related to one another in a simple, straightforward way (Klatt, 1975). Recent demonstrations (Miller and Liberman, 1979; Minifie et al., 1977; Port, 1976, 1977) show that rate of the syllabic context influences the perception of a phonetic unit within the syllable, thus suggesting the influence of remote context on the perception of phonetic units.

In borrowing the term perceptual constancy from the field of visual perception, we are simply stating that just as the perception of an object remains constant over transformations in rotation and distance from the observer, so the perception of a phone remains constant over transformations produced by particular syllabic contexts and talkers. The underlying assumption in vision is, of course, at least for shape and size constancy, that there is a "real" object out there; correspondingly, we must argue that there is some reality to the notion that a set of abstract prototypical acoustic cues can be specified for each phonetic entity, even though we have yet to do so.

Traditional descriptions of the kinds of behavior referred to here as perceptual constancy are to be found in psychology texts under the title of category formation (Bruner et al., 1956; see Burdick and Miller, 1975, for discussion). As these authors review, stimuli that are grouped into specific categories are considered to be "concepts" or "psychological categories." Bruner et al. (1956) describe two types of psychological categories: those in which category membership is *directly perceived*, and those in which category membership is *judged*, that is, attained by rote memory or by application of a rule. Burdick and Miller (1975), arguing that speech-sound categories are directly perceived without "mental gymnastics," suggested that speech-sound categories ought to be considered "auditory concepts."

These notions are particularly interesting from a developmental standpoint. Constancies or auditory concepts are defined by adult listeners, and adult listeners of varying linguistic backgrounds combine different phonetic units into categories. The existing data demonstrate that Japanese listeners, under certain perceptual-testing paradigms, perceive that /r/ and /l/ are similar, whereas English listeners perceive them differently (Miyawaki et al., 1975). We do not as yet understand the levels at which the perceptual change occurs, but it is clear that a change at some level occurs as a result of linguistic experience.

Bruner et al. (1956) note that judged concepts can become perceived concepts as learning occurs. In light of our descriptions of the disjunctive acoustic cues to phonetic categories, this notion may be particularly relevant for speech-sound categories. Stevens (1975), in fact, suggests that there is a set of "prototypical" acoustic cues that differentiate voiced stop consonants (/b, d, g/) and that these primary cues are optimized in certain contexts, such as when these stops occur in the initial position of syllables in the /a/ vowel context. He suggests that these cues be considered primary in that they occur in most contexts; however, there are also secondary acoustic cues that are more in evidence in certain phonetic contexts, such as in high front vowel contexts. Stevens (1975) hypothesized that infants learn to distinguish phonetic categories on the basis of primary cues and then, by association, learn that a set of secondary cues also occurs in certain instances. Is it necessary, then, for the infant to learn to recognize phonetic similarity by exposure to a large set of exemplars from the phonetic category before the infant directly perceives a set of prototypical dimensions that uniquely specify each category regardless of context, position, or talker?

The literature on the perception of speech by infants is not particularly helpful regarding the question of the perception of speech-sound constancies and their possible development. We do know that human infants, by 4 weeks of age, appear to possess sufficient auditory acuity to discriminate the sounds of human speech. This summary statement is based largely on data gathered using the high-amplitude-sucking technique (HAS) (Eimas et al., 1971) demonstrating that very young normal infants (4–16 weeks of age) are capable of discriminating the acoustic cues underlying speech-sound distinctions. That is, infants discriminate consonants that differ with respect to voicing (Eimas et al., 1971) and place of articulation (Eimas, 1974; Morse, 1972); they discriminate among fricatives (Eilers and Minifie, 1975) and liquids (Eimas, 1975). The tempo of spectral change, which, for the adult, is sufficient to cue a change in the manner of articulation from a plosive to a semivowel (Liberman et al., 1956), is also discriminable by the young infant (Hillenbrand et al., 1979). Some of these contrasts (/d/ versus /g/) have been tested in the medial and final positions of syllables (Jusczyk, 1977). Trehub (1973) demonstrated that infants discriminate spectrally dissimilar vowels (/a/ versus /i/; /i/ versus /u/); Swoboda et al. (1976) demonstrated that infants also discriminate spectrally similar vowels (/i/ versus /I/). The list of negative findings is relatively short. Other than for certain fricatives (Eilers and Minifie, 1975; Eilers et al., 1977) that are more difficult to discriminate even by adult listeners, and stimuli in which the discriminable contrast is embedded within the syllable (/atapa/ versus /ataba/; /mapa/ versus /pama/; Trehub, 1973), very few negative findings for speech-sound contrasts that are phonemic in English have been reported. In addition, no attempts to replicate any of these reported failures have been made (for recent review of infant data, see Kuhl, 1979a).

In addition to the fact that current findings demonstrate that infants possess sufficient auditory acuity for speech-sound discrimination, the data also reveal that young infants demonstrate interesting perceptual constraints when listening to speech sounds. Like their English-speaking elders, infants raised in English-speaking environments demonstrate a tendency to discriminate sounds from a computer-synthesized acoustic continuum in a discontinuous way; that is, they discriminate voiceless–unaspirated phones from voiceless–aspirated phones, but fail to give evidence of discriminating two voiceless–aspirated phones or two voiceless–unaspirated phones that are spaced an equal distance apart on the continuum. In other words, equal steps on the continuum are not perceptually equivalent for either the infant or the adult. This has been termed "categorical perception" (Studdert-Kennedy *et al.*, 1970). These perceptual constraints are not unique to the perception of a speech-sound continuum (Cutting and Rosner, 1974; Miller *et al.*, 1976; Pisoni, 1977); nor, to human listeners, if our current data (Kuhl, 1976b; Kuhl and Miller, 1975a, 1978) prove indicative of the general case, but a study of these perceptual phenomena allows comparison among species and provides a metric with which to observe the change produced by linguistic exposure.

However extensive the data on speech-sound perception by infants, we have little information concerning an infant's perception of phonetic similarity for phonemes that appear in different phonetic contexts, different positions in a syllable, or are spoken by different talkers. We might expect this kind of task to present quite a different set of problems to the infant than the typical "discrimination problem." Gibson (1969) describes perceptual constancy as involving at least two processes. First, a listener must discover and focus on the acoustic dimension relevant to the particular phonetic distinction. This may be relatively easy when the phonetic context and "talker" are held constant, such as in the typical experiments run on human infants in which a single token from each of two phonetic categories are to be discriminated (Eilers and Minifie, 1975; Eilers *et al.*, 1977; Eimas *et al.*, 1971; Eimas, 1974, 1975; Morse, 1972; Trehub, 1973), but when a variety of tokens representing a phonetic contrast are used, the critical cues vary, and the listener must abstract a cue that is common to the set. The discovery of a set of abstract configurational properties that typify a phonetic category may depend, then, upon exposure to a set of exemplars that differ with respect to phonetic context and to talker.

The second process related to the perception of constancy is a concomitant of the first. When the phonetic context and the talker are varied, acoustically prominent but phonemically irrelevant acoustic dimensions are introduced. If the infant recognizes that /di/ and /du/ are somehow similar, he or she must ignore the most prominant difference between them, that is, the vowel. Fundamental frequency and timbre differences between the voices of different talkers, and pitch contour, are other prominent characteristics that a listener must ignore because they do not provide critical information concerning phonetic identification. The literature on visual perception demonstrates that some aspects of these two processes are learned.

First, it is clear that infants become increasingly adept at focusing their attention on the critical aspects of a stimulus array. The study of eye movements directed at an unfamiliar design that must be remembered demonstrates that 3-year-olds keep their eyes fixed on a single spot longer, and do not systematically explore figures, whereas 6-year-olds orient to the distinctive features, employ brief and frequent gazes, and systematically explore the figure (Zinchenko et al., 1963). Vurpillot (1968) studied the eye movements of children between 5 and 9 in a same–different comparison task. The data supported the notion that skill in scanning systematically and sampling the relevant features increases with age.

Second, the implication that infants become increasingly selective in their visual attention carries with it the notion that infants become more adept at filtering out irrelevant information. Evidence from experiments on incidental learning support this notion. Gibson (1969) reported experiments run by herself and colleagues on form identification in 5-year-old preschoolers. The task was simply to learn the names of nine roman capital letters of the alphabet. When presented during the learning sessions, the letters were colored, three were red, three blue, and three yellow; these colors, of course, did not differentiate the letters uniquely, and served as an "irrelevant" dimension. After practice sessions, the children were asked to identify the same nine forms that were now colored black. In addition, they were tested for recall of the color of each of the forms. Gibson reported that the children remembered correctly as many or more colors than they did the names of the letters, even though color was an irrelevant dimension in this experiment. The experiment was repeated with 9-year-olds using artificial graphemes rather than letters. The task was identical. For these children, recall of names had improved slightly, but more importantly, color was recalled at a level no better than chance. Some children did not even remember what colors had been presented. In a related experiment, Maccoby and Hagen (1965) presented six picture cards, each with a distinctively colored background, to first- through seventh-graders. Subjects were instructed to remember the order of the colors presented. After repeated trials on color identification, the subjects were asked to recall the picture that had appeared on each one of the colors. The results demonstrated that recall on the main task increased steadily with age but that first- through fifth-graders recalled the correct picture significantly more often than seventh-graders, even though it was an irrelevant dimension.

In summary, then, Gibson (1969) concluded that there was evidence to suggest that the ability to seek the invariant information in a stimulus array is a developmental phenomenon. Both the tendency for greater efficiency at picking up the invariant information in a stimulus array, as well as the increasing tendency to filter out irrelevant information, contributes to this gradual approach to perceptual economy.

Two Early Studies

Only recently have researchers attempted to find out whether infants are capable of recognizing the similarity among sounds that have the same phonetic label when the sounds occur in different phonetic contexts, in different positions in a syllable, or when the sounds are spoken by different talkers. Fodor et al. (1975) examined the acquisition of a head-turn response for visual reinforcement in 14–18-week-old infants under two stimulus conditions. In both conditions, three syllables were randomly presented (/pi/, /ka/, /pu/) but only two of the three were reinforced. In one condition, the stimuli being reinforced were phonetically related (/pi/ and /pu/); in the other condition, the stimuli being reinforced were not phonetically related (/pi/ and /ka/). If infants tend to hear the similarity between two syllables that begin with the same consonant despite the differences in the acoustic cues for that consonant and despite the irrelevant differences between the two syllables that must be ignored, such as their vowels, their tendencies to learn the association ought to differ in the two conditions. The proportion of head turns when phonetically similar sounds were reinforced was significantly greater than the proportion of head turns when phonetically dissimilar sounds were reinforced.

These data demonstrated that infants grouped the syllables beginning with /p/ more readily than they grouped syllables that did not share a phonetic feature, but the data also demonstrated that neither task was accomplished very accurately. Two factors may have made the task inordinately difficult. First, observations in our own laboratory on audiometric testing of infants demonstrated that, until 5.5 months of age, a large percentage of infants do not make volitional head-turn responses for a visual reinforcer with ease. At 5.5 months, or older, infants make head-turn responses easily and about 90% of the infants are conditionable. Second, the task was very difficult; it involved a two-response differentiation. That is, a head turn either to the right or to the left, depending on the position of the loudspeaker from which the reinforced stimulus was presented, was required. Head-turn responses to unreinforced stimuli were not recorded.

Kuhl and Miller (1975b) began a systematic exploration of the infant's predispositions to form acoustic categories that were based on shared phonetic features. The perception of vowel categories seemed an appropriate place to begin. The earliest descriptions of the acoustic cues that govern vowel identity were relatively straightforward. Vowel perception is directly related to the location of formants on the frequency axis, and two or three formants are sufficient to synthesize the full complement of English vowels (Delattre et al., 1952). However, in natural speech, the vowel "nucleus" is coarticulated with one or more consonants, and, in rapid speech, a steady-state value is rarely achieved (Lindblom, 1963). In addition, the acoustic

properties of the vowel nucleus are influenced by the coarticulated consonants (House and Fairbanks, 1953; Stevens and House, 1963). Assuming a
constant vocal-tract length, the formant frequencies directly reflect the res-
onances created as the configuration of the vocal tract changes for different
vowels (Stevens and House, 1961). But most importantly, a dramatic variation in formant frequency occurs when the overall dimensions of the vocal
tract are changed. Thus, when the identical vowel is produced by a male,
a female, and a child, the formant frequencies are quite different (Peterson
and Barney, 1952). These changes in overall vocal-tract dimensions, such
as vocal-tract length, are not proportional (Fant, 1966) so that the resulting
formant frequencies are not related in a multiplicative way, such as in the
transposition of a melody (Ward, 1970). Fant (1973) has demonstrated that
the scale factor relating the formants produced by a male, a female, and a
child are not constant across vowels nor across formants within a particular
vowel. In other words, there is no constant relation between the formants
that can as yet be described as the invariant cue that allows the adult listener
to perceive the similarity among vowels spoken by different talkers.

These facts led a number of theorists to hypothesize that listeners perceive vowel identity by "calibrating" or "normalizing" each utterance, ref-
erencing it to a coordinate system based on that talker's extreme articulations (Gerstman, 1968; Joos, 1948; Lieberman, 1973). Experimental tests of
the notion that listeners require exposure to a talker's calibrating vowels to
correctly identify other vowels spoken by that talker have not been supported (Shankweiler et al., 1975). In fact, there is no evidence that the identification of vowels can be improved by presenting the calibrating vowels
prior to the target vowel (Verbrugge et al., 1974).

As a preliminary step toward testing perceptual constancy, Kuhl and
Miller (1975b, described in Kuhl, 1976a) asked whether 4–16-week-old infants could detect a change in a target dimension if an irrelevant dimension
was randomly varied throughout the experiment serving as a kind of distracting stimulus. The HAS paradigm was employed. A change in the target
dimension occurred at the "shift-point," whereas an irrelevant dimension
was randomly varied throughout both the pre- and postshift periods.

In one condition, the target dimension was a phonemic change in the
vowel and the irrelevant dimension was the pitch contour of the vowel; in
a second condition, the target dimension was the pitch contour of the vowel
and the irrelevant dimension was the vowel color. The choice of pitch contour as a distracting acoustic dimension was particularly appropriate given
that the literature is replete with suggestions that suprasegmental dimensions
such as pitch contour, loudness, and stress pattern are more salient than
segmental (phonetic) dimensions at this age (Crystal, 1973). The stimuli were
two /a/'s and two /i/'s synthesized such that one /a/ and one /i/ had identical
monotone pitch contours and one /a/ and one /i/ had identical rise–fall pitch
contours. Discrimination of vowel color and pitch contour targets were

tested *with* and *without* irrelevant variation in the second dimension. The data demonstrated that infants detect a vowel change regardless of the distraction posed by a random change in the pitch contour of the vowel. In contrast, infants detected a change in the pitch contour of a vowel when all other dimensions were held constant, but failed to respond to a pitch-contour change when the vowel color was randomly changed. In addition, infants responded for a significantly longer period of time before habituating (preshift) when the vowel color was constantly changing than when the pitch contour was constantly changing. Using these stimuli, then, it would appear that the vowel-color dimension captured the infant's attention more readily than pitch contour both when it was the target and when it served as the distractor. This research demonstrated the infant's ability to tolerate some degree of distraction and still make the discrimination, but it did not demonstrate the infant's ability to recognize the phonetic similarity among vowel tokens whose critical acoustic dimensions varied.

To extend these results to a situation in which the infant had to contend with variation in both the critical and noncritical dimensions of the signals, Kuhl (1979b) combined the use of a head-turn technique for visual reinforcement with an experimental format requiring the infant to recognize the similarity among tokens in a category.

The Head-Turn Technique and Its Application to Testing Category Formation

Many laboratories have attempted to develop a head-turn technique for use in speech-sound discrimination testing, but until recently no one had described a technique that had been extensively tested and found to work with a large number of infants. The technique was originally developed for assessing auditory thresholds by a team of clinical audiologists at the University of Washington in Seattle (Wilson *et al.*, 1976). Later, the technique was adapted by Eilers *et al.* (1977) to study speech-sound discrimination. In the Eilers *et al.* study, infants were trained to make a head turn whenever a speech sound, repeated once every second as a "background" stimulus, was changed to a "comparison" speech sound. A head turn that occurred during the presentation of the comparison stimulus was rewarded with the presentation of a visual stimulus, for example, a toy monkey that would clap cymbals when activated.

Two types of trials, change and control, were run. During a change trial, the stimulus was actually changed from one speech sound to another speech sound for the duration of the observation interval (typically 4–6 sec). During control trials, the sound was not changed. For both types of trials, the experimenter and the assistant reported whether or not a head turn had occurred during the specified observation interval. If both judges reported that a head turn had occurred on a change trial, the trial was scored as correct; if one or neither reported a head turn, an error was scored. During a control trial, if either judge reported a head turn, the trial was scored as an error; if neither reported a head turn, the trial was scored as correct. Eilers *et al.* (1977) accepted a criterion of at least five out of six correct responses in six consecutive trials, half of which were change trials and half of which were control trials, as evidence that the infant discriminated the background stimulus from the comparison stimulus.

The experimental-control suite is shown in Figure 4.1. The infant is held by a parent so that he or she faces an assistant. The assistant maintains the infant's attention at midline or directly in front of the assistant by manipulating a variety of silent toys. A loudspeaker is located at a 90° azimuth to the assistant; the visual reinforcer is placed directly in front of the loudspeaker. A toy animal is housed in a dark plexiglass box so that the animal is not visible until the lights mounted inside the box are illuminated. The experimenter is housed in an adjoining control room containing a tape deck and a logic device. The two speech sounds being tested are stored on two separate channels of the tape; the onsets of the sounds are synchronized on the two channels and, on each channel, the sound repeats once every 1–2 sec, depending on the specific experiment.

The basic technique has been improved in two ways since it was originally described (Eilers *et al.*, 1977). First, the logic device controlling the experiment is more sophisticated. In the most recent modification of the

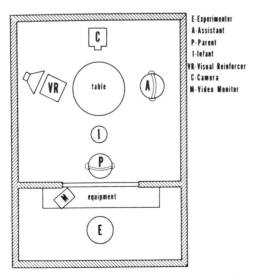

FIGURE 4.1 *Experimental–control suite layout for the head-turn studies; E, experimenter; A, assistant; P, parent; I, infant; VR, visual reinforcer; C, camera; M, video monitor.*

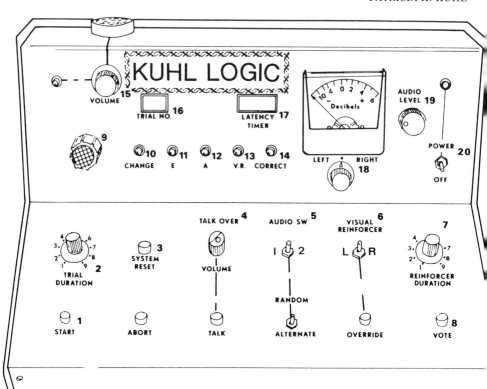

FIGURE 4.2 *Logic device designed and built at the University of Washington to control and time events during the perceptual constancy experiments. The two output channels of the tape recorder are fed to the logic device. A single output from the logic, either the Channel 1 or the Channel 2 signal, is fed to an amplifier. The numbers on the schematic refer to the following:*

    1. The start button actuates a trial for the duration specified.

    2. The trial duration can be varied from 1 to 9 sec.

    3. The system reset returns the signal to the "background" channel and clears the trial number, the latency timer, and all other events that may be recorded.

    4. The talkover system allows the experimenter to talk to the assistant. The experimenter depresses the "talk" button, which intercepts the music being delivered to the assistant's headset. The volume can also be adjusted.

    5. · The audio switch effects the change from Channel 1 (the background channel) to Channel 2 (the comparison channel). A number of options are available: if the upper switch is in the midposition and the bottom switch is in the up position (random), a probability generator set to .5 is activated, and the audio switch will change from Channel 1 to Channel 2 half of the time ("change" trials) and remain on Channel 1 for the remaining half of the trials. If the top switch is in the left position, the probability generator is bypassed and the audio switch will remain on Channel 1 throughout the trial. If the top switch is in the right position, the probability generator is bypassed and the audio switch will automatically change from Channel 1 to Channel 2 for the duration of the trial. The bottom switch can also be forced to the lower technique, Kuhl (1977) described a logic device (see Figure 4.2) containing a probability generator; the state of the probability generator determines whether a change or a control trial will be run. The experimenter begins a trial by depressing a "start" button and has no control over the type of trial that will be run; this ensures that the experimenter cannot inadvertently (or otherwise) start change trials when the infant is restless, or, conversely, start control trials when the infant is visually engaged by the toys. The logic device also times the trial interval, records both the experimenter's and the assistant's votes, scores the trial, activates the reinforcer when it is appropriate, records the latency of the infant's head-turn response, and prints all of the data for each trial. This automatic recording system allows one to assess the agreement between the two judges.

The second improvement in the technique consists of a number of added experimental controls, in addition to those necessitated by the change in the logic, which improve the validity of the technique. For example, Hillenbrand et al. (1977) and Kuhl (1977) reported that both the mother and the assistant wear headphones and listen to music throughout the session; it is adjusted to mask the stimulus change. Neither can differentially change their behavior during change or control trials. Mothers do not know when trials occur, and the assistant is informed that a trial is occurring by a small vibrating pin that is located on the "vote" button, which is held in the assistant's hand. These added controls achieve a situation in which both the mother and the assistant are "blind" and the experimenter does not know ahead of time what type of trial, change or control, will be run.

---

position to produce an alternation between Channel 1 and Channel 2. This latter option is not used at present.

6. The visual reinforcer system has the option of running two visual reinforcers, one to the left of the infant and one to the right of the infant, or, just operating a single reinforcer located to either the infant's right or left. In the present design, a single reinforcer at the infant's left is used. The override switch allows the manual activation of the reinforcer and is used during the "shaping" phase of the experiment.

7. The reinforcer duration can be varied from 1 to 9 sec.

8. The experimenter's vote button;

9. The talkover microphone;

10–14. The five LED lights, when lit, report that: it is a change trial, that the experimenter voted, that the assistant voted, that the visual reinforcer was activated, and that the trial was correct. At the end of each trial this information is printed.

15. The volume control which drives the vibrating pin on the assistant's vote button.

16. The trial number (also printed after each trial).

17. The latency timer (which times from the onset of the first audio signal after the start of a trial until both votes occur or until the trial is complete). The latency (to .1 sec) is also printed after each trial;

18. A decibel meter, which monitors either the left channel, the right channel, or the output of the logic device regardless of the channel.

19. The volume control for the output of the logic device;

20. The power switch.

The technique has been successfully employed with infants as young as 5.5 months (Wilson *et al.*, 1976) and as old as 18 months of age (Eilers *et al.*, 1977). It is ideally suited to infants in the 5.5–10-month age range. Beyond this age, infants tend to be increasingly restless, and they become "object-permanence" wise; that is, the 10-month-old appears to realize that the monkey is still in the box, even if the lights are out and it cannot be seen, causing the infant to want to peer in the box. For a 6-month-old, "out of sight, out of mind" appears to hold.

Recently, Kuhl (1977, 1979b) adapted the basic technique just described to test auditory category formation in infants. In this adaptation of the technique, Kuhl systematically increased the number of tokens in both the background and the comparison categories in a progressive experiment, requiring that the infant achieve 90% correct (9 out of 10 consecutive trials) at each stage in the experiment before advancing to the next stage. To the extent that the infant's learned responses to single tokens from a phonetic category generalized to novel tokens from the same phonetic categories, one could conclude that the infant recognized the similarity among speech tokens sharing a common phonetic feature despite the many ways in which the tokens differed acoustically.

Table 4.1 describes the stimuli in the background category and in the comparison category for each of five stages in one of the category-formation experiments (Kuhl, 1977). In each category, the number of vowels was increased until the two ensembles included six different tokens spoken by

TABLE 4.1

The Stimulus Ensembles for the Background and Comparison Categories for all Five Stages of the Vowel Constancy Experiment[a]

	Experimental conditions			
	Background		Comparison	
Initial training	/a/	(Male, fall)	/ɔ/	(Male, fall)
Pitch variation	/a/	(Male, fall)	/ɔ/	(Male, fall)
	/a/	(Male, rise)	/ɔ/	(Male, rise)
Talker variation	/a/	(Male, fall)	/ɔ/	(Male, fall)
	/a/	(Female, fall)	/ɔ/	(Female, fall)
Talker × pitch variation	/a/	(Male, fall)	/ɔ/	(Male, fall)
	/a/	(Male, rise)	/ɔ/	(Male, rise)
	/a/	(Female, fall)	/ɔ/	(Female, fall)
	/a/	(Female, rise)	/ɔ/	(Female, rise)
Generalization	/a/	(Male, fall)	/ɔ/	(Male, fall)
	/a/	(Male, rise)	/ɔ/	(Male, rise)
	/a/	(Female, fall)	/ɔ/	(Female, fall)
	/a/	(Female, rise)	/ɔ/	(Female, rise)
	/a/	(Child, fall)	/ɔ/	(Child, fall)
	/a/	(Child, rise)	/ɔ/	(Child, rise)

[a] From Kuhl (1977).

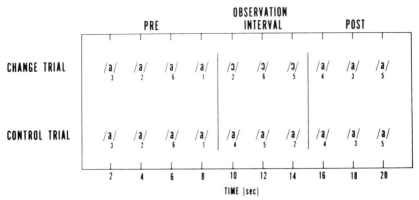

FIGURE 4.3 *An example of the stimulus-presentation format before, during, and after "change" and "control" trials. Prior to and after both kinds of trials, and during the "control" trials, the stimuli in the background category are randomly presented. During a change trial, however, the stimuli in the comparison category are presented. The subscripts (1–6) refer to the six different tokens of /a/ and ɔ/ that are randomly presented in the final stage of testing. The stimulus onsets are separated by a 2-sec interval.*

three different talkers (male, female, and child) each with two different pitch contours (rise and rise–fall). In the initial training stage of the experiment (Stage 1), each of the two categories was represented by a single token, matched in every detail except for the critical cues that differentiate the two categories. In Stage 2, the pitch contour of the vowels in both categories was randomly changed from rise to rise–fall. The pitch contour variation stage was included for two reasons: first, this stage could provide the infant with a cognitive set regarding the rules of this experimental "game." That is, category formation requires a certain "mental set;" the infant has to recognize that he or she is to group stimuli together based on their similarities, even though the stimuli differ in acoustically prominent ways. The pitch-contour variation ought to provide this mental set and also serve as proof that the infant is capable of auditory category formation, so that a failure to generalize to new talkers could not be attributed to an inability to form auditory categories.

In Stage 3, the talker producing the vowels was randomly varied between the male voice and the female voice. In Stage 4, both talkers produced the vowels with a randomly changing pitch contour. In the final stage (Stage 5), the child's tokens (computer-synthesized), also with pitch-contour variations, were added to the ensemble, bringing the total number of tokens in each category to six (three talkers × two pitch contours).

The criterion for progressing from one stage of the experiment to the next was 9 out of 10 consecutive trials correct, 5 of which were change trials and 5 of which were control trials. No more than 3 trials of one kind (either change or control) were allowed to occur consecutively. Typically, 25 trials were run each day in a 20-min session. However, in this case, sessions were always terminated when an infant began to fuss or not attend to the assistant's toys; if an infant was doing well, the session was extended. Infants were tested on consecutive days whenever that was possible.

Figure 4.3 demonstrates the stimulus arrangements for change and control trials. During change trials, the stimulus category changes from /a/ vowels (the six vowels are randomly repeated) to /ɔ/ vowels (again, the six vowels are randomly repeated) for the duration of the observation interval (6 sec). During control trials, the /a/ vowels continue to be repeated randomly.

The Data Obtained in Category-Formation Experiments

General Considerations

The studies completed to date have involved category-formation tasks based on vowel and fricative identity. Studies in which the categories are based on a suprasegmental dimension such as pitch contour or stress, and ones in which the contrastive categories involve the stop consonants /d/ and /g/ are in progress.

In all of these studies, the infants range in age from 5.5 to 6.5 months. Subjects are obtained by mail solicitation and parents are questioned about familial histories of hearing loss and/or treatment for ear infections so that infants who are "at risk" for hearing loss can be eliminated. Subjects are typically paid $5 per visit.

In these studies, the infant's performance is measured in terms of the number of trials until a criterion is met. The criterion has been 9 out of 10 consecutive trials correct (in the vowel studies) or 8 out of 10 consecutive trials correct (in the fricative studies), where half of the trials are control trials and half of the trials are change trials. The ease with which the transfer to new exemplars from the category occurs indicates the degree to which the infant perceives the similarity among the tokens from a given category. "Ease of transfer" in this instance includes the number of trials necessary to meet criterion as well as the response latency when new tokens are introduced. Let us first review the vowel data.

Vowel Experiments

The number of shaping trials and the number of trials to criterion for each of the five stages of the experiment are shown in Table 4.2 for each of four subjects in both the /a/–/i/ (Kuhl, 1979b) and the /a/–/ɔ/ (Kuhl, 1977) experiments. The testing session in which the criterion was met is shown in parentheses.

TABLE 4.2

Trials to Criterion for each Condition of the Experiment in the /a-i/ and /a-ɔ/ Category-Formation Experiments

	/a/ versus /i/				
Condition	S_1	S_2	S_3	S_4	$\bar{X}$
Shaping	12(1)	13(1)	5(1)	9(1)	9.75
Initial training	23(2)	14(1)	32(2)	13(1)	20.5
Pitch	11(2)	11(2)	10(2)	15(1)	11.75
Talker	10(3)	10(2)	10(2)	14(2)	11.0
Talker × pitch	10(4)	29(3)	10(3)	18(2)	16.75
Generalization	10(4)	29(4)	22(4)	19(3)	20.0
Total trials to complete Total days to complete	76(4)	106(4)	89(4)	88(3)	89.75(3.75)

	/a/ versus /ɔ/				
Condition	S_1	S_2	S_3	S_4	$\bar{X}$
Shaping	3(1)	3(1)	5(1)	22(1)	8.25
Initial training	28(2)	103(4)	41(2)	28(2)	50.00
Pitch	20(3)	26(5)	18(3)	45(4)	27.25
Talker	16(3)	10(5)	13(3)	16(4)	13.75
Talker × pitch	15(4)	43(6)	15(4)	23(5)	24.00
Generalization	11(4)	16(7)	24(5)	41(6)	23.00
Total trials to complete Total days to complete	96(4)	204(7)	116(5)	175(6)	147.75(5.5)

The data demonstrate that fairly rapid acquisition of the head-turning response occurs; all eight of the subjects produced three consecutive anticipatory head-turn responses within the first 22 trials during the first session. Two of the eight infants went on to meet the criterion (9 out of 10 consecutive correct responses) for passing the initial training stage of the experiment on the first day of testing; most of the other infants passed initial training on the second day of testing.

It took between three and seven sessions to complete the experiment, and the total number of trials to completion ranged from 76 to 204. The criterion (9 out of 10 consecutive correct responses) mandated a minimum of 50 trials to complete the experiment.

Comparisons of the data obtained in the two experiments suggest, as one might expect, that the /a/–/ɔ/ task was a more difficult one than the /a/–/i/ task. The formant structure for /a/ is very different than that for /i/; the formants are closely spaced or compact for the former and widely spaced or diffuse for the latter. However, the vowel structures of /a/ and /ɔ/ are very similar; in fact, in Peterson and Barney's (1952) data, the absolute frequencies of certain /a/ vowels fall within the /ɔ/ vowel space. In most dialects of American English, the /a/–/ɔ/ distinction is not a phonemic one.

Comparisons reveal that the mean number of trials to criterion during initial training was larger for the /a/– /ɔ/ discrimination than it was for the /a/–/i/ discrimination. The trials-to-criterion measure revealed slightly higher values for this contrast throughout the experiment. For example, no infant met the initial training criteria for /a/–/ɔ/ on the first day of testing, and one subject did not meet criterion until the fourth day of testing. The total number of sessions to completion of the experiment ranged from four to seven sessions for /a/–/ɔ/ versus a range from three to four sessions for /a/–/i/. The mean number of trials to complete the experiment also reflected a greater difficulty for the /a/–/ɔ/ contrast.

The investigation of consonant-based categories like the differentiation of voiced stop categories across vowel context and across position in a syllable should prove to be the most germane from a theoretical standpoint. The acoustic descriptions of these categories have been problematic (although see descriptions by Blumstein and Stevens, 1979), and experiments on the adaptation effect (see Cooper, 1975 for a review) show vowel-contingent effects (Cooper, 1974; Miller and Eimas, 1975) and no adaptation effects when the adapting and test stimuli do not share the same position in the syllable (Ades, 1974).

Experiments on category formation for consonant-based categories has begun with the fricative categories. An easy contrast (/s/–/ʃ/) as well as a difficult contrast (/f/–/θ/) have been investigated in both the initial and final positions of syllables (Holmberg et al., 1977) in two M. A. theses. The five conditions in one of the fricative experiments are illustrated in Table 4.3. One might expect that consonant categories would be more difficult to recognize than the steady-state vowel categories because the infant must ignore prominent differences in the syllables, such as the differences between the vowels. These differences are acoustically prominent but irrelevant to the target distinction being examined.

The number of trials necessary to meet criterion for the six infants tested on the fricatives in the initial position are listed in the top half of Table 4.4. The criterion was 8 out of 10 successive trials correct where 5 of the trials were change trials and 5 of the trials were control trials. There are three noteworthy characteristics of these data. First, the data are more variable, particularly for the /f/–/θ/ contrast, than those obtained previously with the vowel contrasts. Second, the /f/–/θ/ contrast appeared to be more difficult than the /s/–/ʃ/ contrast in that it took more trials, on the average, to pass the initial training phase of the experiment. Third, there was no systematic increase in the number of trials to criterion as the experiment progressed from a single token in initial training to 12 tokens per category in the generalization conditions.

The data for infants tested on the fricatives in the final position are listed in the bottom half of Table 4.4. Here again, the data demonstrate greater average difficulty during the initial training phase of the experiment for the

TABLE 4.3

The Stimulus Ensembles for the Background and Comparison Categories for All Five Stages of the Fricative Constancy Experiment[a]

	Background		Comparison	
Initial training	sa	(Talker 1, token 1)	sha	(Talker 1, token 1)
Token variation	sa	(Talker 1, token 1)	sha	(Talker 1, token 1)
	sa	(Talker 1, token 2)	sha	(Talker 1, token 2)
	sa	(Talker 1, token 3)	sha	(Talker 1, token 3)
	sa	(Talker 1, token 4)	sha	(Talker 1, token 4)
Vowel variation	sa	(Talker 1)	sha	(Talker 1)
	si	(Talker 1)	shi	(Talker 1)
	su	(Talker 1)	shu	(Talker 1)
Talker variation	sa	(Talker 1)	sha	(Talker 1)
	sa	(Talker 2)	sha	(Talker 2)
	sa	(Talker 3)	sha	(Talker 3)
	sa	(Talker 4)	sha	(Talker 4)
Generalization	sa	(Talker 1)	sha	(Talker 1)
	si	(Talker 1)	shi	(Talker 1)
	su	(Talker 1)	shu	(Talker 1)
	sa	(Talker 2)	sha	(Talker 2)
	si	(Talker 2)	shi	(Talker 2)
	su	(Talker 2)	shu	(Talker 2)
	sa	(Talker 3)	sha	(Talker 3)
	si	(Talker 3)	shi	(Talker 3)
	su	(Talker 3)	shu	(Talker 3)
	sa	(Talker 4)	sha	(Talker 4)
	si	(Talker 4)	shi	(Talker 4)
	su	(Talker 4)	shu	(Talker 4)

[a] From Holmberg *et al.* (1977).

/f/–/Θ/ contrast. They also illustrate the variability of the infants; one of the infants tested on the /s/–/ʃ/ contrast was extremely variable. Our impressions were that she could do the task perfectly well, and her data, both in initial training and in vowel variation, bear that out, but tended to get bored in the task after short periods of testing, after which she would simply "refuse to play."

One other interesting analysis is made possible by the use of the new logic device. The latency of response, recorded from the onset of the first syllable occurring within the observation interval to the moment when both the experimenter's and the assistant's votes are detected by the logic, can be reported for trials occurring in each stage of the experiment. Figure 4.4 plots the average latency data for the correct change trials in the five conditions of the experiment for each of the fricative contrasts. Note first, that the latency of response (3 sec) indicates that the head turn is recorded just after the onset of the second syllable, indicating that the infant begins to turn just after the first stimulus presentation. Second, note that even though the number of exemplars increased dramatically over conditions as the ex-

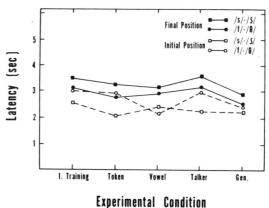

Experimental Condition

FIGURE 4.4 *The average latency of response for correct change trials during each condition of the experiment for infants in the initial /f/–/Θ/, final /f/–/Θ/, initial /s/–/ʃ/, and final /s/–/ʃ/ groups. The latencies indicate that infants made the head-turn response during the second stimulus presentation.*

TABLE 4.4

Trials to Criterion for Each Subject in Each Condition of the /s–ʃ/ and /f–Θ/ Category-formation Experiments

		Initial position						
		s–ʃ					f–Θ			
	S_1	S_2	S_3	$\bar{X}$	S_1	S_2	S_3	$\bar{X}$
Shaping	8(1)	6(1)	14(1)	9.33	6(1)	19(2)	6(1)	10.33
Initial trial	37(1)	16(1)	66(3)	39.66	59(4)	66(4)	48(2)	58.00
Token variation	17(2)	41(3)	17(4)	25.00	26(4)	46(6)	81(4)	51.00
Vowel variation	20(2)	15(3)	55(6)	30.00	19(6)	11(6)	64(6)	31.00
Talker variation	24(2)	30(5)	38(7)	30.66	15(7)	36(9)	38(7)	30.00
Generalization	31(3)	14(5)	53(9)	32.66	17(8)	97(11)	79(9)	64.00
Total trials	129(3)	116(5)	229(9)	157.98	136(8)	256(11)	310(9)	234.00

		Final position						
		s/ʃ					f/Θ			
	S_1	S_2	S_3	$\bar{X}$	S_1	S_2	S_3	$\bar{X}$
Shaping	6(1)	6(1)	3(1)	5	10(1)	5(1)	3(1)	6
Initial trial	20(1)	28(2)	18(1)	22	120(4)	62(2)	52(2)	78
Token variation	28(2)	110(6)	10(1)	49	18(5)	13(2)	19(3)	17
Vowel variation	11(3)	13(6)	15(1)	13	57(7)	19(3)	43(4)	40
Talker variation	10(3)	63(8)	14(2)	29	45(8)	17(3)	27(5)	30
Generalization	16(4)	110(9)	25(3)	50	33(9)	58(4)	56(6)	49
Total Trials	91(4)	330(9)	85(3)	169	283(9)	174(4)	200(6)	219

periment progressed, and the task presumably required a more abstract definition of the target dimension, the latency of response did not increase. This would provide support for the notion that each token in the ensemble attains functional equivalence for the infant, and refutes the notion that the infant "waits" for the training token before responding. Third, note that the average latency for the initial-position contrasts was faster than that for the final-position contrasts.

Comparisons between Category Formation for Vowels and Category Formation for Consonants

To the extent that the data demonstrate rapid transfer-of-learning to the novel tokens of a category, and to the extent that one can rule out alternative hypotheses, one can accept the data as providing a strong suggestion that the infant recognized a similarity between the novel tokens of a category and the training tokens. The data do, in fact, demonstrate that infants are capable of forming categories that correspond to the perceptual categories defined by adult listeners of English. Let us examine closely the possible strategies involved in accomplishing this task.

To succeed at this task, the infant must learn (or perceive) the membership of at least one of the two categories. That is, the infant can either learn the set of stimuli that predict the appearance of the monkey, or learn the set of stimuli that do not predict the monkey's appearance. Recognizing either category, or both categories, would result in correct responses.

The difficulty of any given category-formation task of this kind is related to three factors. First, the task can be made more difficult by increasing the degree of variability for the critical, or target dimension. When the target dimension is vowel color, for example, the critical dimension relates to the formant frequencies. Depending on the degree to which the formant frequencies of the tokens actually do vary, the task could presumably be made more or less difficult. Second, the difficulty in the task relates to the acoustic variables that are not critical to the assignment of a token to its proper category, but, nonetheless, are acoustically prominent in the signal. In this case, acoustic dimensions like fundamental frequency, quality differences in the voices of the talkers, pitch contour, and, in the case of the consonant categories, the vowel context, are irrelevant dimensions with regard to the discrimination. But these dimensions may make it difficult for the infant to recognize the similarity among members of the category due to the potentially distracting qualities of these nontarget dimensions. The literature on the development of visual perception demonstrates that the ability to filter out irrelevant visual dimensions increases with age (Gibson, 1969). Third, the relative difficulty of the task relates to the perceptual distance between the two categories. The closer the two categories lie in perceptual space, the more difficult it should be to form categories based on the target dimension.

It is difficult, then, to directly compare the results in the vowel experiments to those obtained in the fricative experiments. First, it is impossible to equate the tasks on the degree to which the nontarget dimensions distracted the infant. In the vowel experiments, the distractors were the timbre differences in the voices and the pitch-contour variations. In the fricative experiments, the distractors were again the timbre differences in the voices, but this time the voices were those of real talkers (two male and two female) rather than computer-simulated voices, and, to my ear, this makes them much more distracting. Another potent distractor in the fricative experiments was the variation in vowel context. The vowel is longer in duration and more intense than the fricative, so that it is potentially a very noticeable and potentially distracting acoustic event. Second, the number of tokens in the vowel ensembles was much smaller than the number of tokens in the fricative ensembles, 6 tokens per vowel category and 12 tokens per fricative category. A third factor making it difficult to directly compare the vowel and fricative data is the fact that the criterion was changed, though, one might argue, in a direction that attempted to compensate for the more difficult consonantal contrasts. A 9 out of 10 criterion was required in the vowel studies, whereas an 8 out of 10 criterion was required in the fricative studies. I will add, however, that in the fricative studies we calculated the number of trials to criterion using five different criteria (5 out of 6; 6 out of 8; 7 out of 10; 8 out of 10; 9 out of 10) and, with few exceptions, the data were essentially unchanged.

Despite these aforementioned objections to a direct comparison, Figure 4.5 makes global comparisons with fairly predictable outcomes. Measures

	Trials to Meet Shaping Criterion		Trials to Pass Initial Training		Total Trials		Number of Days to Complete	
	X̄	Mdn.	X̄	Mdn.	X̄	Mdn.	X̄	Mdn.
/a/ vs. /i/	9.8	10.5	20.5	18.5	89.8	88.5	3.8	3.8
/a/ vs. /ɔ/	8.3	4.0	50.0	34.5	146.3	145.5	5.5	5.5
/s/ vs. /ʃ/	7.2	6.2	30.8	24.0	168.2	129.5	5.5	4.5
/f/ vs. /θ/	8.2	6.0	68.0	60.5	231.7	237.5	7.8	8.5

FIGURE 4.5 *Performance comparisons on four selected measures for the four groups of subjects tested on the /a/–/i/, /a/–/ɔ/, /s/–/ʃ/, and /f/–/θ/ contrasts. Three of the four variables, trials to pass initial training, total trials to complete the experiment, and the number of days to complete the experiment, suggest the following ranking: the /a/–/i/ contrast is easiest, the /f/–/θ/ contrast is the most difficult, and the /a/–/ɔ/ and /s/–/ʃ/ are of intermediate difficulty. The fourth variable, the number of trials to meet shaping criterion, demonstrated no systematic trends. See text for discussion.*

such as the average number of trials to meet criterion in the initial phase of the experiment when only two tokens were being discriminated, the total number of trials to complete the five stages of the experiment, and the total number of days the infant was tested in the experiment, allow one to rank the contrasts according to their relative difficulty. Using these metrics, one would rank the /a/–/i/ task as the easiest, the /f/–/Θ/ as the most difficult, and the /a/–/ɔ/ and /s/–/ʃ/ as intermediate in difficulty.

Using these descriptions of task difficulty, one can attribute the greater difficulty in the /a/–/ɔ/ task, when compared to the /a/–/i/ task, to the third factor, that is, to the perceptual distance between the two categories. Similarly, one can attribute the greater difficulty in the /f/–/Θ/ task, when compared to the /s/–/ʃ/ task, to the same perceptual distance factor. Comparing either of the vowel tasks to the fricative tasks, however, does not allow one to attribute the relative difficulty to any single factor of the three as the vowel and fricative tasks were not well matched on the other two factors.

Current Experiments

We are currently running experiments on the formation of categories involving the stop consonants /d/ and /g/. The experiment embodies three major changes in the way these experiments are run. First, two groups of infants are run; one group is presented with the task of learning to form categories that are based on a phonetic distinction, in this case, the /d/–/g/, distinction regardless of the vowel context in which it appears and its position in the syllable. The other group of infants is run in a category-formation task in which the categories are not based on a phonetic distinction but are formed by randomly assigning each of the 24 individual stimuli to one of two categories. This format allows statistical comparisons of the two groups of infants and adds the potential for learning how infants cope with the task of learning disjunctive auditory categories.

Second, the criterion for progressing through the experiment still involves passing the 8 out of 10 criterion, but infants are tested for a maximum of 15 trials in each condition, and then go on to the next stage whether or not they passed the previous stage. This ensures that most infants will complete the experiment before the reinforcer loses its effectiveness.

Third, the final stage in these experiments is manipulated in such a way that the infant is presented with a single stimulus, repeated three times, during the observation interval of either a change or a control trial (in Figure 4.3, for example, each stimulus would be repeated three times so that during the observation interval of the change trial, the /ɔ₂/ stimulus would be repeated three times). This means, of course, that the infant bases the response on a single stimulus (See Kuhl, 1979b for an example of the resulting data).

Although the data are not all in, one infant responded correctly on 42 out of 46 consecutive trials in the /d/–/g/ identification task, labeling the category /d/ (by making a head turn) regardless of its vowel context (/i, a, u/) or its position in a syllable (/da, ada, ad/) or any combination of vowel context and position.

Discussion

General Comments

These results on the perception of constancy by young normal infants demonstrate their capability to recognize the abstract dimensions of sound in a task that has considerable "cognitive load." To complete the task, the infant must be capable of abstracting a similarity between phonetic units even though the acoustic components of the exemplars are not identical. In addition to abstracting this similarity, the infant must ignore very prominent, but irrelevant, dimensions such as pitch contour, talkers, and vowel context, as well as constantly monitor the signal and recall the rules of the game (something like, "turn to see the monkey when the sound changes from /a/ to /i/, no matter who says it or how it is said)."

The advantages of this testing format are obvious. Since the multidimensional stimulus sets can be grouped according to a number of dimensions, including segmental (vowel color, for example) as well as suprasegmental (intonation contour, for example) features, one can test the relative ease or efficiency an infant displays at forming acoustic categories based on these dimensions, thereby assessing their relative acoustic salience, and determining whether an infant's auditory proclivities to form categories changes with maturation and/or exposure to a particular language.

Mechanisms–Underlying Processes

Given that the infant demonstrates the ability to recognize certain similarities among members of a stimulus set that share phonetic features, to what do we attribute this expertise? Is the infant recognizing complex configurations, or are we tapping some simple sensitivities that do not require complex explanation?

The question is a familiar one to ethologists studying animal behavior, particularly animal communication, and I think we have something to learn by examining the hypotheses they have generated to account for certain behaviors. An example from animal behavior can be used to illustrate the point. Hailman (1969) has recently reexamined the innateness issue using one of the classic "sign stimuli" originally identified by Tinbergen (1951).

His set of careful experiments suggests a reinterpretation of this supposedly unlearned "instinctual" behavior. The behavioral routine is the feeding behavior of newly hatched herring-gull chicks. Newly hatched chicks peck at the parent's bill to beg for food. Tinbergen identified the critical features of the mother's head by using models and examining an infant's proclivity to peck at them. The red spot on the mother's bill, as well as the shape, orientation, and movement of the bill, proved to be critical features. Tinbergen emphasized the highly configurational aspects of the infant's perception, largely because models in which the red spot was moved to the forehead received very few pecks. Hailman replicated these experiments correcting for the distance the chick had to reach to peck the spot on the forehead, and the extent of the arc through which the spot traveled when it was on the forehead, as opposed to when the head was moved in a pendulum manner. This new forehead-spot model was equally effective in eliciting pecks from the newborns. In another experiment, Hailman examined the pecking responses of newly hatched laughing-gull chicks to the herring-gull models, and found that these infants did not differentiate between models of their real parents and those of the other species. This is interesting because the parents of the two species differ markedly, except for the presence of a prominent red area on each parent's head. The laughing gull has a black head with a red bill; the herring gull has a white head and yellow bill with a red spot on the lower mandible. Hailman interpreted both of the studies to indicate that the infant is innately predisposed to respond to relatively simple stimulus features, and only with experience does the infant develop a schema of the configurational properties of his parent's head. His experiments bear out these suggestions. By examining the infant's proclivities after three and seven days in the nest, he showed that the infant's pecking became increasingly more selective. By one week of age, both species preferred to peck the models that best exemplified their conspecies. The herring-gull chicks preferred the bill-spot model to either Tinbergen's or Hailman's forehead-spot model. In other words, the red spot provided a fairly simple guideline for responding, and only after experience did the infant's response depend upon more configurational properties of the stimulus.

With regard to the infant's innate predispositions toward recognizing speech-sound categories, we simply must reserve judgment. We are accumulating data at a rapid rate, but until we have tested a fair number of speech-sound categories in a constancy format, it is difficult to say how configurational the infant's responses really are, and impossible to attribute their precise nature and origins to special mechanisms. In other words, I think ethology's trend toward conservative interpretation is a good one. It reminds us to restrict our interpretations to the simplest possible mechanisms that will suffice to explain the data we now have in hand. In the interim, we can appease ourselves by realizing that the data we are now collecting should prove germane.

References

Ades, A.E. (1974) "How Phonetic is Selective Adaptation? Experiments on Syllable Position and Vowel Environment," *Perception & Psychophysics*, 16, 61–67.

Blumstein, S.E., and Stevens, K.N. (1979) "Acoustic Invariance in Speech Production: Evidence from Measurements of the Spectral Characteristics of Stop Consonants," *Journal of the Acoustical Society of America*, 66, 1001–1017.

Bruner, J.S., Goodnow, J.J., and Austin, G.A. (1956) *A Study of Thinking*, Wiley, New York.

Burdick, C.K., and Miller, J.D. (1975) "Speech Perception by the Chinchilla: Discrimination of Sustained /a/ and /i/, *Journal of the Acoustical Society of America*, 58, 415–427.

Cooper, W.E. (1974) "Contingent Feature Analysis in Speech Perception," *Perception & Psychophysics*, 16, 201–204.

Cooper, W.E. (1975) "Selective Adaptation to Speech," in F. Restle, R.M. Shiffrin, N.J. Castellan, H.R. Lindman, and D.B. Pisoni, eds., *Cognitive Theory: (Vol. 1)*, Erlbaum, Hillsdale, N.J.

Crystal, D. (1973) "Non-segmental Phonology in Language Acquisition: A Review of the Issues," *Lingua* 32, 1–45.

Cutting, J.E. and Rosner, B.S. (1974) "Categories and Boundaries in Speech and Music," *Perception & Psychophysics*, 16, 564–570.

Delattre, P.C., Liberman, A.M., Cooper, F.S., and Gerstman, L.J. (1952) "An Experimental Study of the Acoustic Determinants of Vowel Color: Observations on One- and Two-formant Vowels Synthesized from Spectrographic Patterns. *Word*, 8, 195–210.

Eilers, R.E. and Minifie, F.D. (1975) "Fricative Discrimination in Early Infancy," *Journal of Speech and Hearing Research*, 18, 158–167.

Eilers, R.E., Wilson, W.R., and Moore, J.M. (1977) "Developmental Changes in Speech Discrimination in Infants, *Journal of Speech and Hearing Research*, 20, 766–780.

Eimas, P.D. (1974) "Auditory and Linguistic Processing of Cues for Place of Articulation by Infants," *Perception & Psychophysics*, 16, 513–521.

Eimas, P.D. (1975) "Auditory and Phonetic Coding of the Cues for Speech: Discrimination of the [r–l] Distinction by Young Infants," *Perception & Psychophysics*, 18, 341–347.

Eimas, P.D., Siqueland, E.R., Jusczyk, P., and Vigorito, J. (1971) "Speech Perception in Infants," *Science*, 171, 303–306.

Fant, C.G.M. (1966) "A Note on Vocal-tract Size Factors and Nonuniform F-pattern Scalings, *Quarterly Progress and Status Report*, Speech Transmission Laboratory, Royal Institute of Technology, Stockholm, Sweden, *QPSR-4*, 22–30.

Fant, G. (1973) *Speech Sounds and Features*, MIT Press, Cambridge.

Fodor, J.A., Garrett, M.F., and Brill, S.L. (1975) "Pi Ka Pu. The Perception of Speech Sounds by Pre-linguistic Infants," *Perception & Psychophysics*, 18, 74–78.

Gerstman, L.H. (1968) "Classification of Self-normalized Vowels," *IEEE Transactions in Audio Electroacoustics*, AU-16, 78–80.

Gibson, E. (1969) *Principles of Perceptual Development*, Appleton-Century-Crofts, New York.

Hailman, J.P. (1969) "How an Instinct is Learned," *Scientific American*, 221, 98–106.

House, A.S., and Fairbanks, G. (1953) "The Influence of Consonant Environment upon the Secondary Acoustical Characteristics of Vowels," *Journal of the Acoustical Society of America*, 25, 105–113.

Hillenbrand, J., Minifie, F.D., and Edwards, T.J. (1979) "Tempo of Spectrum Change as a Cue in Speech–Sound Discrimination by Infants," *Journal of Speech and Hearing Research*, 22, 147–165.

Holmberg, T.L., Morgan, K.A., and Kuhl, P.K. (1977) "Speech Perception in Early Infancy: Discrimination of Fricative Consonants," *Journal of the Acoustical Society of America*, 62, Supplement 1, S99(A).

Joos, M.A. (1948) "Acoustic Phonetics," *Language*, 24, 1–136.

Jusczyk, P.W. (1977) "Perception of Syllable-final Stop Consonants by Two-month-old Infants," *Perception & Psychophysics*, 21, 450–454.

Klatt, D.H. (1975) "Voice Onset Time, Frication, and Aspiration in Word–Initial Consonant Clusters," *Journal of Speech and Hearing Research*, 18, 686–706.

Kuhl, P.K. (1976) "Speech Perception in Early Infancy: The Acquisition of Speech-sound Categories," in S.K. Hirsh, D.H. Eldredge, I.J. Hirsh, and S.R. Silverman, eds., *Hearing and Davis: Essays Honoring Hallowell Davis*, Washington University Press, St. Louis, pp. 265–280. (a)

Kuhl, P.K. (1976) "Speech Perception by the Chinchilla: Categorical Perception of Synthetic Alveolar Plosive Consonants," *Journal of the Acoustical Society of America*, 60, Supplement 1, S81(A). (b)

Kuhl, P.K. (1977) "Speech Perception in Early Infancy: Perceptual Constancy for Vowel Categories /a/ and /ɔ/, *Journal of the Acoustical Society of America*, 61, Supplement 1, S39(A).

Kuhl, P.K. (1978) "Perceptual Predispositions for the Acquisition of Speech-sound Categories: A Comparison of Human Infants and Animals," in R.L. Schiefelbusch and L.L. Lloyd, eds., *Communicative and Cognitive Abilities—Early Behavioral Assessment*, University Park Press, Baltimore.

Kuhl, P.K. (1979a) "The Perception of Speech in Early Infancy," in N.J. Lass, ed., *Speech and Language: Advances in Basic Research and Practice*, Academic Press, New York, pp. 1–47.

Kuhl, P.K. (1979b) "Speech Perception in Early Infancy: Perceptual Constancy for Spectrally Dissimilar Vowel Categories, *Journal of the Acoustical Society of America*, 66, 1668–1679.

Kuhl, P.K. and Miller, J.D. (1975) "Speech Perception by the Chinchilla: Voiced–Voiceless Distinction in Alveolar Plosive Consonants," *Science*, 190, 69–72. (a)

Kuhl, P.K. and Miller, J.D. (1975) "Speech Perception in Early Infancy: Discrimination of Speech-sound Categories," *Journal of the Acoustical Society of America*, 58, Supplement 1, S56(A). (b)

Kuhl, P.K. and Miller, J.D. (1978) "Speech Perception by the Chinchilla: Identification for Synthetic VOT Stimuli," *Journal of the Acoustical Society of America*, 63, 905–917.

Liberman, A.M., Cooper, F.S., Shankweiler, D.P., and Studdert-Kennedy, M. (1967) "Perception of the Speech Code," *Psychological Review*, 74, 431–461.

Liberman, A.M., Delattre, P.C., Gerstman, L.J., and Cooper, F.S. (1956) "Tempo of Frequency Change as a Cue Distinguishing Classes of Speech Sounds," *Journal of Experimental Psychology*, 52, 127–137.

Lieberman, P. (1973) "On the Evolution of Language: A Unified View," *Cognition*, 2, 59–94.

Lindblom, B.E.F. (1963) "Spectrographic Study of Vowel Reduction," *Journal of the Acoustical Society of America*, 35, 1773–1781.

Macoby, E.E., and Hagen, J.W. (1965) "Effects of Distraction upon Central versus Incidental Recall: Developmental Trends," *Journal of Experimental Child Psychology*, 2, 280–289.

Miller, J.D., Wier, C.C., Pastore, R.E., Kelly, W.J., and Dooling, R.J. (1976) "Discrimination and Labeling of Noise–Buzz Sequences with Varying Noise-lead Times: An Example of Categorical Perception," *Journal of the Acoustical Society of America*, 60, 410–417.

Miller, J.L., and Eimas, P.D. (1975) "Studies on the Selective Tuning of Feature Detectors for Speech, *Journal of Phonetics*, 4, 119–127.

Miller, J.L. and Liberman, A.M. (1979) "Some Effects of Later–Occurring Information on the Perception of Stop Consonant and Semivowel," *Perception and Psychophysics*, 25, 457–465.

Minifie, F.D., Kuhl, P.K., and Stecher, E.M. (1977) "Categorical Perception of /b/ and /w/ during Changes in Rate of Utterance," *Journal of the Acoustical Society of America*, 62, Supplement 1, S79(A).

Morse, P.A. (1972) "The Discrimination of Speech and Nonspeech Stimuli in Early Infancy," *Journal of Experimental Child Psychology*, 14, 477–492.

Peterson, G.E. and Barney, H.L. (1952) "Control Methods Used in a Study of the Vowels," *Journal of the Acoustical Society of America*, 24, 175–184.

Pisoni, D.B. (1977) "Identification and Discrimination of the Relative Onset Time of Two-component Tones: Implications for Voicing Perception in Stops," *Journal of the Acoustical Society of America*, 61, 1352–1361.

Port, R. (1976) "Effects of Tempo of the Preceding Carrier on the Perception of "Rabid" and "Rapid," *Journal of the Acoustical Society of America*, 59, S41(A).

Port, R. (1978) "Effects of Word-internal versus Word-external Tempo on the Voicing Boundary for Medial Stop Closure," *Journal of the Acoustical Society of America*, 63, Supplement 1, S20(A).

Shankweiler, D., Strange, W., and Verbrugge, R. (1975) "Speech and the Problem of Perceptual Constancy," in R. Shaw and J. Bransford, eds., *Perceiving, Acting and Knowing: Toward an Ecological Psychology*, Erlbaum, Hillsdale N. J.

Stevens, K.N. (1975) "The Potential Role of Property Detectors in the Perception of Conso-nants," in G. Fant and M.A.A. Tatham, eds., *Auditory Analysis and Perception of Speech*, Academic Press, London, pp. 191–196.

Stevens, K.N. and House, A.S. (1963) "Perturbation of Vowel Articulations by Consonantal Context: An Acoustical Study," *Journal of Speech and Hearing Research*, 6, 111–128.

Stevens, K.N. and House, A.S. (1961) "An Acoustical Theory of Vowel Production and Some of its Implications," *Journal of Speech and Hearing Research*, 4, 303–320.

Studdert-Kennedy, M., Liberman, A., Harris, K.S., and Cooper, F.S. (1970) "Motor Theory of Speech Perception: A Reply to Lane's Critical Review," *Psychological Review*, 77, 234–249.

Swoboda, P., Morse, P., and Leavitt, L. (1976) "Continuous Vowel Discrimination in Normal and At-risk Infants," *Child Development*, 47, 459–465.

Tinbergen, N. (1951) *The Study of Instinct*, Clarendon Press, Oxford.

Trehub, S.E. (1973) "Auditory–Linguistic Sensitivity in Infants," Unpublished Doctoral Dis-sertation, McGill University, Montreal.

Verbrugge, R., Strange, W., and Shankweiler, D. (1974) "What Information Enables a Listener to Map a Talker's Vowel Space?" *Haskins Laboratories Status Report on Speech Research* SR–37–38, 199–208.

Vurpllot, E. (1968) "The Development of Scanning Strategies and their Relation to Visual Differentiation," *Journal of Experimental Child Psychology*, 6, 622–650.

Ward, W.D. (1970) "Musical Perception," in J.V. Tobias, ed., *Foundations of Modern Auditory Theory (Vol. 1)*, Academic Press, New York, pp. 405–443.

Wilson, W.R., Moore, J.M., and Thompson, G. (1976) "Sound Field Auditory Thresholds of Infants Utilizing Visual Reinforcement Audiometry (VRA)," Paper presented at ASHA, Houston.

Zinchenko, V.P., van Chzhi-Tsin, and Tarakonov, V.V. (1963) "The Formation and Devel-opment of Perceptual Activity," *Soviet Psychology and Psychiatry*, 2, 3–12.

Chapter 5

SOME DEVELOPMENTAL PROCESSES IN SPEECH PERCEPTION

RICHARD N. ASLIN AND DAVID B. PISONI

Introduction

We would like to begin by summarizing the main points that we hope to cover in this presentation. First, we will briefly review several theories that have attempted to explain the processes and mechanisms underlying the development of speech perception in young infants. Second, we will present a conceptual framework from which one can evaluate these theories and the numerous alternative explanations that can be applied to the available empirical findings already reported in the literature. Third, we will describe an account of the processes underlying the development of several segmental contrasts with a special emphasis on the perception of voicing in stop consonants, a distinction that has received considerable attention in the speech-perception literature. Finally, we will summarize some recent methodological work from our own laboratory that has been aimed at developing new techniques to investigate the various levels of perceptual analysis that may underlie the perceptual behavior of infants, particularly as these are related to issues surrounding perceptual constancy, feature extraction, and the role of early experience.

In the present chapter, we do not plan to report the details of new experimental findings. Instead, we will focus on some of the general theo-

CHILD PHONOLOGY
VOLUME 2: PERCEPTION

retical issues surrounding the development of speech perception within an organized conceptual framework. In our view, such theoretical efforts are desperately needed at this time, and such an undertaking would seem to be especially appropriate in a volume such as this, which is properly concerned with questions about phonological development. We will concern ourselves primarily with the most extensively studied class of speech sounds—stop consonants, particularly those varying in VOT, although other examples will be referred to from time to time. We believe that our general approach to the problems of perceptual development can be applied to other classes of speech sounds and to other aspects of the phonology of natural languages that must be acquired by children learning language.

Background

The now classic experiment reported by Eimas *et al.* (1971) roused a great deal of interest in the development of speech perception, not only because it demonstrated that prelinguistic infants could discriminate synthetic speech sounds categorically, but also because it provided support for the inference that the perceptual categories found in young infants closely matched the phonetic categories of adults. As Eimas, *et al.* (1971) put it: "The implication of these findings is that the means by which the categorical perception of speech, that is perception in a linguistic mode, is accomplished may well be part of the biological makeup of the organism. . . [p. 306].

This conclusion strongly implied, at the time, that categorical perception was not only unique to the perception of speech signals, but that the discriminative behavior of infants was a consequence of perceptual mechanisms that are innately determined. This view of the development of speech perception, therefore, acknowledged little, if any, influence by nongenetic or experiential factors that might be operative in the early environment of prelinguistic infants.

Although one could argue, as we will shortly, that categorical-like discrimination performance by infants does not necessarily imply the operation of a linguistic mode of processing, there can be little doubt from the available experimental evidence that, for certain classes of speech sounds, discrimination performance is discontinuous. For example, in the case of speech sounds differing in VOT, there is convincing evidence now for the existence of at least one region of heightened discriminability along the VOT continuum. However, the presence of a discontinuity in discrimination performance does not of necessity imply that discrimination is based on a linguistic level of analysis, as at least one major sensory (nonlinguistic) factor, namely, the discrimination of temporal order, has been proposed to account for VOT discrimination performance (see Hirsh, 1959, Pisoni, 1977). Some 7 years later, it is obvious, at least to us, that the implications drawn from Eimas' early experiments were premature.

For example, with regard to the claim that categorical perception is unique to speech signals, several recent reports by Cutting and Rosner (1974), Miller *et al.* (1976), and Pisoni (1977) have demonstrated quite conclusively that several classes of nonspeech signals containing "speechlike" acoustic attributes can be perceived categorically by adults. Moreover, Jusczyk *et al.* (1977) have also demonstrated that young infants show categorical-like discrimination when presented with nonspeech signals differing in rise time. And Jusczyk, Pisoni, Walley, and Murray (1980) have recently shown comparable discrimination data for two tones differing in relative onset time. Thus, the strong contention that categorical perception is unique to the perception of speech sounds because these signals are perceived as linguistic segments does not appear to have the conclusive support that it once had. It follows, then, that the demonstration of categorical-like discrimination of speech signals in infants is not sufficient evidence either to support the view that speech is perceived by "specialized" perceptual mechanisms or to argue that the infant's discriminative behavior is constrained in a principled way by the phonological structure of any particular natural language. It may simply be that infants respond primarily to the psychophysical or sensory properties of speech signals without any subsequent interpretation of these signals as linguistic entities.

The second implication of Eimas *et al.*'s conclusion was that the perceptual categories for at least the stop consonants in initial position are innately specified. The basis for this nativistic claim was twofold. First, Lisker and Abramson (1964, 1967) had previously shown in both analysis and synthesis studies that VOT is sufficient to characterize the voicing and aspiration differences among the stop consonants that exist in a number of diverse languages. From the study of stops in 11 languages, Lisker and Abramson (1964) found that the various tokens were distributed at one of three modal values along the VOT continuum corresponding to long-lead, short-lag and long-lag distinctions in voicing. Although the precise locations of the boundaries between phonological categories for stops differ somewhat from language to language, Lisker and Abramson (1964) suggested that the dimension of VOT was, in all likelihood, a universal and, therefore, was closely tied to the biological basis of language and speech. Second, in their infant study, Eimas *et al.* had found evidence of categorical perception of stops differing in VOT in the short-lag region of the continuum—a region used by all languages, including English, to signal voicing differences. The unusually close correspondence between the infants' discrimination performance on synthetic VOT stimuli and the Lisker and Abramson adult English data permitted Eimas *et al.* (1971) to argue that prelinguistic infants are preattuned to process speech sounds in a linguistically relevant manner, a manner approximating the categorical perception of stops observed in adults. More recently Eimas (1975) has summarized the earlier findings as follows: "Given the considerable overall similarity of the adult and infant discriminability data, infants, apparently, also have access to a phonetic feature code for purposes of deciding whether two speech events are the same or different [p. 341]."

However, despite the apparently sound reasoning behind these nativistic views of Eimas (1975), several important empirical findings were apparently overlooked. First, as noted earlier, the precise locations of the voicing boundaries described by Lisker and Abramson differ somewhat from language to language, suggesting that some fine tuning or alignment will take place during perceptual development. Second, Lasky *et al.* (1975) tested infants raised in a Spanish-speaking environment and found evidence of discrimination of voicing contrasts that were *not* discriminated by Spanish-speaking adults. They also failed to find evidence of discrimination of the contrasts that cross the Spanish adult voicing boundary. These latter findings, therefore, led Eimas (1975) to conclude that "the ability to perceive voicing distinctions in accord with a phonetic feature code during early infancy is independent of the infant's linguistic environment [p. 341]."

Thus, on the one hand, Eimas used the correspondence of the *English* infant–adult discrimination data to support his claim that the voicing categories are linguistically relevant and therefore genetically specified; but, on the other hand, Eimas did not appear to see a conflict in the lack of correspondence between the Spanish infant–adult discrimination data. This line of reasoning raises the interesting question, in our minds, of how past accounts of infant speech perception might have evolved if the Spanish infant discrimination data had been published first. Although the nativistic account of speech perception proposed by Eimas has been a significant advance over previous views of perceptual development, which have assumed that speech production precedes or parallels perception (e.g., Fry, 1966), we still see numerous problems in the logic underlying current conceptualizations of the development of speech perception. Recent empirical findings from a number of sensory and cognitive domains have no doubt broadened the perspective from which researchers can conceptualize the process of perceptual development. However, there is still a very strong tendency toward theoretical simplification of issues in infant speech perception, either in vague terms of learning, or by recourse to nativistic accounts of perceptual development. Our discussion that follows has been motivated chiefly by these theoretical considerations.

The last implication of Eimas' study was that a genetic specification of a perceptual category and its boundaries, although not modifiable during early infancy, may be modified during later childhood. Eimas (1975) obviously realized this modification must occur and even discussed it in light of his earlier results:

A strong genetic determination of phonetic categories and boundaries . . . does not actually preclude modifications of the mechanisms underlying this categorization of speech. Indeed, the data of Lasky et al. demand that modifications in the loci of the phonetic boundary of infants from Spanish environments occur if there is to be effective communication [p. 342].

What has remained unclear even to this time is why the perceptual categories for English infants are specified so accurately by genetics? One possible answer to this question comes from the previously mentioned nonspeech categorical perception findings obtained with adults and from recent research using animal models to study the perception of species-specific acoustic signals.

Kuhl and Miller (1975, 1978) have shown that chinchillas, who obviously do not make use of a human voicing distinction in their own vocal repertoire, can be trained to respond consistently to synthetic labial stop consonant stimuli. Moreover, the perceptual boundaries of the chinchilla correspond quite closely to the category boundaries found for voiced–voiceless stops in English adults. These results have raised the question of what process or level of perceptual analysis might be responsible for the categorical discrimination performance of both human adults and infants, and whether these results can be accounted for in a principled way by recourse to a linguistic mode of processing.

At the present time, it is equally unclear whether the boundaries in human infants and adults undergo a selective modification developmentally as a result of particular linguistic input in their environment and what perceptual mechanisms are responsible for this modification. Clearly, there must be some selectivity in the course of phonological development as evidenced by the fact that different languages have different phonologies, and by the apparent difficulty adults have in recognizing phonetic contrasts that are phonologically irrelevant in their native language. The now classic cross-language work of Lisker and Abramson (1967) has supported the contention that only phonologically distinctive perceptual categories are perceived by adults. A summary of their results for English, Thai, and Spanish subjects is shown in Figure 5.1 to illustrate the significant role that linguistic experience plays in the categorization of speech signals.

More recent cross-language research by Miyawaki et al. (1975) provided support for the view that the phonologically distinctive [r]–[l] contrast in English is perceived by English adults but not by Japanese adults who do not have the [r]–[l] contrast in their language. Furthermore, training studies such as those summarized by Strange and Jenkins (1978) suggest that, although the ability to perceive a phonologically irrelevant contrast may have been present at birth, adults who have lost or failed to develop that contrast are probably incapable of acquiring or reacquiring it. Such findings could be interpreted as evidence that a neural substrate for the perception of pho-

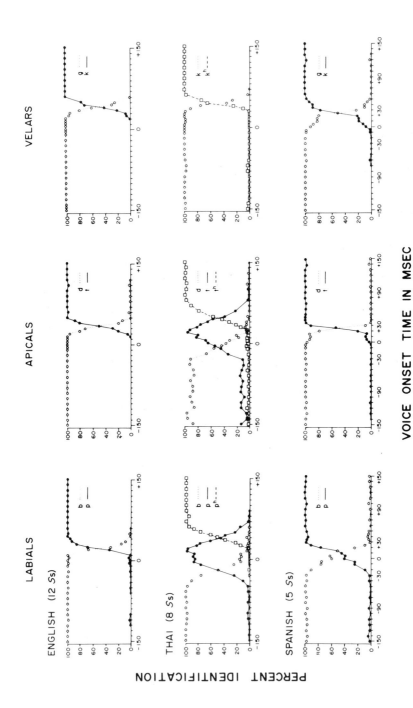

FIGURE 5.1 *Adult labeling functions for synthetic labial, apical, and velar stop consonants varying in VOT obtained from native speakers of English (N=12), Thai (N=8), and Spanish (N=5) (adapted from Lisker and Abramson, 1967).*

nologically irrelevant contrasts either failed to be formed during a critical or sensitive period or atrophied as a result of the absence of experience with that contrast. This neural theory of phonological development is *passive* in the sense that it assumes that little or no involvement, either attentional or productive, is required to maintain or create a particular perceptual ability. As we shall see in a later section, such views of sensory development have not received strong support in recent years.

However, an alternative to this passive or strictly receptive account of the role of early experience in speech perception is the view that the failure to actively engage an attentional or productive system in the use of a particular phonetic contrast only depresses or attenuates subsequent performance on that linguistic contrast. The difficulty shown by adults in discrimination, then, may not be due to any neural process per se, but may be simply a consequence of an attentional deficit similar to the process of acquired equivalence—a perceptual mode that involves learning to ignore distinctive differences among stimuli. This view assumes that perception of the relevant distinctive contrasts is so automatic, as a result of previous processing strategies acquired by the subject, that reacquisition of a phonologically irrelevant contrast is difficult to obtain reliably in untrained adults (see Shiffrin and Schneider, 1977).

To study these questions in more detail, we recently collected some preliminary data from adult subjects that support the predictions of the attentional deficit model just outlined. Figure 5.2 shows labeling data from four adult subjects who were given two repetitions of a synthetic prevoiced /ba/ with a VOT value of −70 msec prior to a forced-choice identification task. In one condition of the experiment, the subjects had three response buttons corresponding to [ba], [pa], and prevoiced [ba]. Note that all subjects were highly consistent in labeling three perceptual categories despite the absence of highly prevoiced stops in initial position in English and the very limited exposure and training experience that preceded the labeling task. These findings are particularly striking when compared with the more traditional two-alternative forced-choice labeling results shown in the right-hand panel for each of these subjects. Note the classic two-category identification functions obtained in this task for /ba/ and /pa/ responses. Our recent findings suggest, therefore, that phonologically irrelevant categories *can* be consistently categorized by adults even without very extensive training and presumably without significant neural loss or atrophy of the feature detectors that have been assumed to underlie phonetic categorization (Eimas, 1975). Such findings call into question the recent conclusions of Strange and Jenkins (1978) concerning the effects of laboratory training studies in speech perception (see Aslin, Pisoni, Hennessy, and Perey, 1979). Moreover, given that subjects could use three responses consistently and without feedback in this task, it is difficult to argue that there was any "selective loss" in perceptual sensitivity of these subjects in processing

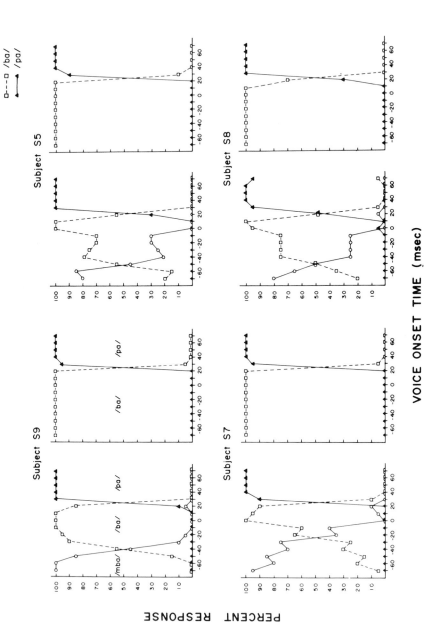

FIGURE 5.2 *Three-alternative and two-alternative labeling functions obtained from four (naive) native speakers of English. The synthetic stimuli were bilabial stop consonants varying in VOT, /mba/, open circles; /ba/, open squares; /pa/, filled triangles (data collected by Beth Hennessy).*

voicing information. The performance decrements observed in earlier studies on voicing discrimination may simply be the result of criteria shifts and response constraints resulting from the use of different subject strategies in these tasks (Carney *et al.*, 1977; Pisoni and Lazarus, 1974).

The Role of Early Experience in Perceptual Development

The need for a coherent framework from which to view the course of perceptual development is of the utmost importance to our understanding of the processes underlying the development of speech perception, especially in light of the many seemingly diverse and contradictory empirical findings that have appeared in the infant perception literature in recent years. Several researchers working in the area of visual-system development have begun to appreciate the many potential and seemingly diverse roles that genetic and experiential factors can play in the development of sensory and perceptual systems. For example, some of the neural mechanisms underlying visual functioning are not present at birth. Moreover, they do not unfold during development as a simple result of a genetically controlled plan or schedule. In other words, early visual experience influences to some extent the course of visual-system development. Yet early experience does not totally control the outcome of visual-system development since some genetically specified limits are clearly placed on how much early experience can influence the course of visual-system development (see Blakemore, 1976; Grobstein and Chow, 1976 for general reviews).

The research of Hubel and Wiesel (1965, 1970) provides a good example of how complex the interactions are between genetic and experiential factors in visual-system development. They have shown that kittens who have been selectively deprived of certain types of early visual experiences fail to develop the normal neural mechanisms subserving binocular vision. Moreover, they have found evidence for a relatively well-defined sensitive period in binocular development, as shown in the top panel of Figure 5.3, during which early visual deprivation exerts its most significant and permanent effects. Yet Hubel and Wiesel (1963) also showed that at least part of the neural mechanism underlying binocular vision *is* present at birth, and this mechanism does not deteriorate if the kitten is reared in total darkness. That is, the absence of visual experience (dark rearing) does not eliminate binocular function, whereas the presence of a binocular imbalance (monocular occlusion) does eliminate binocular function by creating competition between the inputs from the two eyes.

These findings from the animal literature have been extended and generalized to the study of humans who were deprived of certain visual experiences in early life. Banks *et al.* (1975) have reported, as displayed in the lower panel of Figure 5.3, that the development of the human visual system is also characterized by a sensitive period during which selective binocular deprivation can lead to permanent and irreversible deficits in binocular functioning, in particular, depth perception. In contrast, other studies (Banks and Aslin, 1975; Creel *et al.*, 1974) have shown that some humans have genetic anomalies in their visual systems associated with a condition of albinism. These individuals fail to develop normal binocular function irrespective of the presence or absence of binocular deprivation during early life.

Thus, it is clear from the study of visual-system function and its development that a simple dichotomy between nativistic and empiricist accounts of the process of development is inadequate to capture the multiple and seemingly complex genetic and environmental interactions that underlie normal perceptual development. In the next section, we turn to a discussion of some of the intricacies of the genetic–environmental interactions that must be accounted for by any theory of perceptual development, including theories of the development of speech perception.

Gottlieb (1976a,b), a behavioral embryologist, has provided an account of some of the possible roles that early experience can play in the development of sensory systems. His conceptualization of these processes seemed to us to be particularly relevant to discussions of the development of speech

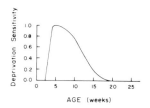

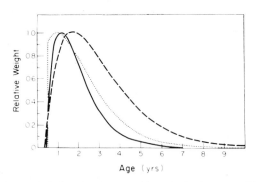

FIGURE 5.3 *Sensitive periods for visual system binocularity in cats and humans as estimated by data from (a) Hubel and Wiesel (1965, 1970) and (b) data from Banks, Aslin and Letson (1975).*

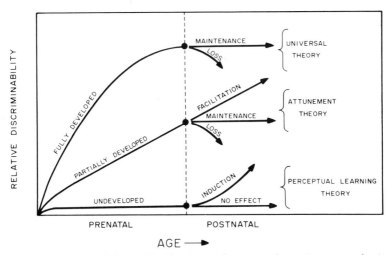

FIGURE 5.4 *Illustration of the major roles that early postnatal experience can play in modifying the relative discriminability of speech sounds. Three general classes of theories are shown here to account for the development of speech-sound discrimination: universal theory, attunement theory and perceptual learning theory.*

perception. According to Gottlieb (1976a,b), there are four basic ways in which early experience can influence the development of a perceptual ability. These possibilities are illustrated in Figure 5.4.

First, a perceptual ability may be present at birth but require certain specific types of early experience to *maintain* the integrity of that ability. The absence or degradation of the required early experience can result in either a partial or a complete loss of the perceptual ability, a loss that may be irreversible despite subsequent experience. For example, as mentioned previously, the work of Hubel and Wiesel (1965, 1970) on the visual system of the kitten showed, among other things, that the full complement of neural cells responsible for binocular vision was present at birth, although those cells lost their function if the kittens were deprived of binocular vision during the sensitive period. Thus, early experience in this case served to maintain the functional integrity of the mechanisms underlying binocular vision.

Second, an ability may be only partially developed at birth, requiring specific types of early experience to *facilitate* or attune the further development of that perceptual ability. The lack of early experience with these stimuli that serve a facilitating function could result either in the absence of any further development or a loss of that ability when compared to its level at birth. As an example of a facilitating function, we can cite the work of Gottlieb himself, who has shown that ducklings modify their subsequent preference and recognition of species-specific calls by their own vocalizations prior to and shortly after hatching (Gottlieb, 1976a). If these self-produced vocalizations are prevented from occurring (through devocalization techniques), while still in the early stages of development, the developmental rate of preference for species-specific calls declines, and the ability to discriminate and recognize particular calls is substantially reduced (Gottlieb, 1975).

Third, a perceptual ability may be absent at birth, and its development may depend upon a process of induction based on specific early experiences by the organism. The presence of a particular ability, then, would depend to a large extent upon the presence of a particular type of early experience. For example, specific early experiences presented to young ducklings leads to imprinting to a particular stimulus object and can be taken as an instance of inducing a behavioral preference (Hess, 1972). Thus, in this case, the presence of a particular early experience is necessary for the subsequent development of a particular perceptual preference or tendency.

Finally, of course, early experience may exert *no* role at all in the development of a particular perceptual ability. That is, the ability may be either present or absent at birth and it may remain, decline, or improve in the absence of any particular type of early experience. Absence of an experiential effect is particularly difficult to identify and often leads to unwarranted conclusions, particularly conclusions that assume that an induction process might be operative. For example, it is quite common for investigators to argue that, if an ability is *absent* at birth, but then observed to be *present* sometime after birth, the ability must have been learned. In terms of the conceptual framework outlined earlier, this could be an example of induction. Yet it is quite possible that the ability simply "unfolded" developmentally according to a genetically specified maturational schedule, a schedule that required no *particular* type of early experience in the environment. This unfolding of an ability may be thought of as an example of the general class of maturational theories of development. As an example, although general motor activity is necessary to prevent the atrophy of particular muscle systems, many of the classic studies by Gesell in the 1930s demonstrated that no particular training experience was necessary for infants to acquire the ability to walk (Gesell and Ames, 1940). Thus, as we have tried to show, the complexity of these numerous possible alternatives—maintenance, facilitation, induction, and maturation—and their possible interactions should caution any rash or premature conclusions regarding the developmental course of specific perceptual abilities.

But what then is the specific relevance of Gottlieb's scheme of the roles of early experience to the development of speech perception? We would like to outline four general classes of theories of perceptual development that are, in our view, appropriate to discussions of phonological development. After we describe the assumptions underlying these four classes of theories, we will select several examples from the available literature on infant speech perception to illustrate the usefulness of this conceptualization. The classes of theories of perceptual development we will consider are what we have called universal theory, attunement theory, perceptual learning theory, and maturational theory.

Universal theory assumes that, at birth, infants are capable of discriminating all the possible phonetic contrasts that may be used phonologically in any natural language. According to this view, early experience functions to *maintain* the ability to discriminate phonologically relevant distinctions, those actually presented to the infant in the environment. However, the absence of phonologically irrelevant contrasts, which are obviously not presented to the infant, results in a selective loss of the abilities to discriminate those specific contrasts. The mechanisms responsible for this loss of sensitivity may be either neural or attentional or both. These two alternatives also make several specific predictions concerning the possible reacquisition of the lost discriminative abilities in adults, a topic of some interest in its own right, as we have mentioned in an earlier section of this chapter.

Attunement theory assumes that, at birth, all infants are capable of discriminating at least some of the possible phonetic contrasts contained in the world's languages, but that the infant's discriminative capacities are incompletely developed and/or possibly quite broadly tuned. Early experience therefore functions to align and/or to sharpen these partially developed discriminative abilities. Phonologically relevant contrasts in the language-learning environment would then become more finely tuned with experience and phonologically irrelevant contrasts would either remain broadly tuned or become attenuated in the absence of specific environmental stimulation.

In contrast with the other two views, perceptual learning theory assumes that the ability to discriminate any particular phonetic contrast is dependent upon specific early experience with that contrast in the language-learning environment. The rate of development could be very fast or very slow, depending on the frequency of occurrence of the phonetic contrasts during early life, the relative acoustic or psychophysical discriminability of the contrast compared with other contrasts, and the attentional state of the infant. According to this view, however, phonologically irrelevant contrasts would *never* be discriminated better than the phonologically relevant contrasts present in the language-learning environment.

Finally, maturational theory assumes that the ability to discriminate a particular phonetic contrast is independent of any specific early experience and simply unfolds according to a predetermined developmental schedule. All possible phonetic contrasts would be discriminated equally well irrespective of the language environment, although the age at which specific phonetic contrasts could be discriminated would be dependent on the developmental level of the underlying sensory mechanism.

These classes of theories of perceptual development make rather specific predictions concerning the developmental course of speech perception in infants and young children, predictions that we think are of special importance to researchers in infant speech perception. It is important to note here that we are *not* claiming that only one of these classes of theories will uniquely account for the development of *all* speech contrasts. Rather, it may be the case that some hybrid of the theories provides the best description of the development of specific classes of speech-sound discrimination. In fact, this view of parallel developmental processes appears to be supported by current empirical findings, as we hope to show. In the remainder of this section, we will first summarize several of the empirical findings already available in the literature and then attempt to provide an account of these findings within the context of the framework we have outlined. However, before proceeding to the empirical findings, it is appropriate to state rather explicitly what our goals are in trying to account for the data in this manner.

One of the key issues involved in a proper understanding of the development of speech perception is the level of analysis presumed to be operative in the processing of speech signals. In our view, the level-of-analysis issue can ultimately be reduced to two basic alternatives, a sensory or psychophysical level, and a phonetic or interpretive level. In the past, a phonetic level of analysis was strongly implicated as the basis for the infant's discrimination of various classes of speech signals, particularly stop consonants. As we noted earlier, the recent findings with adult subjects using nonspeech signals, and the findings from nonhuman animals, have raised the strong possibility that the discriminative behavior observed in the earlier adult experiments as well as in the infant speech perception experiments may be based, to a large extent, on a sensory level of analysis that involves responding to the psychophysical attributes of the speech signals. Although both approaches—the use of complex nonspeech signals with adults and infants and the cross-species comparisons—have helped to broaden our understanding of the adult and infant literature on speech perception, additional evidence for deciding on the particular level or levels of analysis has come from studies of the discrimination of phonetic contrasts that are phonologically irrelevant for a particular group of language-learning infants— that is, the cross-language infant speech perception studies. By comparing an infant's discrimination of both phonologically relevant and phonologically irrelevant phonetic contrasts, we can gain information regarding the specific level of coding of the sensory input and have an opportunity to examine several of the issues surrounding the role of early experience and the processes involved in perceptual development.

Voicing in Stop Consonants

Since Eimas *et al.'s* (1971) study, over 24 VOT contrasts have been studied in infants. Positive evidence of discrimination has been obtained for all contrasts that crossed the English voiced–voiceless boundary. However, for contrasts that crossed a prevoiced–voiced boundary, the only positive evidence of discrimination was obtained with infants whose native language environment contained a phonological contrast between prevoiced and voiced stop consonants.

At first glance, these results on the discrimination of voicing contrasts by infants might appear to provide strong support for a perceptual learning explanation, although certain key findings are clearly in conflict with the predictions of that theory. For example, several contrasts were tested on infants whose native language environment was not English. Discrimination performance on the majority of these contrasts was observed despite the fact that these contrasts were phonologically inappropriate and unlikely to occur in the language-learning environment. That is, infants discriminated a contrast that their parents presumably never used in spoken language. However, other studies of VOT have failed to show evidence that infants discriminate contrasts that are present in their language-learning environment. How can we reconcile these seemingly contradictory results? Within the conceptual framework outlined earlier, we think it is possible to offer a systematic account of these findings in terms of what is currently known about the psychophysical properties of these speech signals and the underlying developmental processes responsible for realizing the discrimination.

We propose the following account of the development of the perception of voicing contrasts as cued by VOT in stop consonants. First, there is now sufficient evidence to suggest that the basis for VOT discrimination by infants is probably *not* directly related to phonetic categorization or to a linguistic mode of analysis (also see Stevens and Klatt, 1974). Rather, we would argue that the discrimination performance of infants tested on VOT contrasts is based on the detection of the relative onsets between two acoustic events; that is, in the case of VOT, the detection of the onset of the first formant relative to the onset of higher formants (Pisoni, 1977). Furthermore, we would suggest that the discrimination of the relative order between these two events is more highly discriminable at certain regions along the VOT stimulus continuum corresponding roughly to the location of the threshold for resolving these differences psychophysically. In the case of temporal order processing, this falls roughly near the region surrounding ± 20 msec, a value corresponding to the threshold for temporal order processing (Hirsh, 1959).

The findings from Pisoni's (1977) study with nonspeech stimuli as shown in Figure 5.5 may be cited as additional support for the claim that a sensory or psychophysical process is probably responsible for the categorical-like discrimination performance found in adults and infants using synthetic speech stimuli differing in VOT. These results showed that adult subjects were able to parse the tone onset time (TOT) nonspeech continuum into three discrete perceptual categories corresponding to leading, lagging, and simultaneous onsets.

Figure 5.6 shows the ABX discrimination data from another nonspeech experiment by Pisoni (1977) with the same stimuli. Note that two distinct

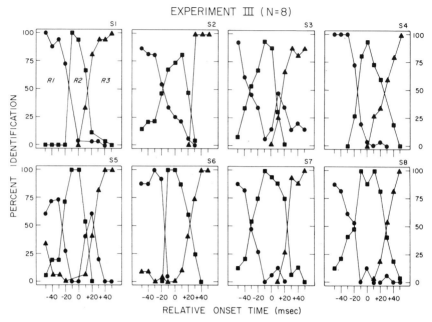

FIGURE 5.5 *Adult labeling functions for tone onset time (TOT) stimuli showing the presence of three labeling categories in adult subjects (N = 8)* (from Pisoni, 1977).

regions of high discriminability are present in the discrimination functions. Thus, it is our contention that evidence of discrimination of VOT contrasts that straddle the -20 and $+20$ msec regions of the stimulus continuum probably results from general sensory constraints on the mammalian auditory system to resolve small differences in temporal order and not from phonetic categorization. However, two questions are immediately apparent from this analysis. First, why is there so little evidence of discrimination of

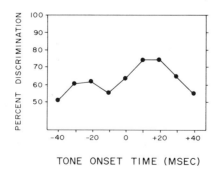

FIGURE 5.6 *Adult ABX discrimination data for tone onset time (TOT) stimuli showing two regions of heightened discriminability* (from Pisoni, 1977).

VOT in the −20 msec region of voicing lead in the infant literature? And second, what role does the environment play in tuning the perceptual mechanism responsible for processing temporal order information?

The first question can be dealt with by a closer examination of the discrimination data shown in Figure 5.6. Note that, even in this figure with nonspeech signals differing in their relative onset time, discrimination of TOT differences is greater in the positive region of the stimulus continuum than in the negative region. These findings are not unique to these particular nonspeech signals as the same relation can be observed in the original Abramson and Lisker (1967) discrimination data obtained with Thai subjects. As shown in the top panel of Figure 5.7, the relative discriminability in the +20 msec region of voicing lag is greater than in the −20 msec region of voicing lead despite the fact that the slopes of the labeling functions for the Thai subjects in these regions are very nearly identical, as shown earlier in Figure 5.1. We propose, therefore, that the smaller incidence of discrimination of VOT differences in the minus region of voicing lead values is probably due to the generally poorer ability of the auditory system to resolve temporal differences in which a lower-frequency component precedes a higher-frequency component.

Lower discriminability of stimuli in the minus region of the VOT continuum cannot account entirely for infants' overall performance, as all three positive instances of discrimination reported in the literature involved infants from linguistic environments that used contrasts between prevoiced and

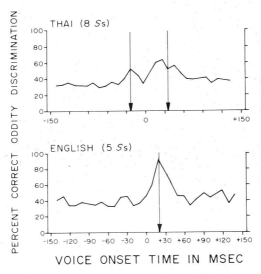

FIGURE 5.7 *Oddity discrimination data obtained from adult speakers of Thai (N=8) and* English (N = 5) for synthetic bilabial stop consonants varying in VOT (redrawn from Abramson and Lisker, 1967).

voiced stops distinctively. Furthermore, we would argue that early linguistic experience *does* play some role in modifying the discriminability of speech stimuli depending on the relative predominance of certain VOT values in the productions of adults.

Differences in the relative discriminability of VOT contrasts along the stimulus continuum may be cited as additional support for the role of early environmental experience as there is evidence of two regions of high discriminability even in the discrimination functions obtained with English subjects, as shown in the lower panel of Figure 5.7. However, the peak in the minus region is substantially reduced when compared with the Thai discrimination data shown in the top panel. A similar result can also be observed in the discrimination data of Williams (1974), which is shown in Figure 5.8, for Spanish and English subjects. Note that the Spanish subjects show a broad region of heightened discriminability extending into the area encompassing the location of the English perceptual boundary.

The evidence on the development of voicing perception therefore appears to provide good support for the attunement theory described earlier.

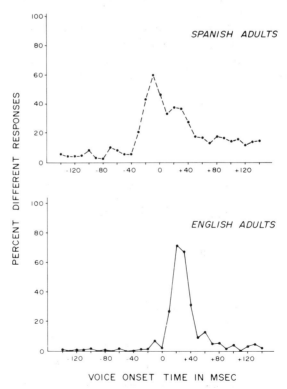

FIGURE 5.8 *A–X discrimination data from adult speakers of Spanish and English for synthetic bilabial stop consonants varying in VOT (redrawn from Williams, 1974).*

That is, a partially specified ability to process temporal order information is assumed to be present at birth. Perceptual sensitivity to temporal order differences such as those present in synthetic VOT stimuli are, however, susceptible to the influence of early experience, thereby selectively modifying the strength and location of the regions of high sensitivity along a stimulus continuum such as VOT.

The course of perceptual development for other classes of speech sounds can also be accounted for in terms of the conceptual framework outlined earlier. To demonstrate the usefulness of our theoretical approach, we will briefly summarize some of the work that has appeared on the discrimination of fricatives, vowels, and liquids by young infants.

Fricatives

In a study by Eilers *et al.* (1977), infants appeared to have great difficulty discriminating between some of the acoustic attributes that differentiate the class of fricative sounds. These perceptual findings parallel the well-documented lag in the articulatory control of fricatives in speech production and suggest that infants probably must undergo a rather long period of perceptual learning to begin to isolate the appropriate acoustic cues for different fricatives. However, an equally plausible explanation of the developmental lag in the perception of fricatives is that the neural mechanisms underlying the perception of fricatives must unfold over a rather long postnatal period before a child is capable of discriminating the acoustic cues for different fricatives. We might suppose, then, that early experience either *induces* the abilities to discriminate fricatives, or that early experience plays *no* particular role in the development of the perceptual mechanisms required for discrimination of fricatives. If the induction or perceptual learning theory account of fricative development is correct, we might expect relatively poor discrimination of fricatives by infants whose native language does not employ specific fricative contrasts distinctively. Alternatively, maturational theory would predict that, at some postnatal age, infants from all language-learning environments would be able to discriminate differences between fricatives, but that early experience reduces the discriminability of the cues for some fricatives if they were absent from the language environment after the neural mechanisms necessary to process these acoustic cues had already reached maturity.

In contrast to these more traditional accounts of the development of fricative perception, an alternative account has been raised in a recent study conducted by Jusczyk, Murray and Bayly (1979). They demonstrated that 2-month-old infants discriminate a /fa/–/θa/ contrast categorically, but that the category boundary is located at the adult /ba/–/da/ boundary. In other words, for infants, the region of heightened discriminability along both the /fa/–/θa/ and /ba/–/da/ continua is approximately coincident. Presumably, an experiential or maturational factor contributes to the developmental shift of the /fa/–/Өa/ category boundary away from the /ba/–/da/ boundary. We would hypothesize on the basis of these data that infants' discrimination of fricatives is initially determined by the psychophysical attributes of the signal, but that a postnatal shift occurs in the manner in which fricatives are categorized. Thus, attunement theory may also provide a reasonable account of the development of fricative perception in infants.

Vowels

The work of Trehub (1976) provides another example of a cross-language comparison that helps to illuminate the possible roles of early experience in phonological development. She reported that infants from an English-speaking environment can discriminate a French vowel contrast, a contrast that was *not* discriminated reliably by English-speaking adults. Thus, it would appear that this vowel contrast is discriminated at birth but that the original discriminative abilities decline postnatally as a result of the absence of particular kinds of early language experiences. This course of perceptual development may follow what we have characterized as the universal theory or, alternatively, may be best described by attunement theory. In the case of vowel perception in adults, there are specific regions of the vowel space that are generally associated with individual vowel classes, although these differ from language to language. The arrangement of the vowel space may, however, initially conform to the acoustic attributes of vowels that are processed most efficiently by the newborn's auditory system, and then only during postnatal development, with environmental experience as input, will the vowel space be rearranged to conform more closely to the phonological categories present in the language-learning environment (see Liljencrants and Lindblom, 1972).

Liquids

Finally, the data on the discrimination of the liquids [r] and [l] as reported by Miyawaki *et al.* (1975) for adults, and by Eimas (1975) for infants suggest that the ability to discriminate differences in the F_3 transitions between the liquids is present at birth. However, the absence of an [r]–[l] contrast in the early postnatal environment of Japanese infants may have prevented the adults in the Miyawaki *et al.* study from discriminating what is now a phonologically irrelevant speech contrast. The universal theory would then appear to be the best candidate to account for this selective loss of a perceptual ability that was initially present at birth.

The perceptual findings briefly reviewed here indicate that early experience may significantly modify the sensory-based perceptual categories presumed to be present at birth. There are several ways in which early experience could selectively modify the perceptual mechanisms and there-fore influence the discriminability of phonetic contrasts found in natural language environments. Figure 5.9 outlines several forms that this selective modification might take with reference to the shape and level of schematized discrimination functions.

First, stimuli in the region of a boundary between two perceptual cat-egories may become either more discriminable or less discriminable, pro-cesses we have called *enhancement* and *attenuation*. The process of en-hancement may account for the heightened discriminability of stops in the prevoiced region of the VOT continuum by Thai speakers. In contrast, the process of attenuation may account for the poor discriminability of VOT differences in the prevoiced region by English speakers, and the apparent decrease in discriminability of the [r]–[l] contrast by Japanese speakers.

Perception of stimuli in the region of a perceptual boundary may also become more finely tuned or more poorly tuned, processes we have called *sharpening* and *broadening*. On the one hand, sharpening may account for the discrete and very well-defined cross-over points in adult labeling func-tions obtained for synthetic stops. On the other hand, broadening may ac-count for the perception of vowels being somewhat more discriminable overall than consonants as well as the wider region of heightened discri-minability of VOT found in Spanish subjects.

Finally, the perceptual boundary may undergo a shift, a process we have called *realignment* that may account for the shifts in the voiced–voiceless boundary observed between English and Spanish stops as reported in studies

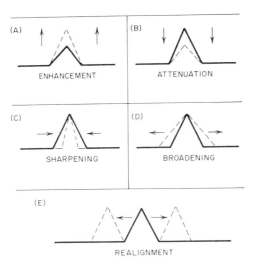

FIGURE 5.9 *Five processes by which early experience in a particular language environment could modify the relative discriminability of speech sounds lying along a particular synthetic continuum.*

by Lisker and Abramson (1967), Williams (1974), and Eilers, Wilson, and Gavin (1977).

From this brief summary of the perception of voicing contrasts in stop consonants, fricatives, vowels, and liquids, it should be apparent that the major roles of early experience that we outlined earlier cannot be uniformly invoked to account for the development of the abilities needed to discriminate *all* speech contrasts found in spoken language. Clearly there are numerous variables that will determine which particular ontogenetic function in Figure 5.4 best characterizes the developmental course of a particular phonetic contrast. For example, the auditory system of humans may well be specialized for processing certain very specific types of acoustic attributes at an early age. If some phonetic contrasts in language happen to have these distinctive acoustic properties in common, the infant should then be able to discriminate these speech signals with practically no experience in the language-learning environment short of sensory deprivation. However, if a certain amount of neural maturation or specific early experience is required for discrimination, we might anticipate a delay or developmental lag in observing discrimination of these contrasts, assuming, of course, that all other things remained constant. This hybrid or parallel view of the role of early experience in the development of speech perception that we are proposing here is not entirely without precedent or empirical support as shown by recent work or visual-system development. For example, most visual cortical neurons are characterized by their simultaneous responsiveness to several aspects of stimulus structure: direction of movement, orientation, and retinal disparity (among others). Yet, the mechanism underlying the development of each of these types of stimulus specificity is quite different. The property of directional selectivity is present at birth and undergoes little improvement or loss, unless the animal is deprived of stimulus movement (see Olson and Pettigrew, 1974, on stroboscopic rearing conditions). The property of orientational selectivity is also present at birth, but the sharpness of each neuron's orientational specificity is dependent upon the quality of early experience (Sherk and Stryker, 1977). And the property of disparity selectivity appears to be nearly absent at birth; the neurons acquire (within broad limits) the range of disparity values provided during early life (Pettigrew, 1974). Thus, the three general theory classes in the speech domain— universal, attunement, and perceptual learning—could be thought of as being analogous to three general mechanisms by which early experience influences visual-system development. Moreover, the foregoing analogy emphasizes the fact that parallel developmental mechanisms can operate upon different aspects of the same sensory input and can underlie the perceptual abilities observed in the adult. It should be obvious now that only a very detailed description of the development of these discriminative abilities will enable us to distinguish between the various types of complex interactions caused by genetic and experiential factors and their contribution to the development of the normal speech-processing mechanisms.

Methodological Considerations

Many of the questions raised in the previous sections about the role of early experience in perceptual development cannot be answered in a completely satisfying manner without new and improved experimental procedures for measuring discrimination and other aspects of perceptual analysis. For example, to answer questions about the discriminative abilities of infants to resolve small differences between speech signals that exist at a purely sensory level, many more data points need to be obtained from each subject so that the shape of the discrimination functions can be examined in greater detail. To study questions surrounding perceptual constancy and categorization of speech signals, some measure analogous to the adult labeling or identification function is needed.

For the past year, we have been working on several techniques for use with infants that would provide us with new and more efficient ways to measure both discrimination and identification of speech and speechlike acoustic signals. The procedures we developed to measure discrimination and perceptual categorization of speech sounds by infants involved several modifications of the operant head-turning paradigm (described by Eilers, Chapter 3, and Kuhl, Chapter 4, this volume). An assistant attracts the gaze of the infant while various signals are presented to the infant who is seated on the mother's lap in a sound-attenuated booth. The mother and assistant both wear tight-fitting headphones during the entire experimental session and listen to a continuous recording of popular music played at a level sufficient to mask the background and target stimuli. A PDP–11 computer is used to present all experimental signals, record responses, and deliver visual reinforcement to the infant. An experimenter, who is unaware of the specific stimulus conditions, as well as the reinforcement contingencies on each trial, is located outside the booth and records head turns directly into the computer, which has been programmed to present the stimuli and to provide the visual reinforcement. In contrast to the head-turning procedure described earlier by Eilers and Kuhl to measure discrimination, in our procedures, the assistant located in the room with the infant does *not* have any control over the stimulus or reinforcement conditions of the experiment and, therefore, is not in a position to provide subtle cues to the infant as he or she is unaware of the exact stimuli because of the masking stimulus in the earphones. Moreover, because the experiment is completely automated, there is no chance of experimenter bias influencing any aspect of the procedure that could affect the infant's behavior in the experiment (See important methodological and conceptual controversy: Aslin & Pisoni, 1980; Eilers, Gavin, and Wilson, 1980).

In one of our studies, we have collected discrimination data from infants using a modified staircase or up–down procedure (Levitt, 1971). Infants were initially shaped to detect a difference between a repeating background signal and a target signal by turning toward the direction of the change. A correct head turn to the left of the midline was reinforced by the presentation of an animated toy monkey, located next to the loudspeaker. This aspect of the head-turning procedure was similar to the method described in Chapters 3 and 4 of this volume by Eilers and Kuhl. However, after this initial shaping phase and a training phase was completed to a criterion level of performance, a series of trials was presented in which the characteristics of the target signal were modified systematically, depending upon the infants perform- ance on the previous trials. An example of the results of this interactive staircase procedure when used to measure VOT discrimination is shown in Figure 5.10.

This particular infant, K. S., was trained on an initial stimulus pair consisting of a +70 msec VOT background signal and a −70 msec VOT

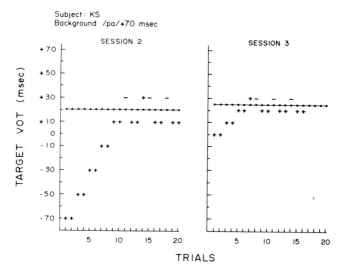

FIGURE 5.10 *Discrimination data from infant K. S. who was tested with synthetic VOT stimuli using a modified staircase procedure. The left-hand panel shows trial-by-trial performance when the full range of stimuli from − 70 msec through + 70 msec was used, whereas the right- hand panel shows performance with a reduced range from 0 msec through + 70 msec VOT. A + indicates a correct response (hit) whereas a − indicates an incorrect response (miss). The VOT value needed to discriminate the + 70 msec background stimulus from the target is quite consistent across both sessions, lying roughly at a value of 25 msec VOT as shown by the horizontal line with filled circles in both panels.*

target stimulus. After reaching a training criterion of 80% correct responses on experimental or change trials *and* 80% correct responses on control trials, the infant was shifted immediately into the staircase discrimination procedure. As currently implemented, the staircase procedure operates according to a very simple algorithm. If the infant discriminates correctly on two consecutive experimental trials (i.e., a hit), the level of the target stimulus is changed on the next trial by some value of VOT so as to make it less discriminable than the previous level of the target. However, if a miss occurs on any trial, the level of the target is then adjusted on the next trial by some value of VOT to be more discriminable. This up–down or staircase procedure typically produces a pattern of oscillation along the stimulus continuum at a value of VOT that can be correctly discriminated 70% of the time from the background stimulus or standard. The results of testing subject K. S. with the full VOT continuum from −70 to +70 msec is shown in the left panel where a VOT value of 20 msec was computed as the boundary value. This same subject was retested a day later on only the 0 through +70 msec range of this continuum, and a VOT boundary value of 25 msec was computed with a smaller step size. Both values agree remarkably well as estimates of the minimum value of VOT that can be discriminated reliably from the +70 msec background stimulus despite the change in the range of stimuli used.

The staircase discrimination procedure has a number of advantages over more traditional psychophysical methods used to measure discrimination, especially when used with young infants. First, it is very efficient, requiring substantially fewer trials than more conventional methods. Second, it offers greater flexibility, thus permitting the infant to continue responding to receive reinforcement, and serves to maintain interest and attention to the experimental situation for longer periods of time. Finally, it provides a rapid and quantitative measure of discriminability of the dimension under study. Such a measure is also less subject to biases resulting from peculiar response strategies than more traditional methods used with infants, which often promote either a high false-alarm rate or a reduction or cessation of responding.

Of course, establishing that infants can discriminate differences between various kinds of speech signals is only one aspect of the speech-perception process as there are numerous acoustic attributes of speech signals that can be used for a discriminative response. Moreover, there is some difficulty in interpreting the results from discrimination experiments alone because it is often unclear, from these studies, which specific acoustic attribute or property was used by the infant for discrimination. In complex acoustic signals such as speech, there are typically a very large number of redundant and irrelevant acoustic cues that may underlie the acoustic realization of a particular phonetic distinction and that may be sufficient for an infant or adult to discriminate this distinction from others.

To examine more directly some of the general questions surrounding perceptual constancy in speech perception and how constancy is maintained despite the wide diversity of physical variability in the sensory input to infants, it seemed necessary to develop a procedure that would provide information on how infants categorize or identify speech signals—signals that are very likely to be acoustically different although, in some cases, phonetically or phonologically equivalent. Identification or labeling functions secured from young infants in this manner could then be directly compared to data obtained with human adults and other species to determine, for example, how early experience with these stimuli in the environment may have tuned or modified the perceptual system to respond selectively to certain criterial attributes and to ignore other noncriterial properties.

We have also been working on several techniques for use with infants that would provide an analogue to the labeling or identification task used in adult speech-perception experiments (see Aslin *et al.*, 1977). We call our procedure a "two-alternative go–no-go"'" categorization task because "go" trials consist of presenting a stimulus, S +, and reinforcing an appropriate head turn toward the left whereas "no-go" trials consist of presenting stimulus S − and *not* reinforcing the head-turn response that was reinforced during S + trials. In essence, we are training the infant to respond *only* to the criterial properties of S + that serve as the discriminative stimulus for a head-turn response and not to respond to S −, the stimulus for which a head-turning response is not reinforced.

Table 5.1 summarizes the performance of four infants tested on the go–no-go categorization task. In each case, the background stimulus, S_B was the synthetic vowel /u/, which was 350 msec in duration and repeated once every second. Stimuli S + and S − were the synthetic vowels /a/ and /i/. As shown in Table 5.1, all infants rapidly learned to turn toward a change from the background stimulus to the target stimulus S +. Correct performance was not as high initially when the infants were required to withhold head turning to a change from the background stimulus to S −. However, the fact that they do turn their heads on the first few trials indicates that they are capable of discriminating S − from the background signal—a fact that is clearly necessary for this procedure to be a meaningful analog of an identification paradigm. Despite the infants' difficulties in initially withholding a head-turn response on S − trials, the data shown in Table 5.1 indicate that infants can learn to respond correctly and consistently, and that they can do this quite rapidly in the span of a small number of trials. Although discrimination paradigms such as those described earlier can provide useful and important information about the abilities of young infants to discriminate or detect small and very subtle differences between various kinds of speech signals, additional information is needed about infants' early abilities to classify or categorize acoustically different sounds that adults perceive as phonologically the same.

TABLE 5.1
Individual Subject Data Using the Two-Alternative Go–No-Go Procedure[a]

Subject	Trials	S+ = go	S− = no go	Percentage correct
R. F. (6.5 months)	1–4		Shaping	
S_B = /u/	5–9	3/3	0/2	60
S+ = /i/	10–19	3/3	3/7	60
S− = /a/	20–29	5/5	3/5	80
J. H. (9 months)	1–5		Shaping	
S_B = /u/	6–15	6/6	1/4	70
S+ = /i/	16–25	5/5	2/5	70
S− = /a/	26–35	4/5	2/5	60
	36–45	4/5	2/5	60
	46–52	4/4	2/3	85
M. B. (6 months)	1–18		Shaping	
S_B = /u/	19–28	6/6	1/4	70
S+ = /a/	29–38	4/5	3/5	70
S− = /i/	39–48	4/5	2/5	60
C. M. (8 months)	1–10		Shaping	
S_B = /u/	11–20	5/5	3/5	80
S+ = /i/	21–30	4/7	3/3	70
S− = /a/	31–40	5/7	1/3	60
	41–50	4/5	3/5	70
	51–60	4/4	1/6	50

[a] From Aslin, Perey, Hennessy, and Pisoni (1977).

We are currently using this categorization procedure in our laboratory to collect labeling data from young infants that should be directly comparable to the data collected with adults and chinchillas. Because all of our experiments are run on-line in real-time under computer control, we are able to present a wide range of different experimental signals for generalization testing, thus permitting us to ask a number of different questions concerning perceptual constancy, feature analysis, and the role of early experience in perceptual development. These categorization results should be particularly relevant to questions of the kind we raised earlier surrounding the existence of species-specific perceptual mechanisms for processing biologically significant acoustic signals such as speech.

Concluding Remarks

Our goal in this chapter has been to organize some of the scattered literature in the area of infant speech perception under a uniform conceptual framework that recognizes the important roles early experience plays in perceptual development. Although there is currently a great deal of empirical data available on infant speech perception, the same cannot be said for theories of development. Previous accounts of speech perception have been very naive, in our view, in their treatment of the role of early experience and the possible interactions between genetic and experiential factors in speech perception. We hope that we have been successful in at least pointing out how complex these interactions can be in the development of speech-perception abilities and in suggesting some possible new ways to examine these interactions. Finally, it is our hope that with new experimental techniques to study infant perception and a more sophisticated conceptual framework, many of the general issues surrounding the developmental course of speech perception can be pursued in a more systematic way than has been true in the past.

Acknowledgments

The preparation of this chapter was supported by grants from NIMH (MH–24027–04 and MH–30424–01) and NIH (NS–12179–03 and HD–11915–01) to Indiana University at Bloomington. We wish to thank Alan Perey, Beth Hennessy, Natalie Olinger and Wendy Crawford for their help in carrying out the research reported here and Jerry C. Forshee for his efforts and expertise in developing and maintaining the computer facilities used in our laboratories. Finally, we thank Dr. Peter Jusczyk for his advice on an earlier draft of the manuscript.

References

Abramson, A.S., and Lisker, L. (1970) "Discriminability along the Voicing Continuum: Cross-language Tests," in *Proceedings of the Sixth International Congress of Phonetic Sciences*, Academia, Prague, Pp. 569–573.

Aslin, R.N., Perey, A.J., Hennessy, B., and Pisoni, D.B. (1977) "Perceptual Analysis of Speech Sounds by Prelinguistic Infants: A First Report," Paper presented at the Acoustical Society of America meetings, Miami Beach, December.

Aslin, R.N., and Pisoni, D.B. (1980) "Effects of Early Linguistic Experience on Speech Discrimination by Infants: A Critique of Eilers, Gavin and Wilson (1979)," *Child Development*, 51, 107–112.

Aslin, R.N., Pisoni, D.B., Hennessy, B.L., and Perey, A.J. (1979) "Identification and Discrimination of a New Linguistic Contrast," in J.J. Wolf and D.H. Klatt, eds., *Speech Communication Papers Presented at the 97th Meeting of the Acoustical Society of America*. Acoustical Society of America.

Banks, M.S., and Aslin, R.N. (1975) "Binocular Development in Human Albinos and Congenital Esotropes," Paper presented at the Midwest Regional Association for Research in Vision and Ophthalmology, Ann Arbor, October.

Banks, M.S., Aslin, R.N., and Letson, R.D. (1975) "Sensitive Period for the Development of Human Binocular Vision," *Science*, 190, 675–677.

Blakemore, C. (1976) "The Conditions Required for the Maintenance of Binocularity in Kitten's Visual Cortex," *Journal of Physiology, (London)*, 261, 423–444.

Carney, A.E., Widin, G.P., and Viemeister, N.F. (1977) "Noncategorical Perception of Stop Consonants Differing in VOT," *Journal of the Acoustical Society of America,* 62, 961–970.

Creel, D., Witkop, C.J., and King, R.A. (1974) "Asymmetric Visually Evoked Potentials in Human Albinos: Evidence for Visual System Anomalies," *Investigative Ophthalmology,* 13, 430–440.

Cutting, J.E., and Rosner, B.S. (1974) "Categories and Boundaries in Speech and Music," *Perception & Psychophysics,* 16, 564–570.

Eilers, R.E., Gavin, W.J., and Wilson, W.R. (1980) "Effects of Early Linguistic Experience on Speech Discrimination by Infants: A Reply," *Child Development,* 51, 113–117.

Eilers, R.E., Wilson, W.R., and Gavin, W.J. (1977) "Perception of VOT by Spanish-learning Infants," Paper presented at the ninety-third meeting of the Acoustical Society of America, December.

Eilers, R.E., Wilson, W.R., and Moore, J.M. (1977) "Developmental Changes in Speech Discrimination in Infants," *Journal of Speech and Hearing Research,* 20, 766–780.

Eimas, P.D. (1975) "Auditory and Phonetic Coding of the Cues for Speech: Discrimination of the r–l Distinction by Young Infants," *Perception & Psychophysics,* 18, 341–347.

Eimas, P.D., Siqueland, E.R., Jusczyk, P., and Vigorito, J. (1971) "Speech Perception in Infants," *Science,* 171, 303–306.

Fry, D.B. (1966) "The Development of the Phonological System in the Normal and Deaf Child," in F. Smith and G.A. Miller, eds., *The Genesis of Language,* MIT Press, Cambridge, Pp. 187–216.

Gesell, A.L., and Ames, L.B. (1940) "The Ontogenetic Organization of Prone Behavior in Human Infancy," *Journal of Genetic Psychology,* 56, 247–263.

Gottlieb, G. (1975) "Development of Species Identification in Ducklings: I. Nature of Perceptual Deficit Caused by Embryonic Auditory Deprivation," *Journal of Comparative and Physiological Psychology,* 89, 387–399.

Gottlieb, G. (1976a) "Conceptions of Prenatal Development: Behavioral Embryology," *Psychological Review,* 83, 215–234.

Gottlieb, G. (1976b) "The Roles of Experience in the Development of Behavior and the Nervous System," in G. Gottlieb, ed., *Neural and Behavioral Specificity,* Academic Press, New York.

Grobstein, P., and Chow, K. (1976) "Receptive Field Organization in the Mammalian Visual Cortex: The Role of Individual Experience in Development," in G. Gottlieb, ed., *Neural and Behavioral Specificity,* Academic Press, New York.

Hess, E.H. (1972). "Imprinting in a Natural Laboratory," *Scientific American,* 227, 24–31.

Hirsh, I.J. (1959) "Auditory Perception of Temporal Order," *Journal of the Acoustical Society of America,* 31 (6), 759–767.

Hubel, D.H., and Wiesel, T.N. (1963) "Receptive Fields of Cells in Striate Cortex of Very Young, Visually Inexperienced Kittens," *Journal of Neurophysiology,* 26, 994–1002.

Hubel, D.H., and Wiesel, T.N. (1965) "Binocular Interaction in Striate Cortex of Kittens Reared with Artificial Squint," *Journal of Neurophysiology,* 28, 1041–1059.

Hubel, D.H., and Wiesel, T.N. (1970) "The Period of Susceptibility to the Physiological Effects of Unilateral Eye Closure in Kittens," *Journal of Physiology* (London), 206, 419–436.

Jusczyk, P.W., Murray, J., and Bayly, J. (1979) "The Perception of Place of Articulation in Fricatives and Stops by Infants" Paper presented at the meeting of the Society for Research in Child Development, San Francisco.

Jusczyk, P.W., Pisoni, D.B., Walley, A., and Murray, J. (1980) "Discrimination of Relative Tone Onset Time of Two-Component Tones by Infants," *Journal of the Acoustical Society of America,* 67, 262–270.

Jusczyk, P.W., Rosner, B.S., Cutting, J.E., Foard, C.F., and Smith, L.B. (1977) "Categorical Perception of Non-speech Sounds by Two-month-old Infants," *Perception & Psychophysics,* 21, 50–54.

Kuhl, P.K., and Miller, J.D. (1975) "Speech Perception by the Chinchilla: Voiced–voiceless Distinction in Alveolar Plosive Consonants," *Science*, 190, 69–72.

Kuhl, P.K., and Miller, J.D. (1978) "Speech Perception by the Chinchilla: Indentification Functions for Synthetic VOT Stimuli," *Journal of the Acoustical Society of America*, 63, 905–917.

Lasky, R.E., Syrdal-Lasky, A., and Klein, R.E. (1975) "VOT Discrimination by Four to Six and a Half Month Old Infants from Spanish Environments," *Journal of Experimental Child Psychology*, 20, 215–225.

Levitt, H. (1970) "Transformed Up–down Methods in Psychoacoustics," *Journal of the Acoustical Society of America*, 49, 467–477.

Liljencrants, J., and Lindblom, B. (1972) "Numerical Simulation of Vowel Quality Systems: The Role of Perceptual Contrast," *Language*, 48, 839–862.

Lisker, L., and Abramson, A.S. (1964) "A Cross Language Study of Voicing in Initial Stops: Acoustical Measurements," *Word*, 20, 384–422.

Lisker, L., and Abramson, A.S. (1967) "The Voicing Dimension: Some Experiments in Comparative Phonetics," *Proceedings of the Sixth International Congress of Phonetic Sciences*, Prague.

Miller, J.D., Wier, C.C., Pastore, R., Kelly, W.J., and Dooling, R.J. (1976) "Discrimination and Labeling of Noise–buzz Sequences with Varying Noise-lead Times: An Example of Categorical Perception," *Journal of the Acoustical Society of America*, 60 (2), 410–417.

Miyawaki, K., Strange, W., Verbrugge, R., Liberman, A.M., Jenkins, J.J., and Fujimura, O. (1975) "An Effect of Linguistic Experience: The Discrimination of [r] and [l] by native speakers of Japanese and English," *Perception & Psychophysics*, 18, 331–340.

Olson, C.R., and Pettigrew, J.D. (1974) "Single Units in Visual Cortex of Kittens Reared in Stroboscopic Illumination," *Brain Research*, 70, 189–204.

Pettigrew, J.D. (1974) "The Effect of Visual Experience on the Development of Stimulus Specificity by Kitten Cortical Neurons," *Journal of Physiology* (London), 237, 49–74.

Pisoni, D.B. (1977) "Identification and Discrimination of the Relative Onset of Two Component Tones: Implications for the Perception of Voicing in Stops," *Journal of the Acoustical Society of America*, 61, 1352–1361.

Sherk, H., and Stryker, M.P. (1977) "Quantitative Study of Cortical Orientation Selectivity in Visually Inexperienced Kitten," *Journal of Neurophysiology*, 39(1), 63–70.

Shiffrin, R.M., and Schneider, W. (1977) "Controlled and Automatic Human Information Processing: II. Perceptual Learning, Automatic Attending and a General Theory," *Psychological Review*, 84, 127–190.

Stevens, K.N., and Klatt, D.H. (1974) "Role of Formant Transitions in the Voiced–voiceless Distinction for Stops," *Journal of the Acoustical Society of America*, 55, 653–659.

Strange, W., and Jenkins, J.J. (1978) "The Role of Linguistic Experience in the Perception of Speech," in H.L. Pick, Jr., and R.D. Walk, eds., *Perception and Experience*, Plenum, New York.

Trehub, S.E. (1976) "The Discrimination of Foreign Speech Contrasts by Infants and Adults," *Child Development*, 47, 466–472.

Williams, C.L. "Speech Perception and Production as a Function of Exposure to a Second Language," Doctoral Dissertation, Harvard University, 1974.

Chapter 6

PHONEMIC PERCEPTION IN CHILDREN

DAVID BARTON

Introduction

This Chapter is an assessment of recent research on phonemic perception. To distinguish this research area from studies of infant perception (reviewed in Aslin and Pisoni, Chapter 5; Kuhl, Chapter 4; and Eilers, Chapter 3; this volume), we need to begin by defining the term *phonemic perception*. Definitions of perception usually contain the two aspects of *sensation* plus *interpretation*, as in the following broad definition of perception as being "the process whereby a living organism receives and interprets information about the surrounding world [Julesz and Hirsch, 1972, p. 285]." These two aspects are important here where we are concerned not just with perceptual discrimination but also with the classification of speech sounds into the categories of phonology. With phonemic perception, then, we are dealing with the classification of speech into the minimal units that signify meaning differences. This emphasis on defining phonemic perception in terms of meaning differences is implicit in Shvachkin's (1948) work. It is also similar to Ferguson's (1975) approach, where it is defined as using sound differences to "identify, store, and recognize lexical items [p. 7]."

We are working at the level of phonemic perception and it should be

CHILD PHONOLOGY
VOLUME 2: PERCEPTION

kept distinct from auditory perception. Obviously some auditory perception is a prerequisite for phonological perception, and it forms the first part of the two part definition of perception; nevertheless, the two can be kept distinct. To take the example of voicing in English, there are many different acoustic cues for the recognition of voicing. We are not concerned here with these cues, but with the use to which they are put: that of classifying oral consonants as voiced or unvoiced in real words in running speech. The perception of some relevant acoustic cues is obviously a prerequisite for this classification. However, there need not be any one-to-one relationship of acoustic cues to phonological features, and phonological features need not be dependent on any invariant set of acoustic features. Thus the work on infant discrimination may demonstrate that infants can discriminate between certain speech categories; however, it obviously does not demonstrate that the infants make use of these categories in their understanding of speech.

There have been many experiments in the past 20 years that have aimed to test the speech-sound discrimination abilities of children. The experiments have come from several different traditions of research, and they have used a variety of discrimination tasks to test different abilities in children ranging in age from less than 1 year to over 10 years. Researchers in speech perception, child development, linguistics, and speech therapy have all been interested in children's speech-sound discrimination. The importance of this work for linguistic theory is that regularities in the production data of children suggest that they make use of greater phonological complexity than a synchronic description of surface regularities would require. In capturing the regularities of production, some child phonologists have used descriptions that, if they are to have any psychological reality, require a child's perception to be well ahead of production (e.g., Smith, 1973). If the data on phonemic perception support this possibility, such descriptions may reflect the cognitive processes of children; if the data do not support this position, such descriptions, though elegant, cease to have the explanatory potential they claim.

The main assessment of these experiments will be in the sections dealing with specific claims and problems. To give these sections substance, we will first describe some of the studies in detail. Of the many studies of children that investigated some aspect of speech-sound discrimination, we have tried to select those that are significant in their results or methodological contributions. We will first describe studies that have been concerned with orders of acquisition and the ages at which children can first make certain discriminations. We will then give examples of other studies, usually with older children, that have been concerned more with accuracy. The sections that follow these each discuss a separate issue that arises from comparison of these studies. Here we concentrate on studies using real speech; for studies using synthetic stimuli, see Strange and Broen, Chapter 7, this volume.

Age of Acquisition

The studies in this section are concerned with plotting the ages at which children can first make these discriminations. There has always been anecdotal evidence on this subject, but there has been little actual experimentation. The classic study is Shvachkin's (1948) investigation of 18 Russian children, some of whom were less than 1 year old at the beginning of the experiments. Shvachkin's method has been adapted by Garnica and has been used in studies of speech-sound discrimination of young English-speaking children (Garnica, 1971, 1973; Edwards, 1974).

In his painstaking experiments, Shvachkin taught children names for objects. In testing any phonemic opposition, there would be three objects and they would each have different CVC names; two would differ minimally in their initial consonants, whereas the third would differ from the first two in all three segments. Thus, the names of three objects might be /mak/, /bak/ and /zub/. When these could be distinguished, all three objects would be tested together. The child would be asked to carry out some task with one of the minimally different objects.

By following children over time, Shvachkin was able to plot an order of acquisition of discriminations for each child. These were analyzed as being an order of acquisition of features, and a general sequence of stages for all children was given. Shvachkin's conclusion was that the children could make all of these discriminations before the age of 2 years. Not all the details of the methodology were reported by Shvachkin; in particular, we do not know how many trials were given to each child for each opposition nor how high the criterion was for accepting that a discrimination could be made.

Garnica (1971) carried out a pilot study on English-speaking children based on Shvachkin's method. Her subjects were eight children aged between 1:9 and 3:5. The objects used in this experiment were wooden blocks with faces painted on them; they were given nonsense CVC syllables as names. Pairs of CVCs differed in their initial consonants and the child was asked to carry out a task with one of the pair. From the results it was established whether or not the child could make each discrimination tested and an overall order of acquisition was constructed. Garnica did not give an overall error rate for the results, but, as she presented the raw data, it is possible to compute an error rate. The mean error rate for the discriminations turns out to be 34.5%.

There are two published studies that have made use of this Shvachkin–Garnica technique. First, Garnica began a main experiment (Garnica, 1973) based on the pilot study. The subjects for this were 15 children aged from 1:5 to 1:10. The experimental procedure and scoring were similar to the pilot study (except that there were some specific training sessions for teaching the words). The order that had been obtained in the pilot study was used as a basis for deciding which pairs the children were tested on. The children were tested over two time periods and their results improved. There was more variation between children than had been observed in the earlier study, and the universal order of acquisition was recast as general trends. Only preliminary results and analysis were given; further results have never been published, and the study seems to have been left unfinished.

The other study that has made use of this technique is a study by Edwards (1974). It is important in that it is one of the few studies that relates perception to production in a systematic way. The subjects were 28 children ranging in age from 1:8 to 3:11 (but only a few of them were used in any one part of the experiment). Some interesting hypotheses were explored in this study; one of these was that the ability to discriminate voicing in stops precedes this ability in fricatives; another suggestive hypothesis was that the ability to discriminate velar spirants would be acquired at a specific point in phonological development, even though such sounds are absent from the English language.

Unfortunately, all the results were vitiated by the statistical treatment. The criterion used for judging whether or not a child could make a particular discrimination was that he should obtain seven correct responses in 10 trials. As explained elsewhere (Barton, 1975a), this low criterion does not give statistically significant results. Using it, approximately one in six of the results thought significant will in fact not be so. This is crucial, because many of Edward's orderings are dependent on very small differences in the results.

In the light of Shvachkin's and Garnica's experiments, I carried out two experiments in phonemic perception. The first experiment (Barton 1975b, 1976, Chapter 3) involved 20 children aged 2:3 to 2:11. This seemed a likely age range for problems of discrimination; in Garnica's study there had been some common discriminations that children of this age apparently could not make. The stimuli were 20 minimally different pairs of words. After an identification stage to assess how well the children knew each word, there was a discrimination stage where the cards were presented repeatedly in a random order. The pairs were illustrated, and there were recorded instructions to point to one of the pair.

The results of this experiment were far better than might be expected from Garnica's findings, and there were only a few cases where children did not discriminate the pairs. Furthermore there was a very high level of unequivocal responding where children consistently discriminated correctly. It was also found that how well the children knew the words seriously affected the results (Barton 1976b). Most of the failures to discriminate occurred when at least one of the pair was a taught word. This was despite the fact that these taught words could be identified correctly in the nonminimal situation. In these cases, it was not possible to know whether the difficulty was with the discrimination or whether it lay in not knowing these taught words adequately.

The second study (Barton 1976a, Chapter 4) investigated the phonemic discrimination abilities of younger children. The subjects were 10 children aged 1:8 to 2:0. Preliminary experimentation showed that the method used with the older children was difficult for these younger children and a method more suited to their demands was used. Just two discriminations, /b–p/ and /g–k/, were investigated; again, they were ones that were thought difficult on the basis of the Shvachkin–Garnica ordering. Toy objects were used and attention was paid to ensuring that the children knew the names of the stimuli.

The minimal pairs chosen were *bear–pear* and *goat–coat*; these gave distinct objects, and there were obvious games that could be played to teach the words in nonminimal pairs: the bear could put on and take off the coat and the goat could nibble at the pear. At least one session was devoted to teaching the nonminimal pairs.

At the beginning of the main experimental sessions, at least 24 hrs after the teaching sessions had been completed, the nonminimal pairs were checked. Until this point, the child had not met the pairs in a minimal situation. Now, all four objects were played with together. The child was asked to get the objects out of the bag before playing with them and to put them away afterward. The instructions now took the form "get out the coat . . . now get out the pear . . . now get out the bear . . . and now the goat." This was done repeatedly and the order in which the objects were requested was randomized. Each set of four requests to take out or put away the objects demanded minimal and nonminimal discriminations from the child. They were analyzed separately. Nonminimal errors on any of the trials were noted, as an excessive number of them indicated that the child was not attending, or that he found this four-object task more difficult than the two-object one.

The four-object task was first carried out with oral instructions. If possible, it was later checked using prerecorded stimuli. Eight of the 10 children could do at least one of the discriminations. Comparison of minimal and nonminimal errors suggested that some of the children were experiencing difficulty with the experimental task. However, it was not clear to what extent failures of discrimination were due to task difficulty rather than to inabilities to discriminate. No lower limit had been set for selecting the children for this experiment and we found that, with the available children, the situation was too difficult for any children under 1:8.

Another study using children under 3 years is reported by Eilers and Oller (1975). Their subjects were 14 children aged from 1:10 to 2:2. The pairs to be discriminated were pairs of objects; one was a familiar object, such as a fish; the other was a nonsense toy that was given a name, [ΘIʃ] in this case. There were eight pairs involving three types of contrast. Five pairs were objects with common substitutions, such as [fIʃ] and [ΘIʃ], two pairs had uncommon substitutions, and the last pair differed in more than one phonological feature.

In the experimental trials, a reward would be hidden under one of the two toys; the child would receive it if he chose correctly when told that it was under one of the pair. Results varied from the good discrimination of the pair that differed by two features [kʰow–pow], down to the pairs [flʃ]–[ΘIʃ] and [mʌkI]–[mʌɲkI] not being discriminated by any of the children. No difference was found between the pairs involving a common substitution and those containing an unlikely one. The authors concluded that, although some discriminations were more difficult than others for 2-year-old children, common substitutions do not necessarily give the most difficulty.

Accuracy of Discrimination

In this section, we will describe some of the studies that have been concerned primarily with the accuracy of speech-sound discrimination in children who have acquired most of the phonological discriminations of the language in their speech, children of at least 3 years of age.

An important study that established norms of language development is that of Templin (1957). The norms were based on the results of an investigation of 480 children aged from 3 years to 8 years. The study covered articulation, vocabulary, sentence development, and speech-sound discrimination. The standard discrimination test used consisted of presenting each child with pairs of nonsense syllables that had to be judged as same or different. An overall score on the test was given, and it was not broken down phonologically. The main result was that children aged between 6 and 8 years improved significantly at the task but that, even at 8 years, their scores were not perfect.

Templin found that this task with nonsense syllables was too difficult for children younger than 6 years, and a different test was constructed. With children from 3 to 5 years, the stimuli were 59 pairs of pictures of objects whose names differed in "one sound element," pairs such as *box* and *blocks*; in this test the children had to point to whichever picture was named by the experimenter. As with the older children, Templin found that these children's accuracy improved gradually with age.

A diagnostic test that uses a same–different judgment for real words is Wepman's (1958) Auditory Discrimination Test. There are 40 word pairs, such as *tub–tug*; they are presented orally, and the children judge whether the two words are the same or different. Each pair is presented once and the test takes about 5 min to administer. The results for a child are in the form of an overall score. This diagnostic test is appropriate for children aged between 5 and 8 years, and it has been used in some of the studies that are mentioned in what follows. In a normative study of the Wepman test, Snyder and Pope (1970) compiled error rates for some of the individual word pairs;

these error rates ranged from 1–2% to 76%. The pairs giving most difficulty were *sheath–sheaf, vow–thou* and *clothe–clove.*

A study contemporary to Templin's and Wepman's that began to look at the results of individual discriminations is that of Pronovost and Dumbleton (1958). This too was used as a diagnostic test. They studied 434 children aged 6 years. The stimuli used were 36 "easily pictured word pairs" where the pairs of words differed in one phoneme. To test each pair, a card containing three pairs of illustrations was used. One of the pairs was the test pair (e.g., *bowl–pole*); the other two were of each of the stimulus words paired with itself, to give *pole–pole*, and *bowl–bowl*, in this example. The experimenter said a pair of words, and the child had to point to the appropriate pair of illustrations. Overall, of a possible score of 72 (36 stimuli tested twice), scores ranged from 16 to 72 with a mean of 65.5.

The scores for all children on each word pair were also examined and an order of difficulty of the word pairs was given. They ranged from *cat–bat*, which was responded to correctly on 98.6% of occasions to *cone–comb*, which was correct only 35.7% of the time. These results were skewed, in that only a dozen pairs were responded to correctly on less than 90% of occasions.

Pronovost and Dumbleton (1958) found that using pairs of real words limited the range of discriminations that could be tested, whereas Templin had found that her task with meaningless syllables was only suitable with children of at least 6 years. Graham and House (1971) managed to use nonsense words with children between 3 and 4.5 years. They did this by training their subjects (30 girls) on tasks with progressively more abstract stimuli. Again, a same–different task was used. The training consisted of beginning with pairs of same or different objects and gradually moving to the more abstract stimuli. In the experimental situation, the task was to judge pairs of nonsense words of the form [hə'Cadə], where C was the consonant that varied.

In their results, Graham and House gave mean error rates for each consonant paired with every other consonant. The error rates for these pairs ranged from 2 to 79%; the mean error rate for these different pairs was 14%, and there were 11 pairs with error rates of greater than 20%. Although individual sound pairs (p–t, p–d, p–k, etc.) showed wide variation in error rates, there was much less variation in total error rates for each sound (/p/ contrasted with all other sounds, /t/ contrasted with all other sounds, etc.)

An ingenious experiment that combined the simplicity of real words with the range of contrasts of nonsense words was the study by Koenigsknecht and Lee (1968). In their experiment, the stimulus for each discrimination was an illustrated "key word," such as *man*. The child heard a recorded list of words, such as *tan, man, ban, kan, han. . .*, where the key word appeared several times. The children had to respond whenever they heard the correct word. The subjects were 20 children aged between 3 and 4 years.

As with other studies, it was found here that there were more errors in contrasts that differed from the key word by only one feature. With such contrasts, there were no errors when the feature was nasal–oral, 17.6% when it was stop–continuant, 30.3% for place of articulation, and 35.8% for voicing. Koenigsknecht and Lee (1968) reported that the children could do the task easily and that they attended well throughout the experiment.

Another study was a short one by Locke (1971). The subjects were 20 children aged from 2:0 to 3:10 with a mean of 3:4. The stimuli were 28 pairs of pictures, the names of which differed from each other in only one segment. Fourteen of the pairs differed from each other in place of articulation, and the other 14 differed in other features. While being tested, the child was shown each pair of pictures in turn and instructed to point to one of the pair. Each pair was presented once, and the child was given an overall score. Locke found that these scores varied in accuracy from 70 to 100%, but that there was no significant difference between the results on the place and the nonplace distinctions. No further analysis was given.

Real Words and Nonsense Words

The problem of whether real words or nonsense words are to be used as stimuli is an old one. The point that we wish to make in this section is that what is more important is how the words are treated by the subjects in the experimental task.

Some studies used pairs of real words, whereas others used nonsense syllables. Often, real words were used in conjunction with pictures of objects; the pictures would be in pairs, and the task would consist of indicating whichever of the pictures was named. Usually, the task with nonsense syllables was to judge whether both members of a pair of spoken syllables were the same or whether they were different. In general, the real-word task was used with the younger children; this was because the judgmental task with nonsense syllables was too difficult for the younger children. Templin (1957), for instance, used nonsense syllables with children of at least 6 years and real words with the younger children. Graham and House managed to use the judgment of pairs of nonsense syllables with children of 3 years; they managed this by training the children to make same–different judgments first with actual objects and gradually with more and more abstract stimuli. Another experiment, by Tikofsky and McInish (1968) used a same–different task with both real and nonsense words as stimuli.

With even younger children, sometimes under 2 years, Shvachkin and Garnica have used nonsense syllables, but they have been taught as words;

therefore, assuming they have been taught adequately, they can be treated by the children as previously unknown words. This makes use of the great advantage of nonsense words over real words, namely that the complete range of phonological discriminations can be tested. Eilers and Oller (1975) have used the interesting approach of pairing real words with invented words.

In some cases, real words are used but, because of the nature of the task, it is possible for them to be treated as nonsense words. In Wepman's (1958) test, for example, real words were used; pairs of them were presented and they had to be judged as same or different. In this situation, it does not necessarily matter whether all the words are known by the children. The test can still be done if they do not know some of the words, and the words can even be regarded as nonsense words. The situation is slightly different in Garnica's experiment. Here nonsense words were taught as names. However, in each trial, both objects were identified by the experimenter, and from the way the instructions to the child were spoken, it was possible for the child to treat them as nonsense words.

There have been studies comparing real and nonsense words. Perozzi and Kunze (1971), for instance, found a high correlation between a real-word discrimination test and a nonsense syllable test. From this they concluded that the two tests involved the same skills, and that one could use either to test children's abilities. However, the high correlation may have arisen from the similar tasks involved rather than from the fact that word tests and nonsense syllable tests in themselves tap the same skills. In both tests, the stimuli were presented in pairs and a same–different judgment had to be made. The word test was essentially similar to Wepman's (1958) test and, as in that test, there was no need for the stimuli to be treated as real words.

Another experiment that compared real and nonsense words (McNeil and Stone, 1965) found nonsense words easier than real words but, again, the important variable was the task involved. In McNeil and Stone's experiment, 60 children aged 5–6 years were asked what sounds they heard in certain words. Half the children were tested on real words and were asked questions like "do you hear /s/ or /m/ in *came*?"; the other half were tested on nonsense words and were asked such questions as "do you hear /s/ or /m/ in *bame*?" It was found that the group that had real words in the stimuli did not do as well at the task as the group that had nonsense words. However, the way in which the question was posed to the children suggests that the skill being tapped in this experiment was that of breaking down words into their components. The skill necessary for this task is separate from speech-sound discrimination and develops later than it (as argued by Zhurova, 1964). McNeil and Stone's (1965) results are of importance to studies on analyzing words in terms of sounds; nevertheless, they do not establish that nonsense words are, in themselves, easier to discriminate than real words.

Perceptual Judgment or Internal Reference

The main difficulty that nonsense syllables bring with them is the problem of interpretation: One tests sound discrimination with nonsense syllables, but it is not always clear that one is testing phonemic discrimination. Whether the discrimination of nonsense syllables taps the same abilities as the discrimination of speech sounds of course depends on the task. In the very common paradigm with nonsense syllables of having to judge two stimuli as the same or different, a perceptual comparison of the two stimuli is possible. The task commonly used with real words involves quite different processes. With real words, there are often two pictures representing the words and only one is named; deciding on the correct one can only be done by reference to some internal representation. Any comparison of this stimulus with any other has to be internal. It is this latter task, where there has to be some reference to internal representation, and that we assume is therefore mediated by the phonological system, which we defined as phonemic perception. However, in some of the studies that have addressed themselves to phonemic perception, such as Garnica's, both words are presented when the child has to respond, and it is possible for the child to make a perceptual judgment and not refer to any internal representation.

Word Familiarity

The main problem with real words is that they have to be known by the children. In the common situation of pairs of pictures, where the children have to choose one of the pictures, they need to be able to relate each word to the appropriate picture. (In some of the two-way forced-choice situations there may be the possibility of "choosing negatively," that is, knowing only one of the pair and always associating the unknown stimulus word with the unknown picture.) The problem of whether or not the children knew the words is mentioned in several of the studies. Templin, for example, tried several methods of scoring items, none of which proved completely satisfactory. In the Wepman test, many of the words would be unfamiliar to young children. The words in each pair were equated for familiarity using the Thorndike–Lorge lists. However, these lists, based on word counts of books for older children, cannot be taken as very accurate here.

Because some researchers were clearly worried by the problem of whether the words were known and made attempts to overcome it, it is surprising that other researchers do not even mention it. Koenigsknecht and Lee (1968) do not mention it; Pronovost and Dumbleton (1953) merely named any unknown words for the children; and Eilers and Oller (1975), with their 2-year-olds, seem to have assumed that the children knew all the stimulus words. Locke excluded one pair from his analysis on the grounds that one member of a pair was "markedly clearer and more familiar than the other" but he does not mention the possibility that knowledge of the words may have affected the results on all the pairs. To the child, nonsense words are equivalent to unknown words and can be taught. In Garnica's study, all the words were unknown, in that they were invented words, and they were taught to the children (although it appears that this was not completely successful). In my first study, how well the children knew the words was assessed at the beginning. The words were classified as *named* (where the child named the word before the experimenter), *prompted* (where the child identified the word when it was named by the experimenter), and *taught*. The number of errors the children made in the discrimination task was found to be closely linked to how well they knew the words.

A "True" Picture of Discrimination Abilities

An important fact about the tasks that were mentioned earlier is that the various tasks may tap different skills—that judging whether two stimuli presented together are the same, for example, requires different abilities from that of choosing the correct picture after hearing one word. Even the various tasks that involve the same types of judgments, such as those that require a same–different response, may be different for the children because of variables such as the training given and the way the child is encouraged to construe the situation. These variables can affect the types of skills used and the overall level of the scores.

An experiment not mentioned so far (Kamil and Rudegeair, 1972) was concerned solely with how experimental variables could affect the level of scores. The subjects in this experiment were 24 children aged from 5 to 6 years. The task was slightly different from any described so far. The stimuli were pairs of contrasting nonsense syllables, and they were presented through two loudspeakers on opposite sides of the testing room. One item was spoken through one speaker; this was followed by the other item through the other speaker. Then *who said X?* was spoken through both speakers, where *X* was one of the two stimuli. The child had to point to the correct loudspeaker.

One experimental variable that Kamil and Rudegeair investigated was testing over time; they tested the children on the same task on 6 consecutive days. It was found that the children improved significantly at the test after the first day and Kamil and Rudegeair suggested that the initial testing be ignored. They also investigated the difference between repeated contrast pairs, such as [bɔb–dɔd], and single contrast pairs, such as [bɔ–dɔ]. Whereas the single contrast pairs, the ones normally used in such tests, gave error rates of around 15%, there were only about 10% of errors with the repeated contrasts. The authors argued that these repeated contrast pairs gave "a truer picture of discrimination abilities . . . uncontaminated by attentional factors [p. 1091]."

The crucial word in this statement is "truer." Their claim is that their lower error rates obtained with repeated contrast pairs were a more accurate reflection of speech-sound discrimination abilities. They successfully reduced the errors that arose from the difficulty of the task and that had interfered with the scores. Given this demonstrated variation in scores, it may be instructive to look at how difficult the tasks in the other studies were.

In Templin's work, it was specifically because the same-different judgment of nonsense syllables was too difficult for younger children that she used the real-word test. The real-word test was used with children from 3 to 5 years, and she suggested that it was too difficult for children younger than that. By training on easier tasks, Graham and House (1971) used a nonsense syllable task with 3-year-old children, whereas Locke (1971), without mentioning any difficulties, used a real-word test with children as young as 2 years. Some experimenters mention that the children found the task in itself simple and interesting; this is true in Koenigsknecht and Lee, for example, and also in my first study. Contrasted with this, Garnica gave the impression that the children in her experiment found the task difficult. Consideration of the difficulties often found when experimenting with young children also makes the results of Shvachkin more remarkable—or more uncertain.

We are arguing here that a difficult task may interfere with the results of a discrimination test and that, in general, the simpler the task the better the test. This is true if one's aim is to get the closest reflection of children's discrimination abilities. However, these studies have varied in their aims and not all of them have wanted to get the highest possible scores. The diagnostic tests, for instance, need to distinguish clearly the children with discrimination difficulties from the normal population. It is useful, in such tests, if the results are skewed towards the top end, so that most children score within a narrow range whereas those with difficulties clearly stand out with lower scores. However, with tests that establish norms, it is best if the scores are spread throughout the whole range of possible results. When results are too bunched up and cover too narrow a range of the scale, differences in performance do not show up clearly. This is the reason that Perozzi and Kunze (1971) argued that some speech-sound discrimination tests should be *more* difficult: to spread out the results of children who would otherwise be bunched up near the top of the scale. This may be necessary for establishing norms, but in phonemic perception studies we are interested in tapping children's actual abilities and so we will want the simplest task that does this; if the results are bunched up near the top, it will indicate that most children can do most of the discriminations (referring to "actual" abilities is deliberately simplistic and will be spelled out as we go on).

Tasks with different aims, then, will bring with them different notions of what constitutes a "truer" picture of abilities. Kamil and Rudegeair (1972) obtained a better result by testing more than once and by repeating the contrast in the stimulus. It may be argued, however, that distinguishing repeated contrasts, though easier, is not the skill required for normal speech discrimination and that this experimental task does not reflect the everyday nonexperimental situation. If that is the case, Kamil and Rudegeair's higher scores do not give a "truer" picture of phonemic perception.

Presentation of the Stimuli

Whatever the aim of the investigation, the task needs to be presented in a well-controlled experiment. The area where these tasks sometimes appear not to be well controlled is the manner of presentation of the stimuli. Whereas some of the studies used recorded stimuli in situations where it was not possible for the experimenters to give nonverbal cues, several of the studies used spoken stimuli and have not considered the possibility of nonverbal cues. Eilers and Oller (1975) compared live and recorded stimuli in their situation and found no difference in the results obtained with them. Their comparison can be faulted as there was a 3.5-month interval between the two tests, and the live tests were always before the recorded tests; it is probably true, though, that a careful live test can be equivalent to a recorded test. In my second study, where the children were willing to carry out the task with recorded stimuli, there was no difference between the results for live presentation and those with recorded presentation. Nevertheless, a spoken test is much less well controlled. Proof of this is found in Pronovost and Dumbleton's (1953) report that they obtained much better results from one of their experimenters who scored 50% of the children tested as having no errors. This was attributed to the one experimenter emphasizing the sound that differentiated the words, when speaking the stimulus words.

The possibility of visual cues from the experimenter helping the subjects was recognized in some of the studies; Graham and House (1971), for example, used live stimuli, but they ensured from the positioning of the experimenter that there was no possibility of visual cuing. However, in some studies, such as Garnica's, these problems did not seem to have been considered. In her experiments, the stimuli were spoken and the experimenter deliberately sat in front of the child. This gave a situation where it was possible that the experimenter unconsciously indicated the correct response by means of such cues as eye movement or body movement. In my second study, for instance, I observed an adult who often put her hand out toward the correct object in anticipation of the child choosing it. For some speech sounds there may also be cues from visible articulation.

Level of Accuracy

The most general result is that obtained by Templin (1957): That children's speech-sound discrimination abilities increase up to 8 years of age, and that even at 8 their scores are not perfect. (There was an error rate of about 6% for 8-year-olds.) This general pattern was supported by the other studies. Given such a task with no masking conditions we assume that adults would get all the discriminations correct. Therefore, even at age 8, children are not as accurate as adults.

It is difficult to give overall error rates for the various ages, however, because the stimuli and tasks were so very different in these studies. One important variable is the position of the discrimination in the word or syllable. Studies have usually kept to one position or they have used only initial and final position. Medial position and embedding in clusters have generally not been tested, and words have usually been presented in isolation or in a fixed frame.

The results support the commonly held view that sounds in initial position are easier to discriminate than those in final position, although often there was not a great deal of difference between the two positions. The initial position was found to be easier in Pronovost and Dumbleton (1953) and in the normative studies of Templin (1957) and Snyder and Pope (1970). Kamil and Rudegeair (1972) found no difference between initial and final position and Koenigsknecht and Lee (1968) found the final position slightly easier. This last result may be explained by the nature of the task in Koenigsknecht and Lee's experiment: it is possible that the children used strategies of attending to rhyme in evaluating the stimuli.

Accuracy of Specific Features

It was a common observation in these studies that pairs that differed from each other in only one feature gave more difficulty than those that differed in more than one feature. This was pointed out by Graham and House (1971), Koenigsknecht and Lee (1968), Tikofsky and McInish (1968), and Eilers and Oller (1975). It was also true in the results of Pronovost and Dumbleton (1953) and Snyder and Pope (1970), although they did not mention the fact. Pairs seemed progressively easier as the number of features separating them increased.

One-feature differences are not all equal in their difficulty. This was made explicit in three of the studies: Tikofsky and McInish (1968) only found errors involving either place or voice in their 7-year-olds; Koenigsknecht and Lee (1968) found that, with one-feature differences, the error rate ranged from 0% with nasality to 35% errors with voicing; Graham and House (1971) reported that their one-feature errors went from 7% in the contrast rounded–unrounded to 30% in the contrast voiced–unvoiced.

Looking more closely at the results, we find that Tikofsky and McInish (1968) reported that all their voicing errors could be attributed to just three of the six voicing contrasts: /v–f, z–s and Θ–ð/. Most of their errors of place could be attributed to the two pairs /f–Θ and v–ð/. This possibility was not mentioned by Graham and House (1971), but their results showed that it was also true that their high error rate for voicing did not reflect a high error rate in all voicing pairs. From their choice of consonants, only two voicing contrasts were tested, /t–d and s–z/. The former had an error rate of 13%, which did not differ significantly from the mean error rate, whereas the latter had an error rate of 52%, the third highest error rate recorded. /s–z/ was the voicing contrast that gave the most errors in Tikofsky and McInish's (1968) study, whereas /t–d/ did not give any errors. Thus different pairs differing only in voicing can vary a great deal in how easy they are to discriminate. My finding that children aged 1:8–2:0 can usually discriminate /k–g and p–b/ cannot, therefore, be assumed to hold for all the voicing contrasts. There is an important parallel here with production where it has also been observed that the acquisition of one feature in a sound does not necessarily imply its acquisition in all relevant sounds (e.g., Ferguson, 1978).

Looking at the individual pairs, Graham and House (1971) found that 11 of their pairs gave error rates of greater than 20%. They were, starting with the most difficult: /f–Θ, r–w, s–w, tʃ–ʃ, l–r, m–n, m–l, l–w, s–ʃ, p–t, p–m/. In Pronovost and Dumbleton's (1953) study, the consonant contrasts that appeared in word pairs that were correct less than 90% of the time (ignoring position in the words), were /n–m, tʃ–ʃ, v–f, p–t, r–l, g–k, and s–Θ/. The pairs that Snyder and Pope (1970) referred to as giving most difficulty, again in word frames, were /f–Θ, and v–ð/; /f–Θ/ was also difficult in Eiler and Oller's (1975) study. In Tikofsky and McInish's results, the only pairs to give errors were /v–ð, f–Θ, z–s, v–f, and Θ–ð/.

Because these studies tested different speech sounds, there are no specific pairs that all studies found difficult. Nevertheless, these lists, obtained in several different types of experiments, have much in common. As noted earlier, many of the paired sounds differ from each other in only one feature. There is not one feature that stands out as being more difficult than the others. Using Chomsky and Halle's (1968) features, coronal, continuant, anterior, strident, and voice all appear as the one feature involved. However, the specific pair that appears to be most difficult is /f–Θ/ and, although similar acoustically, these two sounds differ from each other in two features, coronality and stridency. Not all the consonants of English appear in these lists; all the continuants are there, and a high proportion of the sounds are in fact continuants. One can go further and point out that nearly all the difficult discriminations here are between pairs of continuants.

There is a great danger in interpreting these lists: it arises from the fact that in none of these studies were all the consonants of English compared. The only studies that compared them all were the ones that did not break down their results into individual sound pairs, such as Koenigsknecht and Lee (1968).

With real words, there is the constraint that one can only test pairs of sounds that exist in pairs of minimally different English words (and, frustratingly, English often seems to avoid minimal pairs involving "difficult discriminations)." Where studies used only some sound pairs, the selection was not random but was usually chosen for specific reasons. Templin's (1957) pairs, for instance, were chosen by the criterion that they distinguished most between older and younger children. Wepman (1958) only used pairs that did not differ in manner of articulation. In Graham and House's (1971) study, 16 consonants were studied. The consonants were chosen to represent a wide range of distinctive feature differences. Pairs involving "the most common distinctions in English" such as voicing, were deliberately kept to a minimum. Had they chosen different voicing pairs, they would have obtained different results. In fact, when comparing studies that discuss the difficulty of specific features, much of the difference in error rates can be attributed to the choice of pairs tested. The conclusion to all these results is that one cannot simply refer to certain features as being "difficult to discriminate" without specifying the sound pairs they appear in.

Differences between "Order of Acquisition" and "Level of Accuracy"

All the results discussed so far have been concerned with the level of difficulty of speech-sound discriminations. The results of Shvachkin, Garnica, and Edwards have claimed to have a different aim: the investigation of the order of acquisition of speech-sound discriminations. The two claims, that there is an order of acquisition and that accuracy of discrimination gradually improves are not usually differentiated. However, they are different, although they are clearly not incompatible. The claim that discriminations are acquired in order and acquired early does not make any prediction on the level of accuracy of performance. The other claim, that children do not make their discriminations perfectly even at age 8, does not at any point claim that there are discriminations that the children cannot make (although with the disproportionate contribution of a few discriminations, perhaps this claim ought to be made).

The amount of difficulty and the order of acquisition are conceptually distinct, but one might well hypothesize that the two resultant orders are correlated. There is only slender evidence for evaluating whether the order of acquisition and the order of difficulty are the same. For an order of acquisition that comes from a longitudinal study, we have Shvachkin's (1973) order for Russian, but this is being treated with extreme caution because so little of the methodology is reported by him. Contributing to an order of difficulty, we have the specific sound pairs that were found difficult in several studies. We can therefore examine where these difficult sounds appear in Shvachkin's order of acquisition.

Shvachkin (1973) has a sequence of 10 stages for the discrimination of consonants. As his stages are based on the Russian phonemic system, there are some difficulties of comparison (and one cannot necessarily expect the order of acquisition to be identical in the two languages). Nevertheless, elsewhere (1976a, pp. 61–65), I have attempted to place the pairs that were found difficult in the various studies into Shvachkin's order of acquisition. There was very little relationship between pairs that had been difficult to discriminate and pairs that were late in Shvachkin's order of acquisition: there were difficult sounds that appeared early in Shvachkin's order and there were pairs appearing late in Shvachkin's order that were not found difficult. Therefore, if we accept Shvachkin's order, level of difficulty is not the same as order of acquisition. This may be true; however, as we will see in the next section, there are problems with Shvachkin's ordering, and with Garnica's (1971, 1973) ordering that has claimed to corroborate it.

Problems with Orders of Acquisition

Both Shvachkin and Garnica are claiming that there is a definite order of acquisition of discriminations. However, there is a crucial difference in their claims. Shvachkin argues that the acquisition of discriminations is complete before most discriminations are made in a child's speech production. Garnica, in her pilot study at least, and Edwards (1974) both argued that, even at age 3 there are discriminations that children cannot make; their argument therefore accepts that discrimination develops in important ways as production develops. These two positions have different theoretical implications on the relation between perception and production, and they should be kept separate.

Another difference between Shvachkin's and Garnica's experiments is that whereas Shvachkin followed the children's performance over time, Garnica's pilot study (from which she hypothesized her order of acquisition) was purely a synchronic investigation. In this, Garnica's method does not differ in principle from the investigations of the order of difficulty of discriminations. If the order of acquisition is not identical with the order of difficulty, it is not obvious that Garnica was measuring one rather than the other.

In evaluating Shvachkin's work, we do not know how well controlled his experiments were, how many trials each discrimination was given, nor how many children were tested to set up his order of phonemic development. It seems (Shvachkin, 1973, p. 109) that the order was set up by examining some of the children (perhaps only 4), and not all of these on all the discriminations; the other children were then tested to see if they fitted in with this order. Another doubt arises where much of the discussion of stages of phonemic development is interwoven with statements of phylogenetic orders. Shvachkin appears to assume that these two sources give common orders. This is not always true (e.g., Drachman, 1976; Dressler, 1974). Furthermore, it appears that Shvachkin's phylogenetic statements are not always accurate (see Ferguson and Slobin, 1973, p. 91).

Garnica's order for the acquisition of discriminations in English is very similar to Shvachkin's order and claims to corroborate it. However, the English ordering has been partly taken from the Russian ordering and so cannot be used as independent corroboration of it. To check the English ordering, I have gone back to the English data and reanalyzed it independently of the Russian ordering (Barton 1976a, pp. 66–76). This reanalysis has been done using the Guttman scaling procedure, a straightforward statistical technique that, incidentally, could prove very useful for other orders of acquisition. From the reanalysis, it is evident that, first, Garnica's order is not the best reflection of her results and, second, the best order is nevertheless not a statistically significant order. If we remove the reliance on the Russian ordering, then the English ordering is completely without foundation. Since there are problems with both orderings, we can safely conclude that, in the literature, there is no acceptable ordering of the acquisition of discriminations.

References

Barton, D. (1975) "Statistical Significance in Phonemic Perception Experiments," *Journal of Child Language*, 2, 297–298. (a)

Barton, D. (1975) "The Discrimination of Minimally-different Pairs of Real Words by Children Aged 2:3 to 2:11, "Paper presented at Third International Child Language Symposium. Also in N. Waterson and C. Snow, eds., *The Development of Communication*, Wiley, 1978. (b)

Barton, D. (1976) "The Role of Perception in the Acquisition of Phonology," Doctoral Dissertation, London. Indiana University Linguistics Club. (a)

Barton, D. (1976) "Phonemic Discrimination and the Knowledge of Words in Children under Three Years," *Papers and Reports on Child Language Development*, (Linguistics, Stanford University) 11, 61–68. (b)

Chomsky, N., and Halle, M. (1968) *The Sound Pattern of English*, Harper & Row, New York.

Drachman, G. (1976) "Child Language and Language Change: A Conjecture and Some Refutations," *Second International Conference on Historical Phonology*, Ustronie, Poland.

Dressler, W. (1974) "Diachronic Puzzles for Natural Phonology," in *Papers from the Parasession on Natural Phonology*, Chicago Linguistic Society.

Edwards, M.L. (1974) "Perception and Production in Child Phonology: The Testing of Four Hypotheses," *Journal of Child Language*, 1(2), 205–219.

Eilers, R.E., and Oller, D.K. (1975) "The Role of Speech Discrimination in Developmental Sound Substitutions," *Papers and Reports on Child Language Development*, (Linguistics, Stanford University), 10, 215–226. Also (1976) *Journal of Child Language*, 3, 319–329.

Ferguson, C.A. (1975) "Sound Patterns in Language Acquisition," in D.P. Dato, ed., *Developmental Psycholinguistics: Theory and Application*, Georgetown University Roundtable, 1–16.

Ferguson, C.A., and Slobin, D. eds., (1973) *Studies of Child Language Development*, Holt, Rinehart and Winston.

Ferguson, C.A. (1978) "Fricatives in Child Language Acquisition," in V. Honsa and J.M. Hardman-de-Bautista, eds., *Papers on Linguistics and Child Language*, Mouton, The Hague.

Garnica, O.K. (1971) "The Development of the Perception of Phonemic Differences in Initial Consonants by English-speaking Children: A Pilot Study," *Papers and Reports on Child Language Development*, (Linguistics, Stanford University), 3, 1–29.

Garnica, O.K. (1973) "The Development of Phonemic Speech Perception," in T. Moore, ed., *Cognitive Development and the Acquisition of Language*, Academic Press, New York, 214–222.

Graham, L.W., and House, A.S. (1971) "Phonological Oppositions in Children: A Perceptual Study," *Journal of the Acoustical Society of America*, 49, 559–566.

Julesz, B., and Hirsch, I.J. (1972) "Visual and Auditory Perception—An Essay of Comparison," in E.E. David and P.B. Denes, eds., *Human Communication: A Unified View*, McGraw-Hill, New York, pp. 283–340.

Kamil, M.L., and Rudegeair, R.E. (1972) "Methodological Improvements in the Assessment of Phonological Discrimination in Children," *Child Development*, 43, 1087–1091.

Koenigsknecht, R.A., and Lee, L.L. (1968) "Distinctive Feature Analysis of Speech-Sound Discrimination in Children," Paper presented at The American Speech and Hearing Association.

Locke, J.L. (1971) "Phonemic Perception in 2- and 3-year-old children," *Perceptual and Motor Skills*, 32, 215–217.

McNeil, J.D., and Stone, J. (1965) "Note on Teaching Children to Hear Separate Sounds in Spoken Words," *Journal of Educational Psychology*, 56, 13–15.

Perozzi, J.A., and Kunze, L.H. (1971) "Relationship Between Speech-Sound Discrimination Skills and Language Abilities of Kindergarten Children," *Journal of Speech and Hearing Research*, 14, 382–390.

Pronovost, W., and Dumbleton, C. (1953) "A Picture-type Speech-Sound Discrimination Test," *Journal of Speech and Hearing Disabilities*, 18, 258–266.

Shvachkin, N. Kh. (1973) "The Development of Phonemic Speech Perception in Early Childhood," in C.A. Ferguson and D.I. Slobin, eds., *Studies of Child Language Development*, Holt, Rinehart and Winston, New York, pp. 92–127.

Smith, N.V. (1973) *The Acquisition of Phonology: A Case Study*, Cambridge University Press, Cambridge.

Snyder, R.T., and Pope, P. (1970) "New Norms for and an Item Analysis of the Wepman Test at the 1st Grade 6-year Level," *Perceptual and Motor Skills*, 31, 1007–1010.

Templin, M.C. (1957) *Certain Language Skills in Children*, University of Minnesota Press, Minneapolis.

Thorndike, E.L., and Lorge, I (1944) *The Teacher's Word Book of 30,000 Words*, Columbia University Press, New York.

Tikofsky, R.S., and McInish, J.R. (1968) "Consonant Discrimination by Seven Year Olds," *Psychonomic Science*, 10, 61–62.

Wepman, J. (1958) *Auditory Discrimination Test*, Chicago: University of Chicago Press.
Zhurova, L. Ye. (1964) "The Development of Analysis of Words into their Sounds by Preschool Children," *Soviet Psychology and Psychiatry*, 2, 11–17; and in C.A. Ferguson and D. Slobin, eds., (1973) *Studies of Child Language Development*, Holt, Rinehart and Winston, New York, pp. 141–154.

Chapter 7

PERCEPTION AND PRODUCTION OF APPROXIMANT CONSONANTS BY 3-YEAR-OLDS: A FIRST STUDY

WINIFRED STRANGE AND PATRICIA A. BROEN

Theoretical and Methodological Considerations in the Study of Phonological Development

In this volume, we are generally concerned with the development of both the knowledge and use of a phonological system. A phonological system includes both the individual segments that occur in the language and the rules that combine those segments. In this chapter, we will restrict our attention to an investigation of the perception and production of the individual segments, the phonemes of the language.

It is useful to describe the phoneme inventory as a linguistic classification scheme imposed on a multidimensional phonetic space. In a particular language, this space is divided into a set of equivalence classes that stand in contrastive relation to each other along one or more dimensions. The dimensions along which contrasts occur can be called distinctive features. Variations within an equivalence class are referred to as intraphonemic variation. Systematic variations in phonemes that are predictable from phonetic context are referred to as allophonic variations and are described by phonological rules.

Children acquiring the phonology of a language must learn to differentiate (organize) the phonetic space along the linguistically relevant di-

CHILD PHONOLOGY
VOLUME 2: PERCEPTION

mensions of contrast, that is, the distinctive features. In perception, they must categorize speech segments according to the acoustic parameters that underly the phoneme contrasts, while ignoring those acoustic variations that are linguistically irrelevant. In production, the child must learn to control (use appropriately) the articulatory parameters that distinguish the phonemes of the target language. The child must also learn to produce systematic alternations that are not contrastive (i.e., the allophonic aspects of phoneme production). We conceive of phonological development, then, as a process of differentiation of the acoustic–phonetic space and the articulatory–phonetic space in such a way that linguistically relevant distinctions are preserved, and irrelevant distinctions are ignored. Of special interest in this chapter is the relationship between perceptual differentiation and productive differentiation as the child acquires the adult system.

Theories of the Relation between Perception and Production in Phonological Development

The human newborn is anatomically incapable of producing the full phoneme inventory of any language (Lieberman *et al.*, 1972). Vocal productions during the first months of life, although related in some respects to later articulatory behavior, bear little resemblance to the adult phonological system. The production of speech sounds is not under the volitional control of the child and those productions carry no linguistic meaning. In the course of approximately 4–8 years, most physiologically and intellectually normal children acquire the ability to articulate all the phonemes of the language and to use them appropriately to communicate information linguistically.

The development of articulation involves both the acquisition of a complex motor skill and the acquisition of an understanding of the linguistic relevance of articulatory–phonetic parameters. Students of child phonology generally agree that articulatory behavior reflects a rule-governed system that is refined and reorganized throughout the course of development, approximating more and more closely the adult phonological system.

One unresolved issue in current explanations of phonological development is the relationship of the child's perception of phoneme contrasts to his or her production of those contrasts. Three alternative conceptions have been proposed:

1. The child's perception of the phonological system is complete (fully differentiated) by the time the child begins to acquire productive control of phoneme contrasts (Compton, 1975; Smith, 1973) The child is assumed to perceive all (and perhaps only) the phoneme contrasts of the target language in the same way that adults do. According to this model, there are major discrepancies between perception and production; many contrasts that are

perceived are not produced. These discrepancies have been characterized by a set of "rewrite rules." For example, a child may perceive the contrast between the initial phonemes of the words *wing* and *ring* but produce /wɪŋ/ in both instances. The rewrite rule describing this discrepancy can be written as:

$$\left\{ \begin{array}{c} /w/ \\ /r/ \end{array} \right\} \rightarrow [w] \ / \ \#\underline{\hspace{2cm}}$$

2. Other theorists hypothesize that both the child's perception and production of the phonological system differ from the adult model. At any point in time, the child's system is internally consistent; the child produces all and only the contrasts that he or she perceives. The child's system is described either as complexly related to the adult system (Kornfeld, 1974) or as a reduction or simplification of the adult system (Garnica, 1971). Within this model, the child who produces /wɪŋ/ for the lexical items *ring* and *wing* does not perceive the difference between the initial phonemes of these words. In his or her system, they are homophones.

3. A third theoretical alternative claims that both perception and production develop gradually over the first several years. However, the perception of a contrast generally precedes the production of that contrast (Edwards, 1974; Menyuk and Anderson, 1969; Zlatin and Koenigsknecht, 1976). At first, a given contrast is neither perceived nor produced; later, the contrast is perceived but not produced, and still later, the contrast is both perceived and produced.[1]

These theoretical approaches differ in their characterization of the child's perceptual abilities, specifically in the chronological relationship that is seen to exist between perception and production. Unfortunately, research on phonological perception to date has not produced definitive answers regarding the perceptual abilities of children who are in the process of acquiring their phonological system. In fact, recent research on the perception of

---

[1] Although no current theory of phonological development holds that production of phoneme contrasts might actually *precede* (auditory) perception of those contrasts, this possibility cannot be ruled out on logical grounds. Since there are nonauditory sensory consequences (tactile–kinesthetic feedback) and environmental consequences (reinforcement) of phoneme production, it is possible that children might learn to produce some contrasts before they become able to distinguish the phonemes auditorily. There is no evidence that this relationship is generally found for children acquiring their first language, although individual cases are quite often reported in perception–production studies. However, Goto (1971) reported that adult Japanese who were able to produce American /r/ and /l/ reliably could not perceive the distinction auditorily either in their own speech or in the speech of other Japanese and native American-English speakers. The production of these phonemes, which is notoriously difficult for native Japanese speakers, is often taught by reference to articulatory gestures in Japan (personal communication from Hiroko Tajika to Winifred Strange).

acoustic–phonetic dimensions by infants and adults has produced somewhat paradoxical results.

From one line of research, the evidence indicates that infants as young as 1 month old discriminate contrasts along some acoustic–phonetic dimensions in much the same manner as adults (e.g., Eimas, 1975a; Morse, 1974). That is, speech sounds that are differentiated phonemically (by adults) are also discriminated by the infants, whereas intraphonemic acoustic variations of the same physical magnitude are not detected. These results have been interpreted as supporting the position that the ability to perceive phoneme contrasts is universally present at birth. Some researchers have suggested that the detection of these phonetically relevant acoustic differences is based, at least in part, on the fact that they correspond to "natural" psychophysical boundaries (Miller et al., 1976).

In contrast to the infant studies, research with adults from different language backgrounds demonstrates language-specific perception patterns. Cross-language studies (Abramson and Lisker, 1970; Lisker, 1970; Miyawaki et al., 1975; Williams, Chapter 10, this volume) have each investigated the perception of an acoustic contrast that is phonemic in one language but not in another. Results show that discrimination is accurate only for subjects who know the language in which the distinction is phonologically relevant. Subjects who use a language in which the difference is intraphonemic (or does not occur at all) fail to make the discrimination. A striking aspect of this research is that specificity of adult perception has been demonstrated for some of the same acoustic–phonetic dimensions shown to be discriminated by infants.

We are left with a puzzle. On the one hand, perception of at least some acoustic–phonetic dimensions appears to be determined by biologically given predispositions that are operable shortly after birth. On the other hand, perception by adults of these same acoustic–phonetic dimensions reflects to a high degree their specific linguistic experience. In general, they perceive phoneme contrasts only if they produce them in their language. Clearly, a great deal of modification of perceptual abilities takes place between infancy and adulthood as the individual learns his or her language.

It is important in our understanding of this modification process to document the status of phoneme perception during the years the child is acquiring the phonology in production. However, it is here that our empirical base is most wanting. Until recently, much of the evidence regarding perception was inferential in nature, based on the behavior of one or two subjects and with little systematic control. Some direct perceptual studies have examined only small numbers of children and have utilized informal testing procedures in which the exact nature of the stimuli was not specified. Others (Zlatin and Koenigsknecht, 1975) examined only children who have acquired the contrast that is being tested. Although these sources of data are useful, there is a pressing need for direct experimental evidence on the development of phonological perception. Both cross-sectional and longitudinal studies are needed with groups of children of sufficient size to allow at least preliminary generalizations about normative development. It is of equal importance that these studies utilize stimulus materials that allow for the precise specification of the acoustic–phonetic dimensions that children do and do not differentiate at various stages of development.

Methodological Alternatives in the Study of Phonological Perception and Production

Before proceeding to our own research, let us consider some methodological issues that critically affect the answers to questions about the coordination of phoneme perception and production. These issues concern the definition and measurement of perception and production in the laboratory.

Different kinds of data can be offered in support of the claim that a child "perceives" a certain phoneme contrast or a child "produces" a certain phoneme contrast. Answers to questions regarding the coordination of perception and production will be affected by the kinds of data used in the analysis. For example, any one of the following results might be offered in support of the statement that a child *perceives* a particular phonemic distinction:

1. The child responds differentially to two synthetically generated speech stimuli that differ in only one phonologically relevant acoustic parameter. (The two stimuli are labeled by adults as two distinct phonemes.)

2. When the experimenter articulates a word containing the target phoneme, the child selects the appropriate picture from a pair of pictures representing minimal-pair words.

3. The child demonstrates by appropriate behavior that he or she understands statements containing the target phonemes when they are uttered by adults.

In the same way, the following results might be offered in support of the statement that a particular child *produces* a particular phonemic distinction:

1. Acoustic analysis of words, uttered by the child, that contain the target phonemes show patterns that are "the same" as the patterns shown by adults.

2. The child imitates words containing the target phonemes and a trained listener transcribes them as "correct," that is, equivalent to the adult model.

3. Adults understand the child when he uses words that contain the target phonemes.

These examples reflect only a few of the many kinds of analyses that can be (and have been) used in assessments of phonological development. Most important to our discussion is the fact that these different measures of perception and production often yield inconsistent data regarding the child's ability to perceive and produce a particular phonological contrast. That is, a child may perceive according to one measure, but fail to perceive the same contrast by another measure. Production measured in one way is not always equivalent to production measured in another way. The measures of perception and production used may be critical in determining whether a child perceives a contrast before he or she produces it. Depending on the measures chosen, one may be able to demonstrate any ordering of perception and production, including production preceding perception. In the comments that follow, we outline some of the major experimental variables that, in our opinion, critically affect the interpretation of laboratory assessments of perception and production, and we provide a framework within which it may be possible to reconcile some of the apparently incompatible findings of previous research.

Assessment of Perception

Three classes of variables that influence the outcome and interpretation of experiments on phonological perception are: subject variables, stimulus variables, and task variables. We will focus our attention in this discussion on the latter two classes. The sample of subjects with which we are presently concerned are normal children learning their first (and only) language. The investigation of perception in special populations and in second-language learning involves a separate set of concerns in addition to the issues to be discussed.

Stimulus variables refer to the choice and structure of the set of to-be-perceived items, or more precisely, contrasts among items. Stimulus materials are selected in such a way that they differ along one or more dimensions; each dimension can be specified either as a *criterial dimension* or a *noncriterial dimension* with respect to the to-be-perceived contrast. Because we are interested in testing the perception of a phoneme contrast, the criterial dimensions are those acoustic–phonetic parameters that distinguish one phoneme from another in speech produced by a native speaker of the language. Noncriterial dimensions include phonetically irrelevant acoustic variations, phonotactic parameters, and higher-order linguistic variables.

Research on the acoustic analysis of speech over the last 30 years has demonstrated that, for any phoneme contrast, there are a large number of acoustic parameters that may serve as "cues" to phoneme perception. Furthermore, the interactions among these information-bearing parameters are very complex (see Blumstein, Chapter 2, this volume, on the problem of specifying acoustic invariants for phonemes, and Liberman *et al.,* 1967).

However, investigators have been able to isolate some of the important dimensions that provide sufficient information for the differentiation of some phonemes in some contexts. It is now possible, with the use of computer-generated synthetic speech, to produce a set of stimuli that differ in only one or a few of these acoustic parameters. Adults, for whom the contrast distinguished by the dimensions is phonemic, are able to differentiate the stimuli unambiguously on the basis of these acoustic–phonetic parameters.

In addition to these criterial acoustic parameters, there are also many acoustic variations in natural speech that are not criterial with respect to phoneme contrasts. We refer to these as nonphonetic acoustic parameters. In English, for example, such things as pitch, amplitude, and intonation contour, the specific voice, and rate of speech are not criterial with respect to phoneme contrasts. They may vary independently of the phoneme identity of the speech utterance.

Phonotactic parameters have to do with the phonetic context in which the target phonemes are presented. Consonants may occur in syllable-initial, intervocalic, or syllable-final position. They may precede or follow high or low vowels, front vowels, or back vowels. Often, the phonetic context in which a consonant occurs radically changes the nature of the acoustic–phonetic parameters that characterize a phoneme contrast. We must assume that perception of a contrast may also differ in significant ways, depending upon the phonetic context in which it occurs.[2]

Finally, higher-order linguistic variables can affect the outcome of perceptual experiments in important ways. There is a considerable body of research that explores the effect of such factors as lexical status (words versus nonsense), frequency of usage, and grammatical variables on speech perception in adults (see, for instance, Miller, 1951). In assessing the perceptual skills of young children, these factors must be given special consideration (see Barton, 1976; Barton, Chapter 6, this volume).

There are two ways in which variation in noncriterial dimensions has been treated in studies of phonological perception. In many studies, the stimulus materials are restricted in such a way that all or most noncriterial variables are held constant and only one or a few of the criterial dimensions are varied. This is typically the design used in studies that employ synthetic speech stimuli. In this design, the stimulus set is highly constrained; this allows for the precise specification of the acoustic–phonetic basis for perception. However, it can be criticized on the grounds that it is relatively "unnatural." Since the stimuli do not vary in any but the particular dimen-

---

[2] There is evidence that the voicing contrast in consonants is carried by very different acoustic parameters in word-initial and word-final consonants, and that the perception of those acoustic parameters by adults is qualitatively different (Raphael, 1972). A perceptual study of syllable-initial and syllable-final /r/ and /l/ by McGovern and Strange (1977) used synthetically generated stimuli in which the mirror-image patterns for the syllable-final approximants were atypical of naturally spoken final approximants.

sion(s) along which the subject must differentiate, there is no requirement that he or she *selectively attend* to those criterial dimensions while ignoring irrelevant variations.

The second type of experimental design deals with this problem. A so-called *perceptual constancy* design employs stimulus sets in which one or more of the noncriterial parameters is varied randomly or independently of the criterial dimensions under study. This requires that the subject ignore the noncriterial variation and attend only to the criterial dimensions to respond appropriately.

Task variables have to do with the configuration in which the stimuli are presented and the method by which subjects respond to them. A primary distinction has to do with whether subjects must compare two or more physically present items, or make judgments about each item presented one at a time. We will refer to the former as a *discrimination task*. In the paradigm case, the subjects are presented with a standard and a comparison stimulus and must say whether they are "same" or "different" on the criterial dimensions. "Same" can be defined either as physical identity or as phonetic identity. Common variations of this basic paradigm include the *ABX* and the oddity task in which three stimuli are presented; two are the same and one differs. In the former, the subject must judge whether $X = A$ or $X = B$; in the oddity task, the subject chooses which of three is the different or odd one.

We define an *identification task* as one in which the subjects make judgments about individual items. In this task, the subject must compare the presented item with some nonpresent standard or internal representation. Typically, identification tasks require some kind of "linguistic" response, for instance, assigning an orthographic symbol or pointing to a picture whose "name" corresponds to the stimulus item.

Identification tasks differ as to the number and structure of the response alternatives available to the subjects. The response set can be either (relatively) unconstrained by the experiments (open set) or constrained (closed set). In the latter case, tasks employing only two alternatives can be considered a special subclass; in principle, only one alternative must be explicitly categorized. That is, the subject can respond appropriately on the basis of the classification: X versus not-X.

In a closed set task, the nature of the relationships among response alternatives is important. For instance, if the task is a picture-pointing task, the picture choices can represent minimal-pair names, or they can stand for names that differ on dimensions other than the to-be-perceived contrast.

Other task variables that differ from experiment to experiment and may have important effects on their outcome are such things as the number of trials over which performance is assessed, whether the subjects are given feedback about their performance and, if so, what kind of feedback. We refer to these variables as performance measures.

It is of interest, in light of the preceding discussion, to consider the *categorical perception phenomenon* that has been studied extensively in speech perception research. The phenomenon refers to the close relationship between performance on two types of perceptual tests of synthetic speech series: a perceiver's performance on a discrimination task (requiring the detection of physical differences) is predictable from his or her performance on an identification (labeling) task. In general, it can be said that, for adults tested on a well-constructed synthetic speech series that incorporates a phonemic contrast in their language, subjects discriminate accurately only those acoustic differences that are linguistically relevant. Intraphonemic differences are not discriminated significantly better than chance. We might say that subjects respond in terms of the phonetic identity of the stimuli even when the task does not require a linguistic interpretation, but rather a judgment of physical identity. In other words, subjects find it exceedingly difficult to ignore or to "hear through" the linguistic significance of speech utterances.

These results are borne out by phenomenological experience. A series of synthetic speech stimuli that differ in equal steps over a range sufficient to encompass two phoneme categories is presented in succession. Listeners hear several identical or nearly identical instances of one phoneme; then there is an abrupt change, and they hear instances of the other phoneme category. It is sometimes very difficult to convince listeners that each successive stimulus differs by the same physical magnitude!

A question of empirical interest is whether children acquiring phonological distinctions in production perceive the acoustic–phonetic dimensions underlying those distinctions in a categorical manner. Are children more or less sensitive to intraphonemic variation than adults? There is evidence that at least the voicing distinction may be perceived categorically by children (Williams, 1974; Williams, Chapter 10, this volume; Wolf, 1973).

Combining both stimulus and task variables, it is possible to organize the various measures of perception into a matrix such as the one presented in Table 7.1. Experimental designs in different cells of the matrix can be related in terms of degree of constraints. Moving from left to right, stimulus materials increase in variation (decrease in constraint); from top to bottom, task and response alternatives become less constrained.

The top left ceil of the matrix marks the experimental paradigm that is most constrained: the typical discrimination paradigm with synthetically generated speech materials used to assess phoneme perception in infants and adults. In such a study, the stimuli vary on only one criterial dimension; all other parameters are held constant. The task involves a comparison of two physically present stimuli; no linguistic response is required. Indeed, in most infant studies, the standard is presented repeatedly, followed by a shift to the comparison, which is also repeated. The subject must detect only that a change has occurred.

TABLE 7.1
Matrix of Experimental Materials and Procedures used to Assess Phonological Perception[a]

	Stimulus variables			
	Noncriterial dimensions held constant		Noncriterial dimensions varied	
Task variables	Single criterial dimension tested	Multiple criterial dimensions tested	Nonphonetic acoustic parameters varied	Phonotactic & higher-order parameters varied
Discrimination	Eimas (1975) Morse (1974) Eilers (Chapter 3, this volume)		Graham and House (1970)	Kuhl (Chapter 4, this volume)
Two-choice identification Closed set	*Categorical perception studies* *Adults* Miyawaki *et al.* (1975) McGovern and Strange (1977) Abramson and Lisker (1970) Williams (1974) *Children* Wolf (1973) Williams (1974)	Strange and Broen (Chapter 7, this volume)	Eilers and Oller (1978) Garnica (1971) Edwards (1974) Barton (1976, Chapter 6, this volume)	Monnin and Huntington (1974)
Multiple-choice identification Open set	Zlatin and Koenigsknecht (1975) Menyuk and Anderson (1969)		Menyuk (Chapter 8, Volume 1)	"Natural situations"

[a] Selected examples of research studies are placed in their appropriate cells. Enclosed studies that cross cell boundaries employ both materials–procedures indicated.

In the diagonal corner, we have inserted the term "natural situations." In everyday communication situations, phonological contrasts must be differentiated under conditions of minimal constraint as it is defined here.[3] This can be characterized as an open-set identification task where the stimuli are varying on many acoustic, phonotactic, and higher-order linguistic parameters simultaneously.

Between these two extremes, experimental paradigms that utilize stimuli and tasks of intermediate degrees of constraint have been listed. The experiment reported in this chapter falls in the center of this matrix, and is similar in design to other studies reported in the literature.

Assessment of Production

Two classes of variables that influence the outcome and interpretation of experiments on phonological production are (a) speaker-related variables; and (b) listener-related variables. The *speaker-related variables* reflect real variation in the production of the phonemes of interest, whereas the *listener-related variables* are, in a sense, artifacts of the way in which the experimenter interprets the speaker's productions. (Subject variables also affect the outcome of production experiments. Although the performance of different populations is ultimately of interest, the focus here is on normally developing children acquiring their first and only language.)

The first of the speaker-related variables is the stability of phoneme production. A young child may not always produce a given phoneme in the same way; the nature of the production may vary from one time to another in a single word and from one word to another. For example, a child who is beginning to acquire the contrast between prevocalic /r/ and /w/ may produce both [r] and [w] for /r/. He or she may produce the word *ring* as [wIŋ] on one occasion and as [rIŋ] on another occasion, or produce *ring* as [rIŋ] and *rose* as [woz]. If the procedure examines only one instance of prevocalic /r/, this instability will not be noticed or identified. Ingram *et al.* (Chapter 9, Volume 1) both describes and explores some of this variability in the production of fricatives.

The method of obtaining a sample of the child's production is a critical factor in the assessment of articulation skills. Several different procedures can be used, and the method of obtaining the sample may affect the form of the child's production. In many single-subject studies, a child is observed in a natural setting, and the child's productions are transcribed as they are produced (Leopold, 1949; Smith, 1973). This kind of assessment procedure has a sort of ecological validity that is not matched by other sampling methods, but it is time consuming; it is difficult to check the reliability of the

---

[3] However, the semantic and situational constraints present in natural communication situations help to delimit the possible phonological alternatives the listener must consider.

transcription and some phonemes of interest may not be included in the sample.

Two alternative methods of obtaining a speech sample are (a) elicited naming in which the child is asked to name a set of pictures or complete a set of open-ended sentences; and (b) elicited imitation in which the child is asked to repeat a list of words spoken by the experimenter. In either case, the task can be structured to include instances of the desired phonemes. In naming pictures, the child must call on his or her own internal representation of the phonemes in a word; thus the production obtained by this method is probably similar to the child's production in a nontest situation. However, this method of obtaining information is relatively time consuming because each production must be indirectly elicited. The child may produce the wrong word, he or she may not know the intended word, or words with the desired phoneme may not be picturable. The voiced fricative /ð/, for example, occurs primarily in function words such as *the, that, those,* and *them.* It is difficult to picture and difficult to elicit through an open-ended sentence. If a child is tested often, or if multiple productions of set of phonemes are desired, a picture-naming task can be cumbersome.

The child's phoneme production can be sampled through elicited imitation where the child is asked to repeat words after the examiner, and the word list is constructed so that all of the phonemes of interest are tested several times in appropriate phonetic environments. This is a rapid way to obtain a comprehensive sample of the child's productions, but the task is different from a more spontaneous task and the child's responses may be different. In an elicited imitation task, the child must listen to the word spoken by the experimenter. If the word is familiar, the child will have an internal model of the word and his or her production may reflect the internal model, the external model, or some combination of the two. If the word is not familiar, the child will have to base the production on perception of the word as spoken by the examiner.

It is often assumed that the child's productions will be more accurate in an elicited imitation task, but this has been difficult to prove. In some studies comparing imitation and naming, no systematic difference has been found (Ingram *et al.* Chapter 9, Volume 1); Paynter and Bumpas, 1977; Poluha, 1977; Templin, 1947), whereas in others there is a small but consistent difference with imitated production being more accurate (Siegel *et al.,* 1963; Smith and Ainsworth, 1967; Snow and Milisen, 1954).

A child's production may also vary with the complexity of the utterance in which the phoneme occurs. A word can occur as a single, citation form production, or it can be embedded in a sentence. In adult speech, this difference affects the production of vowels more than consonants with unstressed vowels becoming central and lax. It affects some consonants more than others; modifications in both place of articulation and voicing are common. Any judgment of the accuracy of systematic changes that occur in child speech in conversation should recognize the changes that typically occur in adult conversational speech.

Single-syllable words are usually considered less complex for the child than multisyllable words, and one expects the child's production of single-syllable words to be more accurate. Two factors, however, appear to interact with word length to determine the nature of the child's production: the familiarity of the word, and the location of the target phoneme within the word. Ingram *et al.*'s data (Chapter 9, Volume 1) indicate that word frequency or word familiarity may be as important as word complexity in determining the accuracy of the child's production.

Children typically produce a phoneme correctly at the beginning of a word before they produce it correctly at the end of a word, but the effect of the location of a target phoneme in a word is complex (Templin, 1947). A consonant can occur in a prevocalic position or in a postvocalic position, as a part of a consonant cluster or as a consonant single; it can occur in the first syllable in a word or in subsequent syllables. A child may systematically vary his or her production with the phoneme context in which the target phoneme occurs. For example, in a study of children who misarticulated /r/, Curtis and Hardy (1959) found that 93% of the children produced at least one correct /r/ in an initial consonant cluster, 60% produced at least one correct /r/ as a prevocalic consonant single, and only 43% produced at least one correct /r/ as a postvocalic single. Also, /r/ was more often correct when it followed a front consonant or a front vowel.

The sequence of consonants in a word can also affect the articulation of a particular phoneme (Ingram, 1974; Macken, Chapter 8, Volume 1). For example, children in the early stages of language development tend to sequence the place of articulation of consonants within a word from front to back. In this way, an error on a particular consonant will be a function of its location within a word and of the place of articulation of the other consonants in that word.

Any or all of these speaker-related variables can result in a real difference in the production of a phoneme by a child. Alternatively, listener-related variables may cause an apparent change in the child's production or apparent differences from one study to another that are artifacts of the analysis procedure.

The child's productions must be judged in some way. The judgment is made either while listening to the child at the time that he or she speaks or by recording the child's speech and judging the production at some later time. There is some indication that judgments of recorded speech differ from judgments of live speech (Henderson, 1938). If this is the case, it would seem that live judgments would be more accurate, that is, a better representation of the child's actual production. But live judgments have disadvantages. They can only be heard once and cannot be repeated; when the child repeats, it is a new production. Therefore, differences in transcription between judges in a nonrecorded task are difficult to resolve. Judgments of recorded utterances, although involving some distortion imposed by the recording process, allow for replay and resolution of differences.

The child's production must be judged against some standard. This is true regardless of the level of analysis, but the standard will differ from one level of analysis to another. The level of analysis will depend, in part, on the purpose it will serve, but the standard is ultimately a function of the listener's own internal representation. In production studies that parallel perception studies, the child may be described as making or not making a systematic, productive distinction between two phonemes of interest. Neither phoneme need be correct relative to the adult model, they must only differ from each other in a systematic way (Edwards, 1974). The child's production may be judged correct or incorrect relative to the adult model or it may be transcribed using a broad or a narrow phonetic transcription. In any case, there is no external, objective standard against which the child's production can be measured. The child's production is always judged relative to some standard held by the examiner. That model will be a function of the examiner's training, perception, and language learning. For instance, an /r/ that is judged correct by a speaker of an Eastern dialect may be unacceptable in Minnesota. Trained examiners might agree on the transcription of the [r] but disagree on its acceptability. To take an extreme case, a speaker who learned Japanese as a first language might not be able to judge the distinction between /r/ and /l/, regardless of training, because he or she does not perceive that difference (see Goto, 1971; Miyawaki *et al.,* 1975).

Spectrographic analysis would appear to be the most objective method of analyzing a child's production, but in practice this is not the case. The acoustic patterns that correspond to phonemes are extremely complex and are not well understood even in the case of adult speech. Indices of variation in the acoustic patterns corresponding to correct articulation of a particular phoneme have not been worked out. In short, there are no templates against which a child's production can be judged. In addition, the problems of measurement error for children's voices make it exceedingly difficult to obtain reliable estimates of many phonetically relevant acoustic parameters. (See Kent, 1976, for a discussion of the limitations of acoustic analysis of children's speech.)

The final variable affecting the judgment of production is the transcription system used to record the child's productions and the bias imposed by that transcription system. As Allen (1977) notes, even the most detailed transcription is not just a recording of a production but is an analysis of a production. It is not possible to have a transcription system that is free from the effects of (the transcriber's) phonological theory. The transcription system used by the experimenter imposes a bias on the data that is not always identified but may be important in interpreting the results. For example, prevocalic /r/ is said to function as a consonant glide, whereas postvocalic

/r/ is said to function as a vowel (Allen, 1977). Support for this position comes, in part, from an analysis of the substitutions made for /r/ in misarticulated speech. A common substitution for /r/ is the glide /w/ that begins in the articulatory position of a high back vowel. Some transcription systems allow /w/ to occur both as an on-glide and as an off-glide, that is, both in a prevocalic position and in a postvocalic position (Smalley, 1963). Other transcription systems allow only prevocalic /w/ (Faircloth and Faircloth, 1973). In transcribing substitutions for /r/, it is common to find /w/ recorded in the prevocalic position and a high back vowel (either /u/ or /U/) in the postvocalic position. Curtis and Hardy (1959) argued that this is evidence that prevocalic /r/ is a glide consonant and postvocalic /r/ is a vowel. But if the transcription system used does not allow /w/ to be recorded following a vowel, the identification of postvocalic /r/ as a vowel may be an artifact of the transcription system. Indeed, Delattre and Freeman (1968) found that at least some speakers of American English used the same articulatory gesture for prevocalic and postvocalic /r/.

Comparison of Perception and Production in Phonological Development

From the previous discussion, it is readily apparent that the assessment of phonological perception and production is a multifaceted problem. Any one procedure gives only a partial answer to questions about the perceptual and articulatory skills of the child at any point in development. Until we have a much better understanding of how different procedures that test perception compare with each other, and how different procedures that test production compare with each other, we must be extremely cautious in drawing conclusions about the relationship between perception and production in phonological development on the basis of particular experimental outcomes.

Perception and Production of Approximant Consonants by 3-year-old Children

The study reported here investigates the relationship between the perception and production of contrasts within the class of phonemes called approximant consonants (Ladefoged, 1975), specifically among /r/, /l/, and /w/ in syllable-initial position. These consonants were chosen for several reasons: (*a*) The production of some approximants is mastered relatively late; (*b*) many of the acoustic–phonetic dimensions that distinguish these phonemes have been described; and (*c*) research on the perception of some of these acoustic–phonetic dimensions by infants, children, and adults has already been accomplished. Thus, it is possible to test children who do not yet produce some approximant contrasts but who are old enough to be tested with procedures similar to those employed with adults. These tests can be accomplished using carefully controlled stimulus materials. Our results can be placed in the context of research with infants and adults in an effort to provide a cohesive description of the nature of perception during phonological development.

Research on the Production of Approximant Consonants

Previous studies indicate that, although the glides /w/ and /y/ are produced correctly at a relatively early age, /r/ and /l/ are later in appearance. Sanders (1972) found, in examining data from a number of studies, that /w/ was produced correctly by 90% of 3-year-old children and /y/ was produced correctly by 90% of 4-year-old children. However, the glides /r/ and /l/ were not produced correctly by 90% of the children until age 6. The /r/ is also frequently in error in children identified as articulation-disordered (Winitz, 1969) and is resistant to therapy. The /w/ is a typical substitution for /r/.

Acoustic–Phonetic Parameters that Differentiate Initial /w/, /r/, and /l/

The primary acoustic cues for contrasts among initial approximants are differences in the frequency of the formants during the initial steady-state portion and subsequent formant transitions into the vowel. The contrast between /r/ and /l/ is carried primarily by the third formant (F_3) (O'Connor et al., 1957). The third formant begins at a relatively low frequency for /r/; for /l/ it begins at a high-frequency locus. There are also differences in the starting loci and transitions of that first and second formants (F_1 and F_2, respectively); /r/ is characterized by lower F_1 and F_2 frequencies than is /l/. In addition to these spectral characteristics, the temporal structure of the transitions into the vowel differ for /r/ and /l/. For /l/, the formants remain at the initial steady state longer, and then rise at a more rapid rate (Dalston, 1975).

The distinction between /w/ and /r/ and between /w/ and /l/ is also carried spectrally by the steady state and transitions of the first three formants, primarily by F_2 (O'Connor, et al., 1957). The F_2 locus for /w/ is very low, in contrast to the intermediate values for /r/ and /l/. F_3 falls at a locus intermediate to those appropriate for /r/ and /l/; it is more similar to /l/ than to /r/. In temporal characteristics, /w/ and /r/ are very similar and contrast with the more abrupt transitions typical of /l/ (Dalston, 1975). Figure 7.1 presents schematized spectrographic representations of the words—*wake*, *rake*, and *lake*. (The word *bake* is also included as a comparison between the approximants as a class and a stop consonant. Both spectral and temporal distinguishing parameters can be noted.)

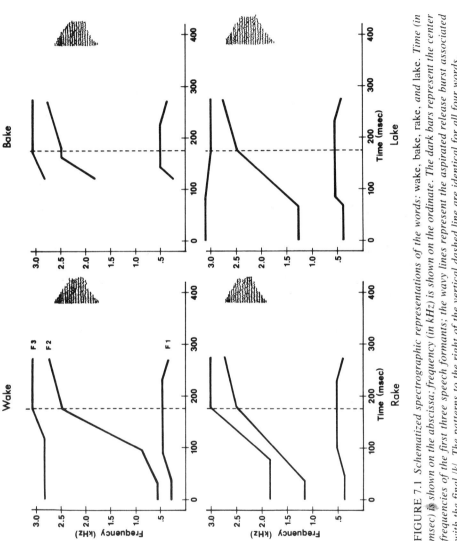

FIGURE 7.1 *Schematized spectrographic representations of the words: wake, bake, rake, and lake. Time (in msec) is shown on the abscissa; frequency (in kHz) is shown on the ordinate. The dark bars represent the center frequencies of the first three speech formants; the wavy lines represent the aspirated release burst associated with the final /k/. The patterns to the right of the vertical dashed line are identical for all four words.*

Having established some of the parameters that differentiate the approximant consonants in initial position, it has been possible for researchers to construct synthetic stimuli that vary these parameters in controlled ways, while holding all noncriterial acoustic parameters constant. Most studies have employed synthetic materials in which only one criterial dimension is varied. A series of stimuli is generated in which values along that criterial dimension are interpolated between the "clear cases" in small, physically equal steps. Thus for instance, a series has been constructed in which CV stimuli differed only in the initial frequency and transition of F_3 throughout a range sufficient to encompass the clear-case syllables, /ra/ and /la/. That is, the stimuli that constituted the end points of the series were synthesized with F_3 values appropriate for /ra/ and /la/; the stimuli between the end points contained F_3 patterns with intermediate values (Miyawaki et al., 1975). Synthetic stimulus series such as these have been used to investigate the perception of the acoustic–phonetic dimensions underlying phoneme contrasts by infants and adults from different language backgrounds.

Previous Research on the Perception of Approximant Consonant Contrasts

A number of studies have investigated the perception of the F_3 acoustic dimension that differentiates /r/ and /l/. When presented to adult speakers of American English, identification and discrimination tests of the /ra/–/la/ series just described produced typical "categorical perception" results (Miyawaki, et al., 1975). Subjects consistently divided the series into two phoneme categories with a relatively sharp boundary between them. Discrimination of pairs drawn from opposite sides of the phoneme boundary was very accurate relative to discrimination of equal-interval pairs drawn from within phoneme categories. In other words, the Americans discriminated well only those acoustic differences in F_3 that marked a contrast between phonemes. Intraphonemic differences were discriminated relatively poorly.

McGovern and Strange (1977) reported the same results for a series of synthetic stimuli that differentiated /ri/ from /li/ and /ir/ from /il/. In both cases, the only acoustic dimension that differed across stimuli was the F_3 steady state and transition. Categorical perception was shown for the /r/–/l/ contrast in both initial- and final-syllable position.

Eimas (1975b) investigated the perception of the F_3 cue for the /ra/–/la/ distinction by 4-month-old infants, using a contingent sucking habituation paradigm (see Eilers, Chapter 3, this volume, for a detailed description of this procedure). Infants from American English homes were able to detect a cross-phoneme-boundary stimulus change (e.g., /ra/–/la/), as measured by a significant release from habituation. When a change of equal physical magnitude constituted a within-phoneme category shift (e.g., /ra$_1$/→/ra$_2$/), infants did not show a significant release from habituation. This suggests that American infants perceived this stimulus series categorically in much the same way as the American adults did.

In light of the preceding findings with infants, the results of discrimination tests of the /ra/–/la/ series by Japanese adults, for whom the distinction is not phonemic, is interesting indeed. Miyawaki and her colleagues (1975) showed that, for adult speakers of Japanese, discrimination performance on all differences in F_3 was quite poor. Pairs that crossed the English phoneme boundary were not discriminated any better than were intraphonemic pairs. In other words, the Japanese adults failed to discriminate differences in F_3 that American infants were able to discriminate. If we assume that infants from Japanese homes would show discrimination performance similar to infants from American homes, it could be said that the adult Japanese "lost" the ability to discriminate an acoustic–phonetic dimension as a result of its not being relevant to the phonology of their language.

Several studies investigating the perception of approximant consonants by normal and articulation-disordered (American) children have been reported in the literature (Aungst and Frick, 1964; Chaney and Menyuk, 1975; Edwards, 1974; Menyuk and Anderson, 1969; Monnin and Huntington, 1974). However, with the exception of Menyuk and Anderson, these studies employed live voice or recorded natural stimuli in which the exact nature of the acoustic variations is not specifiable. It is not possible, therefore, to state precisely the acoustic bases on which the perception might have been accomplished. The studies also differed in the kinds of tasks used to assess perception and the criteria for saying that a particular contrast was perceived.

The study by Menyuk and Anderson (1969) tested identification of three synthetically generated series of stimuli that contrasted /w/ and /r/, /w/ and /l/, and /r/ and /l/. Each series differed on only one criterial acoustic–phonetic parameter. The experimenters reported that, although identification by 4- and 5-year-olds was more accurate than their production (in imitation), only 61% of the children differentiated the stimuli perceptually in the same way as did adults. There is a problem with the interpretation of these results, however. Identification functions for adult subjects showed considerable inconsistency in labeling even for the end-point stimuli that were supposedly the clear case instances of the phonemes under study. This suggests that the synthetic stimuli employed were intrinsically ambiguous, even to adults for whom the contrasts were presumably mastered both in production and perception. The study reported here is similar in design to that conducted by Menyuk and Anderson (1969) but with major differences in stimuli and procedures. The following section outlines briefly the methods we employed.

Method

Twenty-one "normal" children between the ages of 2:11 and 3:5 were identified. All children scored within normal limits on several screening tests including a vocabulary test (PPVT, Dunn, 1965), an articulation test (Templin–Darley Consonant Singles and Templin–Darley Screening Test,[4] 1969), and a hearing screening[5] (Asha, 1975). Further.articulation testing was accomplished using an imitative test developed by Broen that examines the child's articulation of all initial and final consonants in three different vowel contexts.

A score reflecting the accuracy of each child's articulation of initial /r/, /l/ and /w/ was derived from his or her production of these consonants in items from the tests already mentioned. For each phoneme, a score of 1 was assigned if the judge transcribed the production as correct; a score of 2 was assigned to productions transcribed as a distortion of the target consonant; a score of 3 was given to those productions transcribed as a substitution within the class of approximants; and a score of 4 was given to productions transcribed as substitutions other than an approximant. Scores for all productions of each target phoneme transcribed by two experienced judges were averaged to yield an overall score that could range from 1.0 (perfect production) to 4.0 (all nonapproximant substitutions).

With but one exception, all children obtained scores of 1.0 for /w/, (his score was 1.2). Scores for /r/ and /l/ were averaged for the following discussion and three groups of children were identified: (a) those who showed complete mastery of syllable-initial /r/ and /l/ (scores of 1.0); (b) those with few distortions or substitutions for /r/ and /l/ (scores from 1.1 to 1.5); and (c) those with many distortions and/or substitutions for /r/ and /l/ (scores of 1.6 or greater).

The perception of three phoneme contrasts was tested extensively in 4–6 1-hour sessions. We concentrated on only two approximant distinctions: /r/ versus /l/ and /w/ versus /r/. A third contrast, /w/ versus /b/, was employed as a control. The phoneme contrasts were presented using the minimal pair words: *rake–lake, wake–rake,* and *wake–bake,* respectively. All four of these words are easily pictured and within the receptive vocabulary of 3-year-old children.

Each of the minimal pair contrasts was tested using four sets of stimulus materials:

1. A *Live Voice Clear Cases* test consisted of the experimenter pronouncing the members of the minimal pair five times each in a predetermined random order. A set of 10 tokens, 5 of each member of the test pair, is referred to as a block.

2. A *Recorded Clear Cases* test consisted of tokens of the members of the minimal pair spoken by a female speaker and recorded on high fidelity equipment. Using spectrographic analysis, five tokens matched for overall duration, amplitude, pitch, and intonation contour were chosen from a larger

---

[4] Some children were included who satisfied the criterion for Templin–Darley singles but not for Templin–Darley screening.

[5] One child did not pass the hearing screening in one ear.

set. For each minimal pair, a series of five blocks of trials was constructed. Each block consisted of the five tokens of each member of the pair, recorded in random order.

3. A *Synthetic Clear Cases* test consisted of synthetically generated tokens of the members of the minimal pair, constructed on the Haskins Laboratories parallel resonance synthesizer. The stimuli were designed to be as closely matched to the recorded clear cases as was technically possible. Thus, the stimuli differed on several of the criterial dimensions that distinguish these phonemes. However, the four stimuli were adjusted such that the final portion of each word (the constant -ake portion) was identical for all four stimuli. The approximant stimuli were matched on intonation and amplitude contour, pitch, and overall duration. The *bake* stimulus was shorter than the approximants and had a more abrupt amplitude onset (see Figure 7.1). A block consisted of five repetitions of each member of the minimal pair, randomly arranged. Five such blocks were constructed and recorded.

4. A *Synthetic Identification* test was constructed by interpolating on all criterial dimensions between the synthetic clear case tokens. A series of 10 stimuli were generated for each minimal pair. A block consisted of each of the 10 stimuli presented once in random order; 10 such blocks were recorded for each minimal-pair contrast. Thus, each stimulus appeared 10 times in the synthetic identification test.

Perception of these stimulus materials was tested using a two-choice, forced choice identification task that employed a modified "picture-pointing" response. Prior to testing, the children were taught the "names" of the pictures representing the words by using the words in a sentence context (e.g., "*wake* up in the morning"—"*bake* a cake"). Token reinforcers for each response and each block were used to maintain attention. Children were "paid off" in play time with the experimenter. Tests of the /w/–/b/ contrast were interspersed with /r/–/l/ and /w/–/r/ tests to insure continued attention and understanding of the task.

Each child proceeded from the live voice to the recorded to the synthetic clear cases tests upon reaching a criterion of 10/10 correct responses on the first block or 9/10 correct responses on a subsequent block. Each subject was required to complete a minimum of four clear cases blocks on each contrast: one block each of live voice and recorded clear cases and two blocks of the synthetic clear cases. A maximum of five blocks of any one of these tests was presented.

Using these procedures, we asked four major questions about the perception and production of approximant contrasts:

1. Can 3-year-old children differentiate the minimal-pair contrasts /r/ versus /l/ and /r/ versus /w/? Are there differences in performance on spoken versus recorded versus synthetically generated clear cases?

2. How are perceptual and productive differentiation related? Do children who fail to produce a contrast consistently have more difficulty perceiving that contrast?

3. How do 3-year-old children identify synthetic speech series that incorporate acoustic–phonetic contrasts between /r/ and /l/ and between /r/ and /w/? How do their identification functions compare with adults in consistency and boundary placement?

4. How do children's identifications of the synthetic speech series relate to their ability to produce the phoneme contrasts represented by those series?

Results

Identification of Clear Cases

The first question addressed was whether 3-year-old children were able to differentiate the phoneme contrasts under study as measured by our two choice identification procedures. To answer that question, we looked at the overall results of the clear cases tests for the children as a group ($N = 21$). One measure of performance was the number of blocks needed to reach criterion. Recall that a minimum of four blocks was required for each phoneme contrast. It took an average of five blocks for the children to reach criterion on the /r/–/l/ tests. The average number of blocks was five and one-half for the /w/–/r/ tests. Only two children failed to reach criterion in the maximum five blocks on any one of the clear cases tests of /r/–/l/; two other children failed to reach criterion in five blocks on one or two of the /w/–/r/ tests. As expected, children did very well on the /w/–/b/ contrast. The mean number of blocks to criterion was four and one-half; only five children failed to reach criterion in the minimum number of blocks.

Another measure of performance is errors in identification on clear cases tests. Table 7.2 presents the average number of errors children made over all blocks on each type of clear cases test. It is immediately apparent by this measure that children were, in general, able to differentiate all three phoneme contrasts very well; the overall accuracy in identification was better than 90%. The relative difficulty of contrasts was the same by this measure as for the blocks-to-criterion index. The /w/–/r/ contrast was most difficult for children to differentiate, followed by the /r/–/l/ contrast; children performed best on the /w/–/b/ contrast.

A comparison of error rates for live voice, recorded and synthetic clear cases tests is of interest as a check on the quality of the stimulus materials. No consistent pattern of errors was shown across different kinds of tests, although error rates tended to be greater for synthetic stimuli on the /r/–/l/ and /w/–/b/ contrast. Although synthetic stimuli may have produced *rela-*

TABLE 7.2
Identification of Clear Cases[a]

Tests	Phoneme contrasts		
	/r/–/l/	/w/–/r/	/w/–/b/
Live voice	1.3	2.5	.1
Recorded	1.0[b]	1.8	1.3[b]
Synthetic	2.4	1.0	1.0
Overall mean errors	4.7	5.4	2.4
Overall percentage errors	9.3	9.8	5.4

[a] The mean number of identification errors are given for each clear cases test of each phoneme contrast. The overall mean and percentage errors represent the average number and proportion of responses in error out of the total number of responses for all subjects on all trials of each contrast.

[b] These error rates are inflated due to one subject's performance. If the average errors are computed across 20 subjects, deleting this subject's scores, the error rates are .1 for both /r/–/l/ and /w/–/b/ contrasts.

tively more errors in some cases, it is important to note that children were still able to differentiate them with a high degree of accuracy in *absolute* terms. This indicates that the synthetic stimuli were "good" (unambiguous) tokens of the intended phonemes. Performance by adult subjects (18 college students) on the test materials corroborated this conclusion. Adults made no errors on any of the clear cases tests when tested under identical conditions as the children.

We conclude from these results, first, that all the clear case stimuli presented to the children were highly identifiable tokens of the phonemes under study. Second, 3-year-old children were able to perform the identification task with these materials. Finally, the results demonstrate that 3-year-olds, in general, can differentiate "good" exemplars of *rake* from *lake* and *wake* from *rake* in a two-choice identification task with very few errors.

We turn now to the question of the relation between children's ability to perceive the contrasts under study and their ability to differentiate those contrasts in production. Table 7.3 presents the two indices of performance on clear cases tests for children, segregated according to articulation performance. As described earlier, the mastery group (Group 1, $N = 8$) produced all initial /r/ and /l/ phonemes correctly (scores were 1.0). Group 2 children ($N = 5$) produced only a few errors on /r/ and/or /l/ (scores ranged from 1.1 to 1.3). Group 3 children produced many distortions and substitutions in their articulation of words containing initial /r/ and /l/ (scores ranged from 1.7 to 3.4).

It is immediately apparent that identification accuracy was related to the children's ability to produce /r/ and /l/ appropriately. Group 1 children showed almost errorless performance on all contrasts; five of the eight subjects made no errors on any of the clear cases tests. Group 2 children showed small increases over Group 1 in errors and blocks to criterion for /r/–/l/ and

TABLE 7.3

Average Number of Identification Errors and Average Number of Blocks to Criterion on Clear Cases Tests by Children Divided According to their Ability to Produce /r/ and /l/[a]

| Groups | Phoneme contrasts | | | | | |
| | /r/–/l/ | | /w/–/r/ | | /w/–/b/ | |
	errors	blocks	errors	blocks	errors	blocks
1. Mastery $N = 8$, $\bar{X}$ age $= 3.1$	.4	4.0	.3	4.1	.1	4.0
2. Few distortions $N = 5$, $\bar{X}$ age $= 3.3$	1.6	4.8	1.6	4.8	.2	4.0
3. Many distortions and substitutions $N = 8$, $\bar{X}$ age $= 3.2$	10.9	6.1	12.9	7.3	6.1	5.4
Overall average $N = 21$	4.7	5.0	5.4	5.5	2.4	4.5

[a] Live voice, recorded, and synthetic clear cases tests were pooled for this comparison, so a minimum of four blocks to criterion was required of each child.

/w/–/r/ tests only. In contrast, Group 3 children made many more identification errors than either the Group 1 or Group 2 children on all three phoneme contrasts, and especially on /r/–/l/ and /w/–/r/ tests.

These data suggest that there is a relationship between children's perception and production of approximant contrasts. However, there was a great deal of variability among the eight children in Group 3. Four of these children made very few errors in identification, even for contrasts that they did not differentiate consistently in production. All the children, regardless of their articulation proficiency, showed above chance identification of all three contrasts on one or more of the tests.

We conclude, therefore, that for these children there exists an asymmetric relation between production and perception of approximants as those skills were assessed here. Children who produced all initial approximants correctly also perceived contrasts among the phonemes with very high accuracy. For children who did not yet show mastery in production, perception results were heterogeneous. Only some of the children had difficulty perceiving contrasts among approximants they did not correctly produce.

Identification of Synthetic Series

The results of identification tests of the three synthetic series were considered next. Several questions about the children's performance are of interest:

1. How do their overall identification functions compare with those produced by college-aged subjects?

2. Where do the children place boundaries between phoneme categories; how do their boundary locations compare with adults?

3. Are there differences among children in identification functions that are related to differences in articulation performance?

Figure 7.2 compares the overall identification functions for 20 children[6] (solid lines) and 18 adults (dashed lines) on each synthetic series. The functions plot the average number of times (out of 10) each stimulus was identified as the left member of the pair. (Since a two-choice, forced-choice task was employed, the identification functions for the two alternatives in each contrast are exact complements of each other.)

The overall identification functions for adults are characteristic of those obtained in studies of consonant contrasts using synthetic stimuli. For each phoneme contrast, the stimulus series was divided consistently into two phoneme categories with an abrupt crossover in the labeling function that defines the boundary between phonemes. In each series, note that only two stimuli were identified with less than 90% consistency: numbers 4 and 5 for the /w/–/r/ series and numbers 6 and 7 for both the /r/–/l/ and /w/–/b/ series.

For all three phoneme contrasts, the overall identification functions for children were only slightly less consistent than those for the adults. For the /r/–/l/ and /w/–/r/ contrasts, stimuli at both ends of the series were identified with greater than 90% consistency. As with adults, only two stimuli in the boundary region were ambiguously labeled. For the /w/–/b/ contrast, four intermediate stimuli were identified with less than 90% consistency, compared with two for adults.

A comparison of the overall functions in Figure 7.2 suggests that the location of boundaries between phoneme categories may be different for the children and the adults on two of the contrasts, To determine the reasons for these differences in average boundary location, individual functions were inspected. The stimulus or interval between stimuli at which the 50% crossover in identification occurred was defined as the boundary for that contrast for that individual. Figure 7.3 displays the distributions of boundaries for adults (top) and children (bottom) on each synthetic series.

As the figure indicates, children and adults differed in two respects. For /r/–/l/ and /w/–/b/, children showed both increased variability and a shift in the modal boundary location, relative to the adults. For the /w/–/r/ contrast, children differed from adults only in the modal location; the range of locations was the same. The shifted boundaries for /r/–/l/ and /w/–/r/ identification functions indicate that the children were less likely to perceive (or to label) intermediate stimuli as /r/ than were adults. This is interesting in light of the pattern of production shown by these children. In articulation,

---

[6] One child, whose clear cases data was reported, failed to complete the identification tests. She had a great deal of difficulty in the clear cases tests and was among the poorest in production.

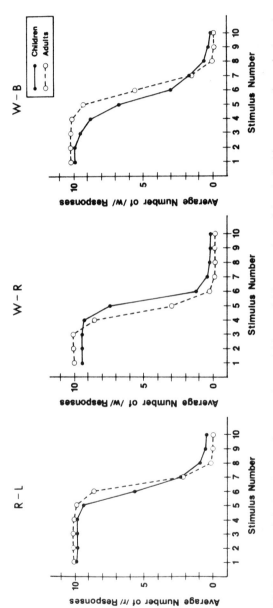

FIGURE 7.2 Pooled identification functions for 20 children (solid lines) and 18 adults (dashed lines) on each synthetic series. The 10 stimuli of each series are displayed along the abscissa; the ordinate indicates the average number of times (out of 10) the stimulus was identified as the left member of each minimal pair.

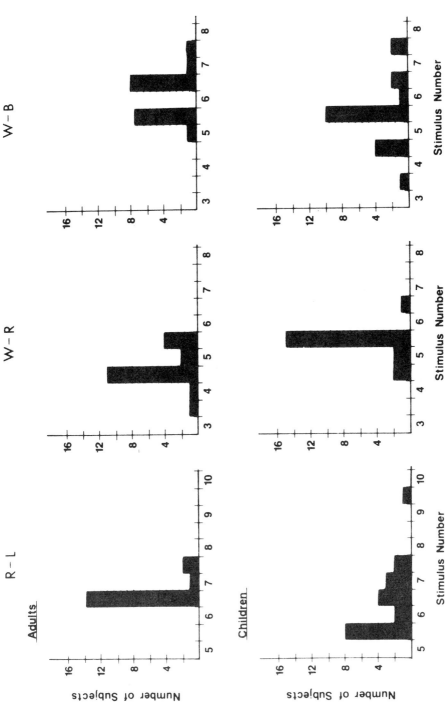

FIGURE 7.3 Distributions of identification boundaries for 18 adults (top) and 20 children (bottom) on each synthetic series. An individual's boundary was defined as the stimulus or interval between stimuli at which the function crossed the 50% point. (In no case did an individual's function cross the 50% point more than one time.)

the phoneme /r/ was the least stable of the three phonemes; furthermore, children who misarticulated /r/ all produced a /w/-like distortion or substituted a /w/ for the intended /r/.

A final question about children's identification of the synthetic series concerns whether or not there were differences in perception that were related to the children's ability to produce these phonemes appropriately. To address this question, we compared identification functions for the eight children who showed articulation mastery (Group 1) with the seven children who most often misarticulated /r/ and /l/ (Group 3). Figure 7.4 compares the average functions for these two groups on each phoneme contrast. (Group 2 children performed very much like Group 1 children.)

As the figure shows, there were some apparent differences in identification performance by Group 1 and Group 3 children. The more gradually sloping functions shown for Group 3 reflect the fact that more of the intermediate stimuli were identified inconsistently both across subjects and across trials for a particular subject. Group 3 subjects also tended to be slightly less consistent even in identifying the extreme /w/ stimuli in the /w/ –/r/ series and the extreme /l/ stimuli in the /r/–/l/ series.

Identification inconsistency can be quantified as the number of stimuli in a series that were labeled as a particular phoneme less than 90% of the time. (In a two-choice task, the probability of selecting the same label fewer than 9 times out of 10 is not significantly different from chance. See Barton, 1975.) Table 7.4 reports the median number of stimuli identified inconsistently by this measure for adults and for the three groups of children. As the table shows, the only differences among children were in the identification of stimuli in the /r/–/l/ series and the /w/–/r/ series by Group 3 children in contrast to Group 1 and Group 2 children. Group 3 children, who misarticulated /r/ or /l/ or both, were less consistent in their identification of series that contained these consonants. For the /w/–/b/ series, where all of the children articulated both members of the pair correctly, the three groups of children did not differ in identification consistency, although all three groups were less consistent than the adults. (The difference between groups of chil-

TABLE 7.4

Median Number of Stimuli in Each Synthetic Series that were Identified with Less Than 90% Consistency

	Phoneme contrast		
	/r/–/l/	/w/–/r/	/w/–/b/
Adults	1	1	1
Children:			
Group 1 (*N* = 8)	1	1	2
Group 2 (*N* = 5)	1	1	2
Group 3 (*N* = 7)	3	3	2

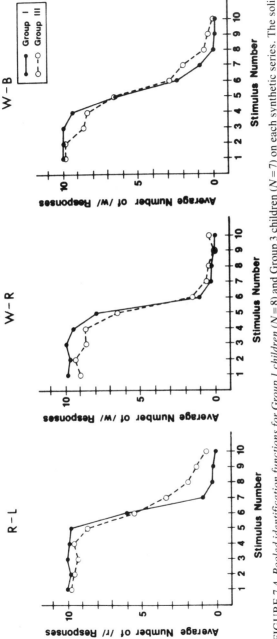

FIGURE 7.4 *Pooled identification functions for Group 1 children (N = 8) and Group 3 children (N = 7)* on each synthetic series. The solid lines represent performance by group 1; the dashed lines show performance by Group 3. The 10 stimuli of each series are displayed along the abscissa; the ordinate indicates the average number of times (out of 10) the stimulus was identified as the left member of the minimal pair.

dren shown in the average functions of Figure 7.4 was due to greater variability among Group 3 subjects in the location of their /w/–/b/ boundary.) Because Group 3 children could identify the /w/–/b/ series as consistently as the other children, we cannot attribute their poorer performance on /r/–/l/ and /w/–/r/ contrasts to general attentional factors. Rather, their performance reflects perceptual difficulty specifically related to those phoneme contrasts that they have not yet differentiated in production.

In summary, the results of identification tests indicate that 3-year-old children, in general, are capable of differentiating series of synthetic stimuli that distinguish /r/ from /l/ and /w/ from /r/ in a manner similar to that shown by adults. Differences in the consistency with which children identified synthetic series was related to their ability to produce initial /r/ and /l/. Discrepancies between "good" and "poor" producers were most evident on the /r/–/l/ and /w/–/r/ series. However, it must be stressed that even the poor producers differentiated these contrasts with far greater than chance accuracy.

Discussion

The results of this study indicate that normally developing 3-year-old children are capable of differentiating among initial approximant consonants, /r/, /l/, and /w/, when tested on a two-choice identification test with both natural and synthetically generated stimulus materials. Previous research by Menyuk and Anderson (1969) on the perception of synthetically generated approximant consonants reported considerably poorer performance for 4-year-old children than that shown here. However, the present study differed from that effort in three ways. A major difference was that the synthetic materials used here were of better quality and contrasted each minimal pair on many acoustic dimensions. Another difference was that Menyuk and Anderson presented all three stimulus series intermixed and required subjects to make one of three responses: *white, right,* or *light.* This increase in response alternatives, coupled with the intrinsic ambiguity of even supposedly clear case stimuli, produced identification functions that failed to show consistency at the extremes even for adult subjects.

Finally, the children in our study were given a great deal of experience with both real speech and the synthetic speech before they were asked to judge stimuli in the synthetic series. This may have had little effect on the performance of children who were "good" articulators. Their performance was almost errorless from the outset. The performance of "poor" articulators, however, may have been affected considerably by the procedures used here. This group of subjects initially made errors on live voice, recorded, and synthetic clear cases. Since our criterion for progressing through the experiment was a stringent one, these children heard and responded to many more instances of the clear cases than the good articulators. This experience may have functioned as pretraining for the identification task, resulting in more consistent performance than would have been obtained otherwise.

What has been demonstrated here is that normal young children, even children who misarticulate /r/ and /l/, *can* differentiate between /r/ and /l/ and between /r/ and /w/ in a highly structured task and after considerable practice that may have "focused their attention" on the criterial dimensions under examination. We have *not* demonstrated that they use these distinctions in interpreting the speech they hear in their environment.

The Development of Phonological Perception and its Relationship to Phonological Production

To provide some perspective, our study of 3-year-olds' perception of contrasts among initial approximant consonants can be compared with some recent results by other investigators. We will restrict ourselves to data obtained on initial approximant contrasts, but the general issues raised in this discussion are applicable to the perception and production of phoneme contrasts in general.

In a recent study on the perception of 20 phoneme contrasts, Barton (1976) tested 2-year-old British-English children using a two-choice identification task and recorded natural voice clear case stimuli. Two contrasts of initial approximant consonants, *wing–ring* and *rock–lock*, are of greatest interest here. Barton reported that seven of eight children (ages 2:6 to 2:11) who knew the lexical items and who completed tests of both contrasts, correctly differentiated the /r/–/l/ pair 100% of the time, and five of these seven children also differentiated the /w/–/r/ pair with 100% accuracy. The other two children made some errors on the /w/–/r/ contrast, but still performed significantly above chance. Only one child failed to differentiate the /w/–/r/ contrast with greater than chance accuracy; this child did differentiate the /r/–/l/ pair significantly better than chance, but made some errors. Although Barton did not explicitly include articulation testing in this study, he reported that two children who differentiated *wing* from *ring* perceptually substituted a /w/ for /r/ in their production of the *ring* test word.

Barton's results corroborate our findings with 3-year-olds on clear cases tests of /r/–/l/ and /w/–/r/ contrasts. It appears that children from 2.5 to 3.5 years old can perceptually differentiate these consonants, even though they may not differentiate them in production.

The task used in both these studies was a highly constrained one. It was "linguistic" in that it required recognizing which of two (known) lexical items was uttered (in contrast to a "same" or "different" response to a discrimination task). However, it presented the minimal-pair contrast in a situation where all phonotactic and high-order parameters were held constant. Thus, in neither study did the children have to *ignore* significant non-criterial variation while *selectively attending* to criterial acoustic–phonetic differences. In our study, only two stimuli and two response alternatives were presented on any one block of trials; this might further focus the subject's attention on the relevant differentia. An increase in the number of stimulus and response alternatives may account, at least in part, for the somewhat surprising and contradictory results reported by Menyuk (Chapter 11, Volume 1) for older normal children (mean age = 4.2 years) on perception and production of initial approximant consonants. Using a three-choice picture-pointing identification task (Show me *X*), and a reproduction task (Say *X*), in which the stimuli were the recorded natural voice items, *right, light,* and *white,* Menyuk reported an overall error rate of 15% on identification and an 11% error rate on reproduction (where an error was defined as a substitution or omission). It is not possible, from her report, to determine how many children contributed errors to the overall error rate or whether the same children produced both perception and production errors. Nevertheless, the average performance was worse than the results we reported for children who were, on the average, a full year younger. Furthermore, the numerically greater number of errors in identification over those reported for reproduction in Menyuk's data suggest a different pattern of results than those obtained for younger children by Barton (1976) and ourselves. It is imperative, however, that these contradictory findings be verified under conditions that allow for the precise determination of their causes. Different stimuli, tasks, amount of familiarization, and the methods of assessing and reporting results make it impossible to conclude confidently which factors contributed most to the differences.

What may we conclude about the perception and production of approximant consonants? Eimas (1975) and Eilers and Oller (1978, see Eilers, Chapter 3, this volume) have demonstrated that infants under 1 year old are capable of detecting an acoustic change in repeated stimuli that marks a phonetic contrast for adult speakers of English (initial /r/–/l/ in Eimas, intervocalic /r/–/w/ in Eilers and Oller). From these data, it can be concluded that the ability to discriminate acoustic differences that are relevant to phonological contrasts among approximant consonants is present from a very early age. That is, human infants show auditory psychophysical sensitivities to acoustic–phonetic dimensions that allow them to perceive these phoneme contrasts far in advance of any indication that they produce these contrasts. Thus, we apparently have evidence in support of the first theoretical alternative listed earlier: By the time children begin to produce lexical items, they perceive (all) phoneme contrasts. Note, however, that the empirical definition of perceive in this case refers to a basic, nonlinguistic sensory capacity, whereas production refers to the intentional, coordinated articulation of meaningful lexical items. It would seem to us more reasonable to compare this kind of perceptual capacity with an empirical assessment of the physiological capacity to produce these sounds (i.e., with motoric capabilities independent of linguistic volition). Such data might come from studies of prebabbling vocalizations such as those reported by Oller (Chapter 6, Volume 1) and Stark (Chapter 5, Volume 1). If we are interested in the perception and production of phoneme contrasts as activities involved in the use of speech as the medium for linguistic communication, we must look further than the infant studies for answers to questions about the relationship of perception and production in phonological development.

Turning to our research and that of Barton (1976) which uses a relatively constrained linguistic task, we find that, although perception is generally very good, performance by some 2- and 3-year-old children shows less than perfect perception.[7] There is an indication of a specific (although asymmetrical) relationship between perception and production. In our study, children who produce initial /r/ and /l/ appropriately never failed to perceive contrasts employing those phonemes with essentially perfect performance. Some children who did not produce the contrasts consistently also showed near perfect perception, but others demonstrated considerable difficulty with the task. These results could be interpreted as providing circumstantial evidence for the third theoretical alternative offered earlier: Both perception and production of phoneme contrasts develop gradually over the first several years, but, normally, perception of contrasts precedes their production. Here, too, however, perception has been assessed in a task that is more highly constrained than is the task used to assess production.

Finally, the experimental data reported by Menyuk (Volume 1) shows less than perfect perception and production of initial approximant consonants by 4-year-old children. Furthermore, perception and production tasks (in which comparable materials and response alternatives were used) yielded about equal proportions of errors. One might be tempted to interpret this as providing circumstantial evidence for the second theoretical alternative stated earlier: Perception and production develop in tandem.[8]

[7] Barton (1976) mentioned that the difference between errorless performance and above chance performance may be an important qualitative one. We concur in this observation. Children who perform without error tend to respond faster and with more assurance; they spontaneously offer the identities of the words during familiarization and otherwise indicate that the task requires little concerted effort on their part. In contrast, children who make errors are often slower; they are more prone to change a response or to look to the experimenter for verification of a response. Their spontaneous comments often indicate that the task is a difficult one. With more sensitive measures of performance, such as response latency measures, we think it would be possible to demonstrate significant differences among children who show errorless performance and those who make some errors on our gross performance measure.

[8] In all these views, a causative connection between perception and production cannot be assumed on the basis of these correlational, cross-sectional data. Experimental tests of whether perception determines production might be possible using perceptual training procedures. This issue becomes especially important when one wishes to extrapolate from normal development to articulation-disordered children.

Clearly, then, differences in the ways perception and production are assessed experimentally can lead to an undesirable situation in which all (and therefore none) of the theoretical alternatives are supported. This suggests to us that the manner in which the theoretical alternatives are posed is wrong, or at least inadequate in that they are essentially untestable. What is needed is a theoretical framework in which perception and production are defined in such a way that makes the explication and comparison of the development of those functions possible.

Perhaps the greatest hiatus in such an effort is a concept of "intentional, coordinated perception" that is comparable to our understanding of speech production as the articulation of lexical items with the intent to communicate linguistically. Phonological perception in this active, purposive sense includes more than the simple detection of acoustic–phonetic differences. It views the listener as an active participant involved in the extraction of the identity of phonetic units from a complexly structured stimulus array to recover the lexical intent of the speaker.

The acoustic patterns that correspond to particular phonemes or to particular phoneme contrasts in different phonetic and prosodic environments are so complex and interdependent that a full description of the invariant acoustic relationships corresponding to phonetic units does not yet exist, despite more than 30 years of research on the problem. Indeed, some investigators have even questioned whether phone-sized units are appropriate segments of analysis (Fujimura and Lovins, 1977; Soli, 1978). Given this great complexity, the task facing the perceiver who must recover the linguistic message from ongoing speech might be likened to the recognition and identification of camouflaged figures, rather than to the detection of objects against a homogeneous contrastive background. As we pointed out earlier in this chapter, the former requires finely attuned *selective* attention to just those aspects of the signal that are relevant to the purpose at hand. It is perception in this sense, then, that we wish to understand and describe in the developing child.

A theoretical orientation that we have found constructive in our own research is to consider the development of phonetic perception as consisting of the "education of selective attention." Gibson (1969) offers a general theory of perceptual learning that is compatible with this view of phonological development:

> What is learned in perceptual learning are distinctive features, invariant relationships, and patterns; . . . these are available in stimulation; . . . they must, therefore, be extracted from the total stimulus flux. The processes which are relevant for extraction include orienting responses of the sense organs; abstraction of relations and invariants; and filtering relevant features from irrelevant stimulation [p. 119].

According to Gibson, perceptual development is marked by increasing economy. Through experience with stimulation, children become more efficient in their ability to abstract information and to filter irrelevant stimulation. If this view of perceptual learning is applicable to phonological development, as we think it is, then experimental work on phonetic perception must seek to describe the development of the ability to extract phonetic information from the speech signal. We must investigate the development of the ability to abstract invariant relations and patterns, while ignoring or filtering out irrelevant acoustic, phonetic, and higher-order linguistic variation. This requires experimental stimuli and tasks with sufficient complexity to tap these abilities, while still being within the general cognitive capacities of the child.

Research to date on the development of phonetic perception has provided only partial answers to questions concerning the attunement of selective attention with experience. Some recent research, notably that of Kuhl (Chapter 4, this volume) is moving in a direction that will enable us to make more precise statements about the development of these perceptual skills, but much more work is needed. Questions to be asked by future research regard the relationship of intentional coordinated perception and intentional, coordinated production. How do the patterns and relations abstracted in perception correspond to the patterns and relations evidenced in production? How does experience with a phonological system, including experience in learning to produce lexical items, shape the child's skills in attending selectively to acoustic–phonetic parameters under various conditions of irrelevant variation? Conversely, how does the attunement of selective attention affect phoneme-production patterns? Answers to these questions have important implications for theories of normal phonological development during first-language learning. They may also provide some important insights into the nature of differences between normal and abnormal phonological development and between first- and second-language learning.

Acknowledgments

The research reported in this chapter was supported by a grant to the authors from the National Institute of Mental Health (MH–30278) and by grants to the Center for Research in Human Learning from the National Institutes of Child Health and Human Development (HD–01136) and the National Science Foundation (BNS–75–03816). The authors wish to thank Dr. Alvin Liberman and the staff of Haskins Laboratories for use of the facilities in constructing stimulus materials under a contract from NICHHD (71–2420). We wish to acknowledge our sincere gratitude to the people who assisted in the conduct of the research reported here: Shirley Doyle, Katharine McGovern, Sharon Penner, Stephen Metz, James Heller, Deborah Landin, Celia Felsenberg Spector, and Jennifer Hoel. James Heller tested the adult subjects reported in the text. We also wish to thank Pamela Young for preparing the figures and Janet Etsokin and Margaret Sherburne for the preparation of the manuscript. Requests for copies of this chapter should be sent to Winifred Strange, Center for Research in Human Learning, 205 Elliott Hall, University of Minnesota, 75 East River Road, Minneapolis, Minnesota 55455.

References

Abramson, A.S., and Lisker, L. (1970) "Discriminability along the Voicing Continuum: Cross-language Tests," in *Proceedings of the Sixth International Congress of Phonetic Science*, Academia, Prague, pp. 569–573.

Allen, G.D. (1977) "On Transcribing the American r," Paper presented at the joint IPS–77/ AAPS Meeting, Miami Beach.

American Speech and Hearing Association (1975) "Guidelines for Identification Audiometry," *Asha*, 17, 94–99.

Aungst, L.F., and Frick, J.V. (1964) "Auditory Discrimination Ability and Consistency of Articulation of /r/," *Journal of Speech and Hearing Disorders*, 29, 76–85.

Barton, D.P. (1975) "Statistical Significance in Phonemic Perception Experiments," *Journal of Child Language*, 2, 297–298.

Barton, D.P. (1976) "The Role of Perception in the Acquisition of Phonology," Unpublished Doctoral Dissertation. University of London.

Chaney, C.F., and Menyuk, P. (1975) "Production and Identification of /w, r, l, j/ in Normal and Articulation Impaired Children," Paper presented at the American Speech and Hearing Association Convention, Washington, D.C.

Compton, A.J. (1975) "Generative Studies of Children's Phonological Disorders: A Strategy of Therapy," in S. Singh, ed., *Measurement Procedures in Speech, Hearing and Language*, University Park Press, Baltimore, pp. 55–90.

Curtis, J., and Hardy, J. (1959) "A Phonetic Study of Misarticulation of /r/," *Journal of Speech and Hearing Research*, 2, 244–290.

Dalston, R.M. (1975) "Acoustic Characteristics of English /w, r, l/ Spoken Correctly by Young Children and Adults," *Journal of the Acoustical Society of America*, 57, 462–469.

Delattre, P., and Freeman, D.C. (1968) "A Dialect Study of American Rs by X-ray Motion Picture," *Linguistics*, 44, 29–68.

Dunn, L.M. (1965) *Peabody Picture Vocabulary Test*. American Guidance Service, Inc., Circle Pines, Minn.

Edwards, M.L. (1974) "Perception and Production in Child Phonology: The Testing of Four Hypotheses," *Journal of Child Language*, 1, 205–219.

Eilers, R.E., and Oller, D.K. (1978) "A Cross-Linguistic Study of Infant Speech Perception," Paper presented at the Southeastern Conference on Human Development, Atlanta, Georgia.

Eimas, P.D. (1975) "Speech Perception in Early Infancy," in L.B. Cohen and P. Salapatek, eds., *Infant Perception*, Academic Press, New York, pp. 193–231. (a)

Eimas, P.D. (1975) "Auditory and Phonetic Coding of the Cues for Speech: Discrimination of the [r–l] Distinction by Young Infants," *Perception & Psychophysics*, 18, 341–347. (b)

Faircloth, S.R., and Faircloth, M.A. (1973) *Phonetic Science*, Prentice-Hall, Englewood Cliffs, N. J..

Fujimura, O., and Lovins, J.B. (1977) "Syllables as Concatenative Phonetic Units," Paper presented at the Symposium on Segment Organization and the Syllable. University of Colorado. Boulder, Colorado.

Garnica, O.K. (1971) "The Development of Perception of Phonemic Differences in Initial Consonants by English-Speaking Children: A Pilot Study," *Papers and Reports on Child Language Development* (Stanford working papers), 3, 1–29.

Gibson, E.J. (1969) *Principles of Perceptual Development*, Appleton-Century-Crofts, New York.

Goto, H. (1971) "Auditory Perception by Normal Japanese Adults of the Sounds "L" and "R." *Neuropsychologia*, 9, 317–323.

Graham, L.W., and House, A.S. (1970) "Phonological Oppositions in Children: A Perceptual Study," *Journal of the Acoustical Society of America*, 49, 559–566.

Henderson, F.H. (1938) "Accuracy in Testing the Articulation of Speech Sounds," *Journal of Educational Research*, 31, 348–356.

Ingram, D. (1974) "Fronting in Child Phonology," *Journal of Child Language*, 1, 233–241.

Kent, R.D. (1976) "Anatomical and Neuromuscular Maturation of the Speech Mechanism: Evidence from Acoustic Studies," *Journal of Speech and Hearing Research*, 19, 421–447.

Kornfeld, J. (1971) "Theoretical Issues in Child Phonology," In *Papers from the Seventh Regional Meeting*, Chicago Linguistic Society.

Ladefoged, P. (1975) *A Course in Phonetics*, Harcourt Brace Jovanovich, New York.

Leopold, W.F. (1949) "Speech Development of a Bilingual Child: A Linguist's Record," (Vol. 4), Northwestern University Press, Evanston, Ill.

Liberman, A.M., Cooper, F.S., Shankweiler, D.P., and Studdert-Kennedy, M. (1967) "Perception of the Speech Code," *Psychological Review*, 74, 431–461.

Lieberman, P., Crelin, E.S., and Klatt, D.H. (1972) "Phonetic Ability and Related Anatomy of the Newborn and Adult Human, Neanderthal Man, and the Chimpanzee," *American Anthropologist*, 74, 287–307.

Lisker, L. (1970) "On Learning a New Contrast," *Haskins Laboratories: Status Report on Speech Research*, SR24, 1–17.

McGovern, K., and Strange, W. (1977) "The Perception of /r/ and /l/ in Syllable-initial and Syllable-final Position," *Perception and Psychophysics*, 21, 162–170.

Menyuk, P., and Anderson, S. (1969) "Children's Identification and Reproduction of /w/, /r/, and /l/. *Journal of Speech and Hearing Research*, 12, 39–52.

Miller, G.A. (1951) *Language and Communication*, McGraw-Hill, New York.

Miller, J.D., Wier, C.C., Pastore, R.E., Kelly, W.J., and Dooling, R.J. (1976) "Discrimination and Labeling of Noise–Buzz Sequences with Varying Noise-lead Times: An Example of Categorical Perception," *Journal of the Acoustical Society of America*, 60, 410–417.

Miyawaki, K., Strange, W., Verbrugge, R.R., Liberman, A.M., Jenkins, J.J., and Fujimura, O. (1975) "An Effect of Linguistic Experience: The Discrimination of [r] and [l] by Native Speakers of Japanese and English, *Perception & Psychophysics*, 18, 331–340.

Morse, P.A. (1974) "Infant Speech Perception: A Preliminary Model and Review of the Literature," in R.L. Schiefelbusch and L.L. Lloyd, eds., *Language Perspectives: Acquisition, Retardation, and Intervention*, University Park Press, Baltimore, pp. 19–53.

Monnin, L.M., and Huntington, D.A. (1974) "Relationship of Articulatory Defects to Speech-sound Identification, *Journal of Speech and Hearing Research*, 17, 352–366.

O'Connor, J.D., Gerstman, L.J., Liberman, A.M., Delattre, P.C., and Cooper, F.S. (1957) "Acoustic Cues for the Perception of Initial /w, j, r, l/ in English," *Word*, 13, 25–43.

Paynter, E.T., and Bumpas, T.C. (1977) "Imitative and Spontaneous Articulatory Assessment of Three-year-old Children," *Journal of Speech and Hearing Disorders*, 42, 119–125.

Poluha, P.C. (1977) "The Effects of Three Tasks on the Articulatory Performance of Articulatory Defective Children," Unpublished Master's Thesis, University of Minnesota.

Raphael, L.J. (1972) "Preceding Vowel Duration as a Cue to the Perception of the Voicing Characteristic of Word-Final Consonants in American English. *Journal of the Acoustical Society of America*, 51, 1296–1303.

Sanders, E.K. (1972) "When are Speech Sounds Learned?" *Journal of Speech and Hearing Disorders*, 37, 55–63.

Siegel, G.M., Winitz, H., and Conkey, H. (1963) "The Influences of Testing Instruments on Articulatory Responses of Children," *Journal of Speech and Hearing Disorders*, 28, 67–76.

Smalley, N.A. (1963) *Manual of Articulatory Phonetics*, Practical Anthropology, Tarrytown, N. Y.

Smith, M.W., and Ainsworth, S. (1967) "The Effects of Three Types of Stimulation on Articulatory Responses of Speech Defective Children," *Journal of Speech and Hearing Research*, 10, 333–338.

Smith, N.V. (1973) *The Acquisition of Phonology: A Case Study*, Cambridge University Press, Cambridge.

Snow, K., and Milisen, R. (1954) "The Influence of Oral Versus Pictorial Presentation upon Articulation Testing Results," *Journal of Speech and Hearing Disorders,* Monograph Supplement 4, 30–36.

Soli, S.D. (1978) "The Role of Distinctive Features and Phonemes in Speech Perception," Unpublished manuscript, University of Minnesota, Minneapolis, Minn.

Templin, M.C. (1947) "Spontaneous versus Imitated Verbalization in Testing Articulation in Preschool Children," *Journal of Speech Disorders,* 12, 293–300.

Templin, M.C., and Darley, F.L. (1969) "The Templin-Darley Tests of Articulation. Bureau of Educational Research, University of Iowa, Iowa City.

Williams, L. (1974) "Speech Perception and Production as a Function of Exposure to a Second Language," Doctoral Dissertation, Harvard University, Cambridge, Mass.

Winitz, H. (1969) *Articulatory Acquisition and Behavior,* Appleton-Century-Crofts, New York.

Wolf, C.G. (1973) "The Perception of Stop Consonants by Children," *Journal of Experimental Child Psychology,* 16, 318–331.

Zlatin, M.A., and Koenigsknecht, R.A. (1975) "Development of the Voicing Contrast: Perception of Stop Consonants," *Journal of Speech and Hearing Research,* 18, 541–553.

Zlatin, M.A., and Koenigsknecht, R.A. (1976) "Development of the Voicing Contrast: A Comparison of Voice Onset Time in Stop Perception and Production," *Journal of Speech and Hearing Research,* 19, 93–111.

Chapter 8

SPEECH PERCEPTION OF LANGUAGE-DELAYED CHILDREN

PAULA TALLAL AND RACHEL E. STARK

Introduction

To investigate the mechanisms involved in processing speech at the neural level, one might look to procedures that have proved successful in investigating the neurological bases of other perceptual functions. Using such an approach, it becomes apparent immediately that speech perception differs in some respects from other perceptual processes. In most other areas of perception, animal research has already suggested mechanisms underlying the specific function in question, which may lead to hypotheses for further study in animals and/or humans. This is not generally the case for speech perception.

Until very recently, it was thought that speech perception was unique to humans. However, recent work has indicated that animals have greater capacities of speech perception than has been assumed (Miller and Kuhl, 1976). If we can assume that animal speech perception, such as it is, does not lead to language comprehension, then, for speech perception, there seems to be a dichotomy between (a) perception of the acoustic aspects of speech signals in the absence of comprehension; and (b) perception of the acoustic speech signal in the context of being understood. The finding that young infants perceive some acoustic and phonemic aspects of speech well before they can comprehend language (Eimas, 1971) also leads to proposing this dichotomy. Whether there are distinct processes involved in these aspects of speech perception, whether acoustic analysis precedes linguistic analysis in a hierarchical manner, or whether parallel processing is occurring are questions that still remain to be answered. It is clear, however, that if we are interested in speech perception, as it eventually relates to linguistic processing and comprehension, we must look to humans for our answers.

In the area of speech perception in humans, four basic subject populations have been studied: (a) normal adults; (b) brain-damaged adults; (c) normally developing children; and (d) language or communication-disordered children. Of these, the speech perceptual abilities of normal adults probably have received the greatest amount of experimental attention. Other studies have concentrated on investigating the speech-perceptual abilities of adults who have sustained specific brain-damage. In both cases, such studies can tell us about the mechanisms involved in maintaining speech-perceptual functions. However, different mechanisms may be involved in developing a function than are involved in maintaining that function once it has been developed fully. Similarly, the effect of disordered speech perception on language comprehension may be quite different in the child who has not yet fully developed language than in the adult, who has had many years of successful language experience. Take, for example, the effect of impaired hearing on language comprehension. The same degree of hearing disability that may result in a profound language disorder in the developing child, often will not seriously disrupt expressive language when the hearing loss occurs for the first time in adulthood. One can hypothesize that the same might be true of some auditory-perceptual disability.

One additional example may be helpful here. Most adults with adequate reading skills read almost exclusively without having to analyze phoneme to grapheme relationships. Resorting to this kind of analysis is only employed by most adults when reading an unfamiliar word. Therefore, a minor deficit affecting phonetic-analysis ability may not significantly affect the reading ability of most adults. However, the same deficit would, most likely, result in considerable difficulty in learning to read, particularly if a phonics approach is stressed.

As in reading, acoustic and/or phonetic analysis is likely to play a different role in language comprehension from childhood to adulthood. To understand this interaction, it is necessary to do developmental studies that look carefully at the mechanisms involved in speech perception and their role in language development. One further technique that can be applied is that of looking at delayed or disordered development as compared to normal development. Such an approach may yield new insights into mechanisms involved in the neurological bases of speech and language processing. In addition, this approach may lead to a better understanding of the etiology of specific devleopmental language disabilities that could result in improved diagnostic and therapeutic techniques.

Auditory-Perceptual Deficits in Language-Delayed Children

Nonverbal auditory-perceptual deficits have been reported in various groups of children with speech, language, and/or reading disorders (Benton, 1964; Critchley, 1964; Eisenson, 1966; Hardy, 1965). Perceptual deficits ranging from low-level temporal summation through higher-level memory and pattern integration have been reported. Rosenthal (1972) reported that developmentally dysphasic children showed abnormal auditory temporal summation functions. A later study (Rosenthal and Wohlert, 1973) reported finding masking level differences for this same population as compared to normally developing children. However, other investigators have reported that language-delayed children do not differ significantly from normally developing children in auditory temporal summation abilities. Lowe and Campbell (1965) experimentally investigated the abilities of children whom they called "aphasoid" to judge auditory succession (auditory fusion), the point at which two rapidly presented signals are heard as a single continuous tone. These authors found no significant differences between the asphasoid and normal children's performance on this task. Similarly, Kornet *et al.* (1977) also failed to demonstrate differences between language-delayed and normal children's auditory temporal resolution abilities.

Hirsh (1959) demonstrated with normal adults that perception of two acoustic events required that first they be identified as two discrete signals, rather than a single continuous event (temporal resolution or auditory fusion). Having determined that two discrete signals had occurred, Hirsh suggested that the listener next had to determine whether the two signals were the same as or different from each other (discrimination). For those signals that were different from each other, the listener must also determine their order of occurrence (temporal order or sequencing). For language-delayed children, although the data pertaining to temporal resolution continues to be equivocal, there is no doubt that these children consistently show deficits in their ability to perceive the temporal order or sequence of acoustic events. Lowe and Campbell (1965) showed that the same aphasoid children that were unimpaired in their ability to judge auditory fusion were impaired in their ability to indicate which of two tones occurred first, when they were presented in rapid sequence. In this study, two different 15-msec pure tones (400 Hz and 2200 Hz) were presented in rapid sequence with brief intersound intervals, (ISIs). Subjects were required to indicate which of the two tones occurred first. The normal control subject made correct temporal order judgments with a mean of 36 msec (15–80 msec). In contrast the aphasoid children required intervals of 55–700 msec (mean = 357 msec) to achieve the same level of performance as the controls (75% correct). Lowe and Campbell concluded that disturbed temporal ordering might be a major factor in the communication difficulties of these children.

It has also been noted that children with specific reading disorders are impaired in their sequential processing abilities (see Bakker (1967) for review). In a study of patterns of impairment in a large sample of children with reading disabilities, Doehring (1968) found that deficits of sequential processing of auditory and visual stimuli were important factors underlying reading disorders. He found that such sequential deficits were particularly marked when items to be sequenced were presented rapidly.

Similar difficulty in sequencing rapidly presented auditory stimuli has been documented in experimental studies with adult aphasics (Carpenter and Rutherford, 1973; Edwards and Auger, 1965; Efron, 1963; Holmes, 1965; Sheehan et al, 1973; see Swisher and Hirsh, 1972, for review). Efron (1963) concluded that "we should not look upon aphasia as a unique disorder of language, but rather as an inevitable consequence of a primary perceptual deficit in temporal analysis, in placing a 'time-label' upon incoming data [p. 418]."

We can conclude from these studies that a deficit in the performance of sequencing tasks certainly appears to be concomitant with communication disorders in both children and adults. Clinical case reports have also stressed the predominance of auditory temporal processing and memory disabilities in children and adults with communicative disorders (Benton, 1964; Eisenson, 1972; Hardy, 1965; McGinnis, 1963; Monsees, 1961; Orton, 1937). However, whether a deficit in sequencing is a primary impairment in some communication disorders, is specific to the auditory modality, or is positively correlated with the degree and type of communication impairment remains to be determined. Furthermore the relationship, if any, of these nonverbal auditory perceptual deficits to speech and language perception cannot be established from these studies.

Tallal and Piercy (1973) investigated in detail the nonverbal auditory-perceptual abilities of developmentally dysphasic children. To investigate the auditory-perceptual abilities of these children in a systematic manner, a new operant experimental procedure that enabled the subjects to report in detail in a nonverbal manner exactly what they perceived, was devised. This method allowed for several different aspects of perception to be investigated by changing only one variable at a time. Using this procedure, auditory detection, association, discrimination, temporal order, and serial memory were investigated as a function of rate of stimulus presentation and sensory modality. This method was designated the "repetition method" and has been described in detail in previous publications (Tallal and Piercy, 1973; and Tallal, 1980). In brief, subjects were operantly trained to respond to stimulus presentations by pressing either of two, identical panels mounted side by side on a response box. Subjects were required to "repeat" (motorically) precisely what they perceived by pressing the appropriate panels on the response box (hence repetition method).

The results of Tallal and Piercy's studies using these new experimental methods, demonstrated that a well-defined group of children with specific developmental language delay (the criteria for inclusion as language-delayed as well as a detailed clinical description of these subjects has been given in a previous publication, Tallal and Piercy, 1973) were not significantly different than normally developing control subjects in their ability to detect, discriminate, or sequence auditory nonverbal complex tones (incorporating frequencies within the speech range) that were presented relatively slowly. However, when these same stimuli were presented more rapidly, the language-delayed children were significantly impaired in their ability to discriminate between the signals and also to sequence them. This deficit was demonstrated by systematically varying demands made on auditory processing by altering the duration of the ISI between two complex nonverbal tones, presented in sequence, while holding the duration of the tones themselves constant. Whereas the normal children required only 8 msec between two 75 msec tones to respond correctly to their temporal order (75% correct) the language-delayed children required an average of 300 msec to even *discriminate* between the tones. Furthermore, the same amount of time (300 msec) was required by the language-delayed children to *discriminate* between two tones as was required to sequence those tones. Thus, the results of this study indicated that these language-delayed children were specifically impaired in their ability to respond correctly to rapidly presented nonverbal auditory stimuli, regardless of whether or not temporal order perception was required. A deficit in discrimination at rapid rates of presentation would be primary to, and thus account for, a sequencing deficit. Discrimination between items to be sequenced at rapid rates of presentation was not tested in other studies that reported deficits in temporal order perception. Thus, it is possible that previous reports of temporal order or sequencing deficits for subjects with communicative disorders can be attributed to more primary deficits in discrimination. This may be the case for all the studies reviewed. Thus, the critical factor underlying these subjects' impaired performance on auditory perceptual tasks may have been discrimination at rapid rates, rather than temporal order or sequencing, as was reported.

In another study (Tallal and Piercy, 1973) the same language-disordered subjects and controls were tested for their ability to perceive sequences of nonverbal stimuli of various durations in the auditory as well as in the visual modality, using the same operant techniques. These subjects' performances were studied in relation to the duration of the stimulus elements, the interval between elements, and the number of elements in the sequence. The results of this study showed that there was no significant difference between the language-delayed and the control group's performance on any of the visual tests given. In contrast, on the auditory test, the language-impaired subjects, but not the controls, were adversely affected by decreases in the duration of the stimulus elements and intervals between elements as well as by increases in the number of elements in a series. That is, the language-impaired subjects' performances decreased when auditory stimulus items were presented more rapidly (by decreasing the duration of the stimulus elements themselves or the interval between elements) and when more items were included in a series of tones that had to be remembered. The total duration of the stimulus patterns was found to correlate significantly ($rho = .89$) with the performance of these children. Furthermore, these children could respond correctly to two- and three-element sequences presented with long-duration tones (250 msec), but were unable to respond correctly to the same two- and three-element sequences when they were presented with shorter-duration tones (75 msec). It was suggested that these children with developmental language delay were incapable of responding correctly to acoustic information presented at rapid rates, and the possibility was considered that this auditory-perceptual impairment might underlie their language impairment.

Curtiss (1978) studied older language-impaired children (9–10 years old) than those studied by Tallal and Piercy (7–9 years old). This sample was given the repetition test using 75-msec duration nonverbal tones. Curtiss reported replicating the findings of Tallal and Piercy (1973). That is, she found the language-impaired children's performance to be significantly impaired, in comparison to that of the controls, in both discriminating and sequencing rapidly presented nonverbal stimuli.

Speech-Perceptual Deficits in Language-Delayed Children

To suggest that a nonverbal auditory-perceptual deficit might be related to the language disabilities of language-impaired children, it is necessary to demonstrate how the specific pattern of nonverbal perceptual abilities is related to the speech-perceptual abilities of these children. Investigating the speech signal as an acoustic, rather than as a linguistic event, may yield some insight into the auditory-perceptual mechanisms involved in speech perception. This, in turn, may also provide a link between nonverbal and verbal-perceptual deficits.

The results of Tallal and Piercy's studies (1973) with developmentally dysphasic children indicated that these children had specific difficulty in responding to rapidly presented acoustic signals. If this deficit were related in some way to these children's language disabilities, one might hypothesize that they would have more difficulty processing speech sounds that incorporated rapid acoustic changes, than they would speech sounds that were steady-state or unchanging in nature. To investigate this hypothesis, Tallal and Piercy (1974) studied the same language-impaired children's ability to process computer-synthesized stop CV syllables (such as /ba/ versus /da/, which incorporate rapid acoustic changes) and also synthesized steady-state vowels (such as /ɛ/ versus /æ/, which do not incorporate rapid acoustic changes). The results of these experiments showed that the language-impaired subjects' ability to respond correctly to vowel stimuli did not differ significantly from their ability to respond correctly to nonverbal auditory stimuli, of the same duration, on any of the perceptual or serial memory tasks studied. Clearly, these children's performances did not deteriorate simply as a consequence of changing from nonverbal to verbal auditory stimuli, when both were steady-state. However, the results with synthesized stop CV syllables were entirely different. On all tasks studied, the language-impaired subjects' discrimination of consonant stimuli was significantly inferior both to their own discrimination of vowel and nonverbal stimuli of the same duration, and to that of their matched controls.

These studies showed, for the first time, a direct relationship between the acoustic characteristics of speech signals and their discriminability for language-delayed children. As such, a method of linking auditory-perceptual abilities directly to speech-perceptual abilities of individuals with communication disorders was developed. Thus, using similar techniques, it should be possible to pose more specific questions concerning the detailed pattern of perceptual abilities, both nonverbal and verbal, of patients with communication disorders. It should also be possible to investigate further the mechanisms underlying these abilities, as well as their role in the communication disorder.

Tallal and Piercy (1974) reported that language-delayed children were impaired in their ability to discriminate between stop CV syllables that incorporated rapidly changing formant structures, and were unimpaired in their ability to discriminate between steady-state vowels. It could not be determined from that study, however, exactly which aspects of the acoustic spectra of the CV syllables were misperceived, and thus resulted in the language-delayed children's impaired discrimination. That is, did these children have difficulty in processing the rapid frequency change over time, the brevity of the formant transition, or some other aspect of the spectrum? To investigate these questions in more detail, Tallal and Piercy (1975) carried out two additional experiments with these same children. Again, using the computer to provide precise control of the acoustic spectra, two additional pairs of stimuli were synthesized. In one pair, the duration of the initial formant transition within the stop CV syllables /ba/ and /da/ was extended, from the traditional 40, to 80 msec. In this pair, the acoustic information critical for discrimination continued to be transitional in nature but occurred over a longer duration. A different pair of stimuli was synthesized so that the duration of the critical cues for discrimination remained at 40 msec. However, in these signals, the 40 msec was steady state rather than transitional in nature. The resulting stimuli for this second pair were "diphthong-like." They commenced with a 40 msec steady-state period, that was different between the two signals, and ended with a 210 msec steady-state period, that was the same between the two signals. In this way, as in the traditional stop CV syllables, only 40 msec of the signal contained acoustically different information. However, unlike the stop CV syllables, this 40 msec period was steady state rather than transitional in nature. The language-delayed and normal children's ability to discriminate between these two additional stimulus pairs was investigated. The results indicated that the control children were virtually errorless in discriminating between both of the new stimulus pairs. The language-delayed children, however, were significantly impaired in their ability to discriminate between the second, but not the first, stimulus pair. That is, these children were unable to discriminate between the "diphthong-like" syllables, which incorporated brief, but steady-state, acoustic cues. Importantly, these children's ability to discriminate between the stop CV syllables, with the extended duration formant transition (80 msec), was significantly improved over their own previous discrimination performance with the same stop consonants, with 40 msec duration transitions. Thus, for the same speech sounds, these language-impaired children's discrimination improved markedly as the result of changing a single acoustic cue.

Tallal and Piercy's findings of specific nonverbal and verbal auditory-perceptual deficits all resulted initially from studies with the same twelve language-delayed children, between the ages of 7–9 years. These children were all attending a special school in England for language-delayed children. It is possible that selection criteria, specific to this school, influenced the results obtained, and that they may not be representative of other groups of language-delayed children. Therefore, Tallal and Stark have undertaken a broad-based developmental study, including many of these same experiments, with a much larger group of selected language-delayed children in the United States.

Development of Auditory- and Speech-Perceptual Capabilities in Language-Delayed and Normal Children

The subjects participating in Tallal and Stark's studies were selected from several different schools for language-delayed children on the basis of the following criteria: (a) performance (nonverbal) intelligence was 85 or above; (b) receptive language age (as measured by a battery of standardized receptive language tests) was at least 6 months behind performance mental age; (c) expressive language was at least 1 year behind performance mental age; (*d*) composite language age (averaged from receptive and expressive language age) was at least one year behind both performance mental age and chronological age; (*e*) articulation age was within 6 months of expressive language age; and (*f*) reading age was within 6 months of expressive language age. A control group, matched for age, IQ, and socioeconomic status, was also carefully selected. Subjects included in the control group had to be within 6 months of both their performance mental age and chronological age in the areas of receptive and expressive language, articulation, and reading skills. Control subjects performance IQ also had to be 85 or above. For each group, subjects between the ages of 5 and 9 years old were included. Between four and six subjects were included in each half-age group.

One of the specific aims of Tallal and Stark's studies was to try to replicate the findings of Tallal and Piercy (1973, 1974, 1975) with another, larger group of language-delayed and control children, covering a wider age range. In addition, the following research questions were posed for these studies:

1. It has been demonstrated that language-disordered children are impaired in discriminating speech sounds that incorporate rapidly changing acoustic spectra. Which specific aspect of the acoustic spectra (temporal features, spectral features, or a combination of temporal and spectral features) are most difficult for language-delayed children to discriminate.

2. For the normal listener, more complex acoustic stimuli that carry information about several acoustic features at once, are easier to discriminate than simple stimuli, that differ along only a single dimension. Does this relation hold for language-disordered children? This question is of particular importance when comparing the results of studies that used synthesized speech signals (where there may have been very little acoustic redundancy in the signal) to those that used natural speech signals (containing a good deal of redundancy).

3. Can we use the foundation of knowledge we have begun to build, concerning the basic perceptual capabilities of language-delayed children, to ask more precise questions concerning these children's cognitive linguistic abilities? For example, if a child can discriminate between certain stimuli, can he perform generalizations, segmentation, or cross-modal integration tasks that were based on those discriminations?

4. Do specific patterns of speech-perception impairment correlate positively with specific patterns of speech-production impairment?

5. Are specific patterns of perceptual and perceptual–cognitive impairments modality specific?

6. Are there any direct relationships between patterns and levels of performance on these sensory, perceptual, and cognitive tests and the degree and/or type of language impairment?

7. Are different patterns of performance characteristic of different subgroups of impaired children?

Specific test procedures were developed to ask these specific questions. These procedures were similar in most cases to those used previously by Tallal and Piercy (1973). However, many additional speech-sound contrasts were used so that the acoustic and phonetic abilities of this group of children might be more specifically described. A large program was undertaken to investigate these areas of interest. Children were tested at their own schools twice a week during 30 min sessions. Testing continued approximately 3–4 months. Each subject participated in over 50 experimental test procedures. The order of presentation of these procedures was counter-balanced between subjects by means of a computer randomization program. Auditory-perceptual, visual-perceptual and cross-modal (auditory–visual, visual–tactile) tests were included in this battery. It is not within the scope of this chapter to describe all of the theoretical questions underlying the development and the specific methods used for each test in the experimental battery, or to present all of the results. The initial phase of data analysis has now been completed and some of the general results obtained from these studies will be discussed in what follows. However, more detailed analysis will be needed before a complete description of the data can be made.

One hundred and twenty eight language-delayed children were referred by the speech pathologists from four special schools for language-impaired children, as potential subjects for this study. Of those children, only 40 fulfilled all of our criteria for inclusion as subjects. The major reasons for exclusion from the study were performance IQ being too low, receptive language being too high, and articulation being too low (in relation to expressive language) to meet our criteria. Eighty-nine normally developing children were referred from four public schools in the same counties as the special schools for language-delayed children. Of the 89 normal children referred, 48 met the criteria for inclusion in the study. The major causes for exclusion from the study were performance IQ being too high, articulation being too low, and families moving away before testing had been completed.

The overall results of between-group univariate analysis performed on the data obtained from the language-delayed and control children for each of the experimental test procedures in this test battery, in general, continue to support the hypothesis that language-delayed children are specifically impaired in their ability to discriminate between acoustic signals that incorporate rapid acoustic change regardless of whether those changes are verbal or nonverbal. The major findings of Tallal and Piercy's previous studies (1973, 1974, 1975) were replicated with this new group of children. That is, this group of language-delayed children also was significantly impaired, in comparison to normally developing children, in their ability to respond correctly to rapidly presented nonverbal tone sequences. In fact, these children proved to have even more difficulty than that reported previously by Tallal and Piercy (1973). That is, these language-delayed children showed impaired performance at even slower rates of presentation than had been found to be necessary to demonstrate breakdown in Tallal and Piercy's group. This difference in degree of impairment, however, probably can be attributed to the fact that younger children were included in the language-delayed group participating in this study (5–9 years old) than had been included in Tallal and Piercy's group (7–9 years old). Additional analysis will be needed to assess the contribution of age in these data.

One of the questions posed in this study was whether or not language-delayed children, like normal children, respond better to more complex acoustic stimuli that carry information about several acoustic features at once than they do to simple stimuli that differ along only a single dimension. To investigate this question, the ability to discriminate between stop CV syllables synthesized with three formant transitions (F_1, F_2, F_3) was compared to that for the same syllables synthesized with only two formant transitions (F_1, F_2). The results of these studies clearly indicated that the language-delayed children, like normally developing children, find acoustic stimuli that carry information about several acoustic features at once (three formants) easier to discriminate than the same syllables carrying less acoustic information (two formants). Similarly, both the language-delayed children and the normally developing children made fewer errors in discriminating between stop CV syllables that were produced naturally than they did those that were synthesized. Naturally produced syllables are also more complex acoustically than are synthesized syllables. However, even with the naturally produced stop CV syllables, the language-delayed children's performance was significantly impaired in comparison to that of the normally developing children. It has been suggested for language-delayed children, as well as for deaf children, that reducing the redundancy of acoustic information within speech sounds may aid these children in perception (Danaher and Pickett, 1975). The results of our studies, at least for language-delayed children, do not support this suggestion. Conversely, these language-delayed children appear to benefit from complexity and redundancy in the acoustic signal, as do normally developing children.

Visual-Perceptual Abilities Of Language-Delayed Children

Tallal and Piercy (1974) reported finding that the language-delayed children in their study were not significantly impaired in their ability to respond to any of the visual-perceptual tests that were included in their test battery. However, they reported reservations about extending these findings to other groups of language-delayed children. These reservations derived from the fact that the Raven's colored progressive matrices test (1965), which is heavily loaded in visual perception, was used to assess nonverbal intelligence in their population of language-delayed children. As children who failed to perform in the average or above average range on this test were not included in this study, children with visual-perceptual deficits may have inadvertently been excluded.

Other authors have reported finding visual-perceptual deficits as well as auditory-perceptual deficits in language-delayed populations (Furth and Pufall, 1966; Stark, 1966, 1967; Withrow, 1964). These authors studied language-delayed, deaf, and normally developing children. They found that, whereas there was no difference between the language-delayed and the deaf children in their studies, both of these groups of children were impaired as compared to normal children on tasks requiring them to reproduce a temporal, spatial sequence of visual stimuli.

In another study, Poppen *et al.* (1969) investigated the visual-sequencing abilities of developmentally aphasic children. Subjects were required to press three identical panels in the order in which these panels had previously been illuminated. In one condition, subjects were allowed to respond immediately after the stimulus had been presented. In a second condition, response was delayed between 2 and 27 sec after the stimulus had been presented. These authors reported that, whereas the aphasic children were able to perform at a level of 75% correct or better on the first condition, they were significantly impaired in comparison to controls on the delayed-response condition. However, the delayed-response condition placed additional demands on memory. It is possible that the control subjects were able to make use of verbal mediation strategies to help them in this task to an extent that was not available to the language-delayed children. Thus, it is unclear whether these results reflect specific visual-perceptual impairments.

Furth (1964) investigated developmentally aphasic, deaf, and normal children's ability to respond to sequences of nonsense figures presented in a visual spatial display, either simultaneously, or in succession. Although Furth hypothesized that the developmentally aphasic subjects would be more impaired in indicating which sequence pattern had been presented than would deaf or normal subjects, this hypothesis was not sustained. No significant differences between groups were observed.

The results of previous studies that have investigated the visual-perceptual abilities of language-delayed children have been equivocal. Thus, the status of the visual-perceptual abilities of such children required further study. Therefore, the language-delayed and control children participating in our present developmental studies were given a battery of visual-perceptual tests. The same methods that were used in the auditory modality, were used again in the visual modality. Nonverbal as well as verbal visual stimuli were presented. The results of these studies indicated that the language-delayed children as a group made more errors in the auditory modality than they did in the visual modality.

In addition, unlike their performance in the auditory modality, the language-delayed children were virtually errorless in their ability to discriminate between any of the visual stimulus pairs. However, the language-impaired children were significantly impaired, in comparison to the normally developing children, on both nonverbal and verbal sequencing and memory tests presented in the visual modality.

In addition to tests presented in either the auditory or the visual modality, cross-modality perceptual tests were also given. In these tests, subjects were trained to press one button on the response panel whenever a tone was presented, and the other button whenever a light-flash was presented. The tone and the light-flash were both presented for 75 msec. Each of these signals had previously been used in the within-modality tests. The cross-modal test was given to all subjects last. The results of this study were similar to those reported for the visual modality. That is, the language-delayed group made more errors on the repetition test in the auditory modality, alone, than they did in the cross-modal tests, even though the same test procedures were used. Similarly, these children were unimpaired in their ability to learn the correct button association (and hence discriminate between) the cross-modal stimuli. However, the language-delayed children were impaired, in comparison to the controls, on the cross-modal sequencing and serial memory tests. Thus, we can conclude that, although the language-delayed children studied here were more impaired in the auditory modality than they were in the visual modality or cross-modality, they did demonstrate some impairment in visual- and cross-modal perception as well. Although they could discriminate stimuli adequately both visually and cross-modally, the younger language-impaired subjects (5- and 6-year olds) were impaired on higher-level tasks such as sequencing and serial memory with these stimuli. Additional analyses have demonstrated that the modality specificity of perceptual deficits in aphasic children is significantly related to age (Tallal *et al.*, 1980a).

Higher-Level Perceptual and Cognitive Capabilities of Language-Delayed Children

Another question of particular interest in these studies concerned the effect of deficits in basic perceptual analysis on subsequent cognitive linguistic abilities. That is, what effect does impaired phoneme discrimination have on higher-level concept formations, generalization, or segmentation tasks. These questions were investigated in several additional experiments (Tallal *et al.*, 1980b,c). Concept generalization was investigated in a study that tested children for their ability to (*a*) group several acoustically different syllables, each containing a similar phoneme segment, together; and (*b*) differentiate members of this category from other syllables that were acoustically different, but did not contain the same phoneme. For example, the syllables /ba/, /be/, /bi/, /dɛ/, /dæ/ and /di/ were presented singly in random order. Each of these syllables is acoustically different from all of the others. However, half of the syllables contain the phoneme /b/ and the other half contained the phoneme /d/. Children were trained to assign each of these syllables to one of two categories (by pushing the appropriate button on a two-button response panel). They were not instructed verbally how to formulate the categories. They were told to listen to each sound and to try to learn which sounds were correctly paired with each of the two buttons. Correct responses were reinforced. The language-delayed children as a group were significantly impaired, in comparison to the controls, in their ability to respond correctly on this task. For those children in each group, however, who did reach criterion on this concept-formation task, an additional test was given. Having learned that the lower button on the response panel should be pressed for all syllables containing the phoneme /b/ and the top button for all syllables containing the phoneme /d/, two syllables were presented in sequence. In each case, the two syllables presented, when· blended together, formed a real word (ba-by, da-ddy, De-bbie, bo-dy). In Condition 1, the two syllables that were presented in sequence were separated by a 500 msec ISI (ba-by, da-ddy, etc.). In Condition 2, a 50 msec interval separated the two syllables as occurs in natural speech; the syllables were presented as a single word (baby, daddy, Debbie, body). It was of interest to determine, for those children who had already demonstrated their ability to discriminate between phonemes and isolated syllables, what the status of their perceptual abilities were as it became necessary to use these abilities to process larger linguistic units. The results of this study showed that the language-delayed children, who had performed adequately on the previous phoneme-discrimination and concept-formation tests, nonetheless, were significantly impaired in their ability to make use of this information in performing the higher-level perceptual and cognitive–linguistic skills required in this task. These children were significantly impaired in their ability both to sequence the two syllables when they were presented with a brief ISI and also to segment syllables within words (Condition 2). Whereas there was no significant difference on the two conditions for the controls, the language-delayed group's performance was significantly poorer on Condition 2 (which had briefer silent intervals between the syllables) than on Condition 1. It should be stressed that the results of this study only pertain to those language-delayed children who did *not* show difficulty with phoneme discrimination and/or concept formation. Those children who were unable even to discriminate between the phonemes used in this task, were obviously at a much greater disadvantage. Without the ability to discriminate adequately even at the acoustic and phonemic levels, attaining higher-level linguistic skills must be very difficult indeed.

Conclusions

Studies investigating the auditory-perceptual and speech-perceptual abilities of language-delayed children have been reviewed in this chapter. The current studies that we have been doing with this group of children could only be summarized in brief, at the present time. There is growing evidence that language-delayed children as a group are significantly impaired in specific aspects of acoustic and phonetic analysis in comparison to normally developing children. These lower-level acoustic and phonetic disabilities also appear to affect directly these children's ability to perform higher-level perceptual, cognitive, and linguistic tasks. It is hoped that through additional analysis of the data obtained from our studies of language-delayed and normally developing children, as well as from those of other researchers in this field, it will be possible to begin to determine more directly the relationship between these lower-level acoustic and phonetic deficits and higher-level linguistic abilities. It is also our intention to begin to look for subgroups of children who are characterized by different types and degrees of perceptual and linguistic abilities.

It is not our intention to suggest that all language-delayed children show the same pattern of perceptual deficits or even that such deficits are a necessary and/or sufficient cause of the disorder. Rather it is our purpose to demonstrate that, by investigating nonverbal perception and also the acoustic aspects of the speech stream in a systematic and detailed manner, consistent data can be derived that might further our understanding of how speech and language are processed. In addition, this line of research may help us to determine which aspects of acoustic and phonetic analysis are critical for normal language development. Finally, it is our hope that speech-perceptual research will lead to a better understanding of some types of developmental language disabilities that, in turn, may lead to improved diagnosis and treatment for these children.

Acknowledgments

The work reported in this chapter was funded by a grant from the American Association for University Women (Ida Green Fellowship) and by NINCDS (Contract Number 25353).

References

Bakker, D.J., (1967) "Temporal Order, Meaningfulness, Reading Ability," *Perception and Motor Skills*, 24, 1027–1030.

Benton, A.L. (1964) "Developmental Aphasia and Brain Damage," *Cortex*, 1, 40–52.

Carpenter, R.L., and Rutherford, D.R. (1973) "Acoustic Cue Discrimination in Adult Aphasia," *Journal of Speech and Hearing Research*, 16, 534–544.

Critchely, M. (1964) *Developmental Dyslexia*, Heinemann, London.

Curtiss, B.C. (1978) "A Study of Auditory Processing and Speech Perception in Language-impaired Children," Unpublished Doctoral Dissertation, Johns Hopkins University, Baltimore, Maryland.

Danaher, E.M., and Pickett, J.M. (1975) "Some Masking Effects Produced by Low Frequency Vowel Formants in Persons with Sensorineural Loss," *Journal of Speech and Hearing Research*, 18, 261–271.

Doehring, D.G. (1968) *Patterns of Impairments in Specific Reading Disability*, Indiana University Press, Bloomington.

Edwards, A.E., and Auger, R. (1965) "The Effect of Aphasia on the Perception of Precedence," *Proceedings of the Seventy-Third Annual Convention of the American Psychological Association*, 207–208.

Efron, R. (1963) "Temporal Perception, Aphasia and Deja Vu," *Brain*, 86, 423–424.

Eimas, P., *et al.*, (1971) "Speech Perception in Infants," *Science*, 171, 303–306.

Eisenson, J. (1966) "Perceptual Disturbances in Children with Central Nervous Dysfunction and Implications for Language Development," *British Journal of Disorders of Communication*, 1, 21–32.

Eisenson, J. (1972) *Aphasia in Children*, Harper & Row, London.

Furth, H.G. (1964) "Sequence Learning in Aphasic and Deaf Children," *Journal of Speech and Hearing Disorders*, 29, (2), 171–177.

Furth, H.G., and Pufall, P.B. (1966) "Visual and Auditory Sequence Learning in Hearing-impaired Children," *Journal of Speech and Hearing Research*, 9, 441–449.

Hardy, W.G. (1965) "On Language Disorders in Young Children; A Reorganization of Thinking," *Journal of Speech and Hearing Disturbances*, 8, 3–16.

Hirsh, I.J. (1959) "Auditory Perception of Temporal Order," *Journal of the Acoustic Society of America*, 31, 759–767.

Holmes, H.L. (1965) "Disordered Perception of Auditory Sequences in Aphasia," Unpublished Thesis, Harvard University, 1965.

Kornet, R.H., Thal, D., and Maxon, A. (1977) "Temporal Interpretation in Dysphasic Children," *The Working Papers in Experimental Speech Pathology and Audiology*, Vol. VI, 73–94.

Lowe, A.D., and Campbell, R.A., (1965) "Temporal Discrimination in Aphasoid and Normal Children," *Journal of Speech and Hearing Research*, 8, 313–314.

McGinnis, M. (1963) *Aphasic Children*, A.G. Bell Association for the Deaf, Washington, D.C.

Miller, J.D., and Kuhl, P.K. (1976) "Speech and Perception by the Chinchilla: A Progress Report on Syllable-initial Voiced-plosive Consonants," *Journal of the Acoustical Society of America*, 59, 554 (a).

Monsees, E.K. (1961) "Aphasia in Children," *Journal of Speech and Hearing Disorders*, 26, 83–86.

Orton, S.T. (1937) *Reading, Writing and Speech Problems in Children*, Chapman and Hall, London.

Poppen, R., Stark, J., Eisenson, J., Forrest, T., and Wertheim, G. (1969) "Visual Sequencing Performance of Aphasic Children," *Journal of Speech and Hearing Research*, 12, 288–300.

Rosenthal, W.S. (1972) "Auditory and Linguistic Interaction in Developmental Aphasia: Evidence from Two Studies of Auditory Processing," *Paper and Reports on Child Language Development.*, Committee on Linguistics, Stanford University 19–34.

Rosenthal, W.S., and Wohlert, K.L. (1973) "Masking Level Differences (MLD) Effects in Aphasic Children," Paper presented at ASHA Convention, Detroit.

Sheehan, J.G., Aseltine, S., and Edwards, A.E. (1973) "Aphasic Comprehension of Time Spacing," *Journal of Speech and Hearing Research*, 16, 650–657.

Stark, J. (1966) "Performance of Aphasic Children on the ITPA," *Exceptional Child*, 33, 153–158.

Stark, J. (1967) "A Comparison of the Performance of Aphasic Children on Three Sequencing Tests," *Journal of Communication Disorders*, 1, 31–34.

Swisher, L., and Hirsh, I.J. (1972) "Brain Damage and the Ordering of Two Temporally Successive Stimuli," *Neuropsychology*, 10, 137–151.

Tallal, P. (1975) "An Experimental Investigation of the Role of Auditory Temporal Processing in Normal and Disordered Language Development," in A. Caramazza and E. Zuriff, eds., *Acquisition and Breakdown of Language: Parallels and Divergencies*, Johns Hopkins Press, Baltimore, Md.

Tallal, P. (1980) "Perceptual Requisites for Language," in R. Schiefelbusch, ed., *Non-Speech Language and Communication*, University Park Press, Baltimore, Maryland, pp. 449–467.

Tallal, P., and Piercy, M. (1973) "Defects of Non-verbal Auditory Perception in Children with Developmental Aphasia," *Nature*, 241, 468–469.

Tallal, P., and Piercy, M. (1973) "Developmental Aphasia: Rate of Auditory Processing and Selective Impairment of Consonant Perception," *Neuropsychologia*, 11, pp. 389–398.

Tallal, P., and Piercy, M. (1974) "Developmental Aphasia: Rate of Auditory Processing and Selective Impairment of Consonant Perception," *Neuropsychologia*, 12, 83–94.

Tallal, P., and Piercy, M. (1975) "Developmental Aphasia: The Perception of Brief Vowels and Extended Stop Consonants," *Neuropsychologia*, 13, 69–74.

Tallal, P., Stark, R., and Curtiss, B. (1976) "The Relation between Speech Perception Impairment and Speech Production Impairment in Children with Developmental Dysphasia," *Brain and Language*, 3, 305–317.

Tallal, P., Stark, R., Kallman, C., and Mellits, D. (1980) "A Reexamination of Some Non-Verbal Perceptual Abilities of Language-Impaired Children as a Function of Age and Sensory Modality," *Journal of Speech and Hearing Research*, in press. (a)

Tallal, P., Stark, R., Kallman, C., and Mellits, D. (1980) "Perceptual Constancy for Phonemic Categories: A Developmental Study With Normal and Language-Impaired Children," *Applied Psycholinguistics*, 1, 49–64. (b)

Tallal, P., Stark, R., Kallman, C and Mellits, D. (1980) Developmental dysphasia: The Relation between Acoustic Processing Deficits and Verbal Processing. *Neuropsychologia*, in press. (c)

Withrow, F.B. (1964) "Immediate Recall by Aphasic, Deaf and Normally Hearing Children for Visual Forms Presented Simultaneously or Sequentially in Time," *Asha*, 6, 386.

Chapter 9

TWO HYPOTHESES FOR PHONETIC CLARIFICATION IN THE SPEECH OF MOTHERS TO CHILDREN

BATHSHEBA J. MALSHEEN*

A number of studies have shown that mothers' speech to children has different syntactic, semantic, and phonological characteristics from mothers' speech to adults. In general, it has been found that mothers' speech to children is clearer and simpler than mother's speech to adults along a number of different syntactic, lexical, and prosodic dimensions, such as mean length of utterance (MLU), concreteness of nouns, and others (Snow and Ferguson 1977). Moslin (1977, 1978) made an acoustic analysis of the speech of mothers to children to determine whether phonological segments (i.e., stop consonants, produced in mother–child (M–C) speech differ phonetically from those produced in adult–adult (A–A) speech). It is known that normal A–A speech is not carefully articulated, and that many segmental acoustic cues that are present in careful, deliberate speech are diminished or absent when the segments are produced in conversational contexts. The principal acoustic dimension measured in this study was VOT, which has been shown to effectively distinguish initial voiced and voiceless stops in English (Lisker and Abramson, 1964). VOT is defined as the interval between the release of stop occlusion and the onset of vocal-fold oscillation. In normal A–A speech, which contains many unstressed syllables and polysyllabic words, VOT distributions for voiced and voiceless stops show considerable overlap. It was of interest to determine whether the VOT distributions for voiced and voice-

---

*The author formerly wrote under the name of Barbara J. Moslin.

CHILD PHONOLOGY
VOLUME 2: PERCEPTION

less stops produced in M–C speech showed less overlap than they did in A–A speech. That is, do mothers "clean up" the phonetic environment for their children, or do they present them with a data base of sloppy phonetics from which to learn a phonological contrast?

The subjects were six middle-class mothers, each of whom was recorded in her home over a six-month period, while engaged in verbal interaction with her child. At the beginning of the study, the two youngest children, aged 0;6 and 0;8, were babbling their first CV syllables and had not yet acquired a first recognizable word. The two "middle" children, 1;3 and 1;4 at the beginning of the study were producing their first words. The two oldest children, aged 2;5 and 5;2, were producing three- to five-word sentences containing a large inventory of lexical items. All occurrences of word-initial /b/, /d/, /g/, /p/, /t/, and /k/ were measured on an oscillographic display of a PDP–9 computer. Stops produced in both stressed and unstressed words, and in both open- and closed-word-class items were analyzed.

Results of sign tests showed that there were no significant differences in VOT overlap between the speech of A–A speech and M–C speech ($p > .05$), nor were there any differences found in VOT overlap between A–A speech and M–C speech to the two oldest children, who were producing relatively sophisticated syntactic structures ($p > .05$). However, the stop consonants produced by mothers to children acquiring their first words showed a significant overlap reduction ($p < .01$). This was effected primarily through an increase in the mean VOT value of the voiceless stop. The mean VOT value of the short-lag voiced stops also showed a slight but significant increase in M–C speech.[1] Since prevoicing was extremely difficult to measure for stops produced in running speech, only voiced stops with "positive" VOT values were included in this analysis.[2]

Figure 9.1 compares VOT distributions for one mother's production of word-initial alveolar stops to another adult, and to her 18-month-old child. Note the reduction in overlap of VOT values for /d/ and /t/ from 52.7% in the A–A condition to 11.4% in the M–C condition.

Two Hypotheses

The data on segmental phonetic modification in the speech of mothers to children acquiring their first words were consistent with two distinct hy-

---

[1] It should be noted, however, that there is no a priori reason to assume that VOT differences of the same magnitude along the short-lag and long-lag ranges of the continuum are perceptually equivalent. It could certainly be the case that a 2-msec shift in mean VOT value for the voiced stop is as perceptible a change as the larger (13 msec) shift in mean VOT value for the voiceless stop. There is no reason to believe that the model of VOT presented by the mother to the child for the voiced stop will have any more or less influence on the child's subsequent articulatory behavior than the VOT model for the voiceless stop.

[2] A detailed discussion of prevoicing in M–C speech is presented in Moslin (1978).

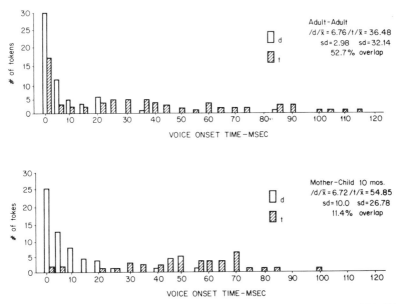

FIGURE 9.1 *Comparisons of VOT distributions of alveolar stops, A–A (a) and M–C (b), of the mother of an 18-month-old child. The number of tokens is indicated along the ordinate, and VOT in sec along the abscissa.*

potheses. The first hypothesis will be referred to as the *independent phonetic clarification* hypothesis (IPC). This hypothesis states that mothers tailor their speech to their children on the phonetic level, and that this tailoring occurs independently of any stylistic modification on other linguistic levels. That is, the phonetic clarification phenomenon may occur *in parallel* with M–C speech modifications on different linguistic levels, (i.e., semantic, syntactic, prosodic, etc.); it may also occur either before mothers have begun, or after they have terminated, modification on another level. For example, it was found that, although mothers of babbling children do not significantly alter the phonetic characteristics of their speech along the VOT dimension when talking to their children, they reduce their MLU's. However, mothers of the middle two children showed both a reduction in MLU *and* phonetic modification.

The IPC hypothesis implies that a mother is sensitive to her child's attempts to articulate phonologically relevant phonetic distinctions, and consequently assists her child on the phonetic level by providing him or her with a maximally distinct phonetic input. Moreover, this hypothesis implies that mothers employ a special phonetic style of speech or a special "phonetic mode" when they talk to their children. This mode would be independent of the phonological component of the adult grammar and would be characterized by a set of low-level phonetic rules; one of these rules would consist of a set of articulatory instructions, specified in phonetic features, for effecting a VOT increase. Presumably, this rule would apply to all word-initial stops produced by the mother to the child.

An alternative to the IPC hypothesis is a more integrative, multilevel explanation of the M–C clarification phenomenon. This will be referred to as the *accidental by-product clarification* hypothesis (ABC). The ABC hypothesis states that the VOT differences discovered in M–C speech are predictable, indirect results, or accidental by-products of higher-level, functionally motivated semantic alterations.

The ABC hypothesis is based upon Newport's (1976) functional interpretation of the syntactic modification phenomenon in M–C speech. Briefly, Newport argues against the claims, made by other experimenters, that syntactic modifications in M–C speech are specific attempts on the part of the mother to reduce the syntactic complexity, or "derivational history" of their sentences to their children. These experimenters have suggested that mothers, in general, are very sensitive to their children's levels of semantic and syntactic competence, and are adjusting their syntactic and semantic input to their children to provide them with linguistic instruction.

Newport offers the following alternative explanation of the syntactic, simplification phenomenon in M–C speech. Adults normally have a very restricted set of messages to convey to a child. Most of these messages are geared toward directing the activity of the child, instructing him, or of having him demonstrate his linguistic competence to others. It has been observed that the behavior directives, or word elicitations, are ordinarily communicated through *short sentences*. These short sentences are usually imperatives, "Give me the ball" or *questions*, "Is that a doll?" or deictic *statements* "That's a peach." Newport suggests that the syntactic modifications discovered in M–C speech are an accidental consequence of the interaction of two primary factors: (*a*) the restricted set of messages a mother has to communicate to her child; and (*b*) the presentation of these messages in a form that is optimally suited to a young child's limited processing capabilities (i.e., limited memory, attention span, etc.). Messages that are presented in a form tailored to match the cognitive capacities of a child (e.g., short sentences) would be more likely to produce the proper response from the child. Incidentally, Newport notes that the interaction of the two factors that shape syntactic structure of M–C speech may not always result in sentences that are "transformationally" simple, as exemplified by the large number of questions and imperatives in M–C speech.

Newport's explanation of the syntactic differences that appear in M–C speech implicitly rules out the notion of a special syntactic style, or mode, or an independent syntactic component, for M–C speech. All reductions in complexity that occurred along a syntactic dimension would be only by-product simplifications of higher-order, functionally motivated alterations.

The basic principles behind Newport's explanation of syntactic modifications in M–C speech can be extended to account for the differences between VOT characteristics of A–A and M–C speech. The limited set of short syntactic structures used as a vehicle for conveying a restricted set of messages to a child would also tend to include a very large proportion of *stressed* words, larger than that found in A–A speech. First, it was observed that, when mothers talk to children, they tend to produce more words in isolation than they do when talking to others adults. Mothers tend to point to objects, and to name them repetitively for their children, for the purposes of instruction. These words are always stressed. Second, since sentences produced in M–C speech are typically very short, they rarely include unstressed modifiers, which are very commonly used in A–A speech. Third, although prepositions, conjunctions, auxiliaries, and other function words, or closed-class items occur very frequently in A–A speech (Kučera and Francis, 1967), they are very often deleted from M–C speech (Phillips 1973). In addition, Newport has found that mothers tend to substitute catenatives, such as "wanna" for phrases containing auxiliaries and prepositions, such as "Do you want to?" Also, in this study, sentences such as "Mommy goes sleepie," were produced for "Mommy is going to sleep."

Lisker and Abramson (1967) have shown that unstressed words that occur in sentence contexts are produced with much lower VOT values than stressed words produced in isolation. One would predict, therefore, that, in general, closed-class items, which are almost always unstressed in sentence contexts, would have significantly lower VOT values than open-class items, or content words, which tend to be stressed. To test this hypothesis, mean VOT values were computed for a sample of 325 word-initial alveolar stops produced by a mother of one of the middle children in both A–A and M–C conditions. The stops were then divided into *closed-class* and *open-class* categories. The mean VOT value for word-initial /d/ produced in closed-class items was 0 msec, whereas the mean value for /d/ in open-class items was 4 msec. The mean VOT value for word-initial /t/ in closed-class items was 17 msec, whereas for open-class items it was 62 msec. These results reflect the mean VOT values computed for A–A and M–C conditions *together*; they confirm the hypothesis that stops in closed-class items have lower VOT values than stops in open-class items. This is especially true for the voiceless stop /t/—the difference between mean VOT values for open- and closed-class categories was 45 msec.

The ABC hypothesis of M–C simplification states that VOT modifications found in M–C speech are correlated with a reduction of unstressed words, particularly closed-class items, which normally have low VOT values. In other words, this hypothesis predicts that target voiceless stops (e.g., the /t/ in *to*) that are produced with either (*a*) VOT values on the lower end of the voiceless range of the continuum (35 msec or greater); or (*b*) VOT values that fall well within the voiced range of the continuum (0–30 msec), will be significantly reduced, or eliminated in M–C speech. As a consequence of this reduction of *low* VOT values, the *mean* VOT value for the

M–C voiceless stop would be higher than the A–A value. The ABC hypothesis also predicts that voiced stops in unstressed utterances (e.g., the auxiliary *do*) that tend to show no break in phonation when produced in running speech, will be significantly reduced or eliminated in M–C speech. This elimination of very low VOT values (mostly 0 msec) at the voiced end of the continuum would result in a slightly higher VOT value for voiced stops in M–C speech.

The evidence presented in what follows shows that the overlap reduction and high mean VOT values that have been shown to occur in M–C speech cannot be explained by a low frequency of occurrence of unstressed items, or more specifically, a lack of "very low" VOT values. It will be argued in the following sections that neither a strict IPC nor an ABC hypothesis is sufficient *by iteslf* to explain M–C VOT modifications; however, the data more strongly support the basic tenet of the IPC hypothesis—that there is a special phonetic style or mode for M–C speech, and a special articulatory rule component that produces this style of speech, irrespective of whether or not modifications are being effected on other linguistic levels.

Testing the Hypotheses

Closed-class Comparisons

To determine whether or not there was a significant difference between A–A and M–C conditions for the percentages of stops that were produced in *closed-class* items, the following analysis was performed. For one middle child's mother, the word-initial alveolar stop productions were divided into open- and closed-class categories, for A–A and M–C conditions. The M–C sample consisted of the mother's stop productions to her child over the 6-month taping period; it was subdivided into three separate 2-month data samples. Percentages of measurable voiced and voiceless stops that appeared in closed-class items were computed for each data sample, and comparisons were made of the differences in A–A and M–C conditions. Results showed that, overall, there was a slightly higher percentage of voiced and voiceless stops in closed-class items for the A–A condition (35%), than in the M–C condition (29%). However, this difference between speaking conditions was not significant according to 2-tailed t-tests ($t = .63$, $df = 5$, $p > .20$). This finding sheds considerable doubt on the ABC hypothesis, which predicts a significantly greater number of closed-class word-initial stops in the A–A condition than in the M–C condition.

However, the nonsignificant result found here could be attributed to the following fact: in normal A–A English speech a "flapping rule" is usually applied to word-initial stops of closed-class items that are embedded between two vowels, as in "Go *to* the store." It has been shown by Laferriere and

Zue (1977) that flaps are often produced without complete articulatory closure; that is, the tongue only approximates the alveolar ridge, and an incomplete closure is effected, resulting in some frication noise, but no visible burst. In addition, it was found, in the present study, that when the voiceless stop of a closed-class item was followed by another voiceless consonant after an intervening vowel, as in "hard *to* carry," the vowel tends to be voiceless; hence, there is no visible periodicity. In both of the cases mentioned—flaps without burst, and voiceless vowels—VOT is impossible to measure. Consequently, these utterances would have been discarded from the data base. It is possible that most of the voiceless stops of closed-class items that were produced in rapid A–A speech lacked the acoustic cues necessary for VOT measurement; hence, there would appear to be similar percentages of closed-class items containing initial stops produced in the two conditions.

It is also quite possible that mothers, in an effort to articulate more clearly to their children, avoid the production of flaps in M–C speech (Braine, 1974). A number of instances were observed in which mothers produced words such as "butter," which is normally produced with a flap, as [bʌtʰɜ], with an aspirated medial stop. One might hypothesize that there is a set of articulatory rules and constraints for M–C speech that function together in a "clarity conspiracy" (Kisseberth, 1970) to ensure maximum distinctiveness for the voiceless stop. One rule would increase VOT in voiceless stops having normal adult-like values; another rule would block the production of flaps that have shorter VOT than regular voiceless stops; an additional rule would ensure that stops are always produced with complete closure, and so on. In sum, the nonsignificant result for A–A and M–C percentage differences, for stops produced in closed-class items, may be a consequence of the fact that more stops were measurable in M–C speech than in A–A speech.

A basic corollary of the IPC hypothesis of VOT modification is that a context-blind VOT increase rule applies to all word-initial stops produced in M–C speech, including those that appear in closed-class items. However, the ABC hypothesis predicts instead that higher-level modifications reduce the occurrence of unstressed closed-class items in M–C speech.

To test the two hypotheses, a comparison was made of the mean VOT values of the production of word-initial /t/ by the mother of a middle child in A–A and M–C conditions, for closed-class items only. Results of 2-tailed *t*-tests indicate a significant difference between A–A and M–C conditions ($t = 3.03$, $p < .05$). The mean VOT value for the A–A condition was 14 msec, and the mean VOT value for the M–C condition was 19 msec.

Specific A–A and M–C comparisons were made of identical or nearly identical closed-class items said by the same mother in similar phonetic environments in running conversational speech. The VOTs of word-initial /t/ of unstressed, closed-class *to* in A–A "It's a mistake *to* confuse them," and in M–C "You want a book *to* read" were compared.[3] In the A–A production, the /t/ had a VOT of ~15 msec; there appeared to be no break in phonation during the burst, and no aspiration period. The target voiceless stop was essentially produced as a voiced stop, with the VOT being a measure of the burst frication (cf. Klatt, 1975). The /t/ of the M–C production had a VOT of ~55 msec, and had a clear aspiration period.

A comparison was also made of A–A *to* in the phrase "*to* go" and M–C *to* in "*to*day." In this case, they hardly differed in VOT, but they showed different acoustic patterns. For the A–A production of *to*, there was no break in phonation; burst frication was slowly released while vocal-fold vibration was maintained. Again, as in the previous case, the A–A /t/ was produced as a voiced stop, with no aspiration period. The VOT was ~29 msec, again a measure of the burst duration. The M–C production had a VOT of ~27 msec, but it was clearly produced as a voiceless stop with an aspiration period.

A third comparison was made, between A–A *to* in "Go *to* sleep," and M–C *to* in "go *to* bed." Unlike the productions in the previous two cases, these unstressed items were both produced in a slower, more "deliberate" style. The VOT for the A–A production was ~30 msec and for the M–C production, ~80 msec.

All three cases supported the IPC hypothesis of M–C VOT modification, and more specifically, the notion of a clarity continuum in M–C speech. Except for the few rare cases in which the items were emphasized, the A–A voiceless stops produced in closed-class items showed no break in phonation and manifested the same acoustic characteristics as a voiced stop. The M–C productions almost always showed a break in phonation and an aspiration period, which was usually shorter than that in open-class items, but still clearly voiceless.

---

[3] It is important to point out that, in this study, all closed-class items (i.e., prepositions, conjunctions, auxiliaries, were treated as a uniform group of morphemes). As the focal point of this analysis was to determine whether or not differences exist between A–A and M–C conditions for the mother's production of unstressed utterances, the class of grammatical morphemes, which is almost always unstressed, was chosen for measurement. However, it is yet to be determined whether there are any nonphonetically conditioned, systematic differences in VOT between types of grammatical morphemes (i.e., prepositions, conjunctions); or between instances of the same grammatical morpheme (the preposition (*to*) that appear in the same phonetic contexts on the surface (both may be preceded by a stressed syllable), but that appear within constructions produced by different syntactic transformations. For example, the preposition *to* of the A–A production "It's a mistake *to* confuse them" appears within a complement; whereas the *to* of "you want a book *to* read" appears within an infinitival relative construction. In addition, the two prepositions differ in their relative positions within a constituent. *A book to read* is a single NP constituent, whereas *a mistake to confuse them* is not a constituent; *to confuse them* is an extraposed sentential subject. Consequently, in the first case *to* appears in the middle of the constituent, and in the second case, it appears in initial position. The possible effects of constituent structure, as well as derivational history on VOT have yet to be investigated thoroughly.

The finding that closed-class items were exaggerated by mothers questions the basic assumption of the ABC hypothesis—that the mean VOT values in the M–C condition are higher than the mean A–A values because of the small number of unstressed words produced by mothers to children. The data were again consistent with the IPC hypothesis, which also attributes VOT increases to an elimination of low VOT values; however, according to this hypothesis, they are eliminated through a special phonetic rule component, which serves to clarify utterances by increasing VOT. This rule component would have as its surface phonetic "goal" for an underlying voiceless stop a segment with a clear burst and aspiration.

Other Evidence

An additional piece of evidence that is consistent with the IPC hypothesis is the following: It was found that in A–A speech, voiceless stops were rarely, if ever, produced with especially long VOTs. That is, even in slow, deliberate A–A speech, VOT values for voiceless stops rarely exceeded 100 msec. But, when mothers of middle children talked to their children, they occasionally produced voiceless stops with VOT values over 125 msec. For example, although in A–A speech, the mother of a middle child did not produce any tokens of /k/ with values higher than 90 msec, she produced 14 tokens of /k/ to her child with values higher than 125 msec (4.4% of her total number of M–C /k/ productions). The highest VOT value for that mother's production of /t/ in A–A speech was 115 msec, but she produced 7 tokens to her child with VOT values exceeding 125 msec (3% of her total number of M–C /t/ productions). These data supported the notion of a special VOT increase rule for M–C speech.

The ABC hypothesis of VOT modification in M–C speech predicts a reduction in closed-class items in M–C speech, which will result in fewer low VOT values for voiced and voiceless stops. One would, therefore, expect to find a significant decrease in standard deviations for the two stop categories in M–C speech to children acquiring their first words. The results of sign tests showed the opposite, that there were no significant differences between standard deviations for the two speaking conditions for either voiced ($p > .05$) or voiceless stops ($p > .05$).

This result supported the IPC hypothesis, which predicts that a VOT increase rule that applies to all occurrences of word-initial stops in M–C speech would eliminate some of the lower VOT values of each category, but would also raise some of the higher ones. Consequently, one would expect A–A and M–C speech to have similar variability in their VOT distributions, unless additional clarification strategies, such as variability reduction, were employed.

Because there are no closed-class items beginning with /p/ in the English language (Kučera and Francis, 1967), the ABC hypothesis of VOT modification for M–C speech would predict no significant differences in mean VOT values of word-initial /p/ between A–A and M–C speaking conditions. This study found that the mother of a middle child was producing voiceless bilabial stops to her child with higher VOT values than she produced to other adults. Again, this finding argues for a VOT increase rule that applies to all initial stops, and, therefore, supports the IPC hypothesis.

Although there were no significant differences in VOT between A–A and M–C speaking conditions for mothers of the youngest or of the oldest children, the mothers were significantly shortening the sentences they produced to their children, as measured by MLU. One would expect a reduction in MLU to result in fewer closed-class items and consequently fewer low VOT values. The finding that there was no direct correlation between lowered MLU and higher VOT values in M–C speech is not consistent with the ABC hypothesis.

Open-class Comparisons

The ABC hypothesis of VOT modification predicts no significant differences in the VOT characteristics of A–A and M–C stop productions in stressed, open-class items. To test this hypothesis, 50 tokens of voiceless alveolar stops that exhibited very high VOT values in the speech of a mother to her middle child were collected, together with the sentences in which they originally appeared. These sentences were then incorporated into a humorous story, preserving the original stress and position of each token in its sentence. After ample practice, the mother was instructed to read the story as if she were telling it to another adult. The VOT values were then measured and compared to the originals, which had been addressed to the child. The M–C values, with a mean value of 85 msec, were found by a 2-tailed t-test to be significantly higher than the A–A values ($p < .001$). The mean VOT value for the A–A productions was 61 msec. In sum, we must conclude that the higher mean VOT value for the voiceless stop found in M–C speech cannot be attributed to a mere reduction of VOT values along the lower end of the continuum. It appears that a stylistic phonetic rule, peculiar to M–C speech is increasing VOT in M–C word-initial stops. Although a reduction of unstressed items in M–C speech may contribute somewhat to the overall reduction in overlap and increase in mean VOT values, it cannot be the primary factor responsible for the clarification phenomenon.

A final argument in favor of the IPC hypothesis, and for the notion of a special phonetic rule component for M–C speech that generates clearly articulated, maximally contrastive utterances is the following: It was found that even when no difference in VOT was found between stops produced in A–A and M–C conditions, the voicing distinction appeared to be maximized, or clarified, through enhancement of other potential cues for the contrast. Thus, in A–A and M–C productions of word-initial /p/ in unstressed syllables in the words *particular* and *pajamas*, the VOT of the A–A utterance was approximately 35 msec, and that of the M–C utterance approximately 28 msec. Nevertheless, although the stops in the two unstressed syllables did not differ significantly with respect to VOT, they did differ in amount of overall energy—this greater energy was particularly apparent during the burst release and aspiration period of the M–C production. An utterance produced with greater overall energy, or higher amplitude, would result in a louder, more voiceless, percept.[4]

This finding contradicts the basic tenet of the ABC hypothesis. The increase in energy found in the M–C production cannot be attributed to higher-level modifications. This finding fits in well, however, with the notion of a special set of rules for M–C speech. These rules would all be functioning together to achieve maximal distinction in the voicing contrast. However, certain rules would focus on a VOT increase, and other rules on an increase in overall amplitude.

Summary

In conclusion, it has been reported in this chapter that the overlap in VOT between voiced and voiceless initial stops is reduced in mother's speech to her child, in comparison to her speech to another adult, and that this reduction takes place when the child is at the stage of producing his or her first words, not when the child is in the babbling stage or at the stage of producing three- to five-word sentences.

It was demonstrated that this reduction does not depend on the lower incidence of unstressed words, particularly closed-class, function words in the speech addressed to children. Two hypotheses were tested: the independent phonetic clarification (IPC) hypothesis, which states that the VOT differences result from mothers tailoring their speech to their children on the phonetic level, independently of any stylistic modifications on other levels, and the accidental by-product clarification (ABC) hypothesis, which states that the VOT differences are indirect results of higher-level, functionally motivated semantic alterations. Closed-class comparisons, open-class comparisons, and a variety of other evidence supported the IPC hypothesis over the ABC.

---

[4] It was observed that mothers of middle children tended to speak more loudly to their children than they did to other adults; this phenomenon was observed in almost every M–C interaction. It is doubtful, due to the consistency of this effect across M–C taping sessions, that the overall increase in signal amplitude was solely a consequence of mothers speaking at varying distances from the microphone, or of interactions taped at different recording levels in A–A and M–C conditions. Recording conditions were kept as uniform as possible in A–A and M–C conditions.

It appears that as soon as the child first attempts to articulate phonological segments that contrast in voicing, the mother begins to issue phonological instructions, through a special set of phonetic cue-enhancement rules. Consequently, the mother is presenting her language-learning child with an idealized corpus of voiced and voiceless phonetic segments—one that contains fewer less carefully articulated, categorially ambiguous segments than does normal A–A speech.

Acknowledgments

This research has been made possible by Grant #5R01–HD–09197 from the National Institute of Child Health and Human Development.

References

Braine, M.D.S. (1974) "On What Might Constitute Learnable Phonology," *Language*, 50, 270–299.

Kisseberth, C.W. (1970) "On the Functional Unity of Phonological Rules," *Linguistic Inquiry*, 1, 291–306.

Klatt, D. (1975) "Voice Onset Time, Frication, and Aspiration in Word-initial Consonant Clusters," *Journal of Speech and Hearing Research*, 18, 686–706.

Kučera, H.W., and Francis, W.N. (1967) "Computational Analysis of Present-day American English," Brown University Press, Providence, R.I.

Laferriere, M., and Zue, V. (1977) "The Flapping Rule in American English: An Acoustic Study," Paper presented at the ninety-third meeting of the Acoustical Society of America, University Park, Pennsylvania.

Lisker, L., and Abramson, A. (1964) "A Cross-language Study of Voicing in Initial Stops: Acoustical Measurements," *Word*, 20, 384–422.

Lisker, L., and Abramson, A. (1967) "Some Effects of Context on Voice Onset Time in English Stops," *Language and Speech*, 10, 1–26.

Moslin, B. (1977) "On the Role of Phonetic Input in a Child's Acquisition of a Phonological Contrast," *Papers of the Regional Meeting of the Chicago Linguistic Society*, 13, 428–439.

Moslin, B. (1978) "The Role of Phonetic Input in a Child's Acquisition of the Voicing Contrast: A VOT Analysis," Unpublished Doctoral Dissertation, Brown University.

Newport, E.L. (1976) "Motherese; the Speech of Mothers to Young Children," in N.J. Castellan, D.B. Pisoni, and G.R. Potts, eds., *Cognitive Theory* (Vol. 2). Erlbaum, Hillsdale, N.J.

Phillips, J.R. (1973) "Syntax and Vocabulary of Mothers' Speech to Young Children: Age and Sex Comparisons," *Child Development*, 44, 182–185.

Snow, C.E. and Ferguson, C.A. (1977) "Talking to Children; Language Input and Acquisition," Cambridge University Press, Cambridge.

Chapter 10

PHONETIC VARIATION AS A FUNCTION OF SECOND-LANGUAGE LEARNING

LEE WILLIAMS

Introduction

Research in the field of visual perception has demonstrated the flexibility of the human perceptual system in response to changes in sensory input. The system seems to have the capacity to modify its use of environmental "information" to arrive at an appropriate interpretation of sensory stimulation. It is surprising that relatively little research has been carried out to study perceptual modification that may also take place in the auditory modality, such as in the perception of speech.

In recent years, research in speech perception has made substantial progress in revealing the manner in which acoustic characteristics of the speech signal provide linguistic information to the listener (e.g., cues for phonetic distinctions). The results of a series of studies being reported here deal with modifications or adjustments in acoustic–phonetic properties as they are relevant to receptive (speech perception) as well as expressive (speech production) language performance in bilingual speakers of Spanish and English. Questions relating to modification are addressed in two ways:

1. By comparing patterns of production and perception from Spanish and English monolingual adults with similar patterns from adult Spanish–English bilinguals who are fluent in each language. According to

a theory that perceptual modification takes place in second-language learning, results from these bilinguals should show the effect of perceptual modification *already accomplished.*

2. By comparing patterns of production and perception in Spanish and
English monolinguals with those of Spanish-speaking children from two age
groups who have had different amounts of exposure to English as a second
language. According to the perceptual modification theory, the results from
second-language learners should reflect the *process* of modification in the
form of changes in patterns of performance that vary with exposure to English. According to theories supporting a critical period for second-language
learning, perceptual modification should interact with age.

A number of empirical questions can be formulated that are related to
issues surrounding perceptual modification:

1. Do patterns of perception and production in bilinguals reflect sensitivity to acoustic–phonetic characteristics of both languages?
2. During second-language learning, do formerly monolingual speakers
   learn the new acoustic–phonetic distinctions in their second language?
3. If there is acquisition of a new acoustic–phonetic distinction, what
   is the time course of this learning, the relationship between changes
   in patterns of perception and patterns of production, and the relationship between acquisition and the age of the learner?

Demonstration of Reliable Cross-Language Differences in Patterns of Voicing Perception and Production

To demonstrate changes in the perception and production of acoustic–phonetic properties as a function of second-language learning, it is clearly
important to first demonstrate that there are reliable differences in performance between monolinguals of the two languages being represented in the
learning process. Therefore, the experiments described in this section were
undertaken to document cross-language differences in the realization of the
voicing distinction in both perception and production with monolingual
speakers of Spanish and English.

When the voicing distinction applies to word-initial stop consonants,
it has been customary to describe the voiced consonant by the presence of
glottal vibration (voicing) during the closure period of consonant articulation
and the voiceless consonant by the absence of glottal vibration during that
period (Heffner, 1969; Hockett, 1960). However, close examination of the
articulatory process reveals that such a description does not suffice for all
languages. An example can be found by comparing the voicing contrast in

word-initial stops in Spanish and English. The voiced stop in Spanish is produced with voicing during consonant closure, whereas the voiceless cognate is not (Lisker and Abramson, 1964; Williams, 1974). However, both voiced and voiceless categories in initial position in English may be produced without voicing during closure (Lisker and Abramson, 1964; Williams, 1977b; Zlatin, 1974). Thus, a traditional definition of voicing can distinguish homorganic stops in word-initial position in Spanish but not in English.

Failure of a traditional phonetic description to account for cross-language differences in the realization of the voicing distinction has led to the formation of an alternative descriptive system by Lisker and Abramson (1964, 1971) in which the contrast is realized by the relative timing of voicing onset with reference to the release of articulatory closure, called by these investigators voice onset time or VOT[1]. All of the synthetic speech stimuli used in the perceptual studies discussed here employed a VOT continuum based on the original series prepared by Lisker and Abramson[2]. In this series, the onset of the low-frequency first formant (F_1) buzz source was varied in equal 10 msec steps with reference to the onset of energy in higher formants. By convention, negative VOT values stand for voicing lead (onset of glottal vibration prior to articulatory release), and positive values, voicing lag (onset of glottal vibration following release).

The VOT series is not a simple continuum in which only VOT is varied parametrically. Several other acoustic variables are included in the stimuli in accord with the characteristics of natural speech. Figure 10.1 shows spectrographic patterns of three stimuli from the labial or [b]–[p] series.

---

[1] Another system has been devised that relies on the presence or absence of four different articulatory states to describe cross-language differences in voicing (Chomsky and Halle, 1968; Halle and Stevens, 1971). The relative usefulness of these two systems has been discussed (Lisker and Abramson, 1971) and to some extent, subjected to empirical testing (Bell-Berti, 1975; Lisker et al., 1967; Sawashima et al., 1970).

[2] The speech stimuli were CV syllables, each made up of an initial stop consonant with formant transitions appropriate for a labial release, [b] or [p], followed by three formant patterns appropriate for the steady-state vowel [a]. Stimuli spanned a range of VOT values centered at the point of release, which was assigned the value of zero. The stimulus series varied in 10 msec steps of VOT, except for the range between − 50 and + 50, which varied in 5 msec steps. To represent voicing lead, only the low-frequency harmonics (F_1) of the periodic source were used. Voicing lag was represented by the onset of a periodic source at F_1, F_2, and F_3. During the interval between release and the delayed onset of the periodic source, F_2 and F_3 were excited by a noise source with suppression of F_1. All stimuli were approximately 600 msec long.

The stimuli were recorded directly from the Haskins Laboratories speech synthesizer onto audio tapes for use in the labeling and discrimination tasks. The 31 labeling test stimuli, which covered a VOT range of − 100 to + 100 msec, were arranged in eight random orders. There were 4 sec between each stimulus and 10 sec between every block of 10. The discrimination test was made of 34 different stimulus pairs covering the range of VOT from − 150 msec to + 150 msec. Pair members were separated by an interval of 1 sec, and each pair was separated from the following by 4 sec, with a 10 sec interval between every block of 10 pairs.

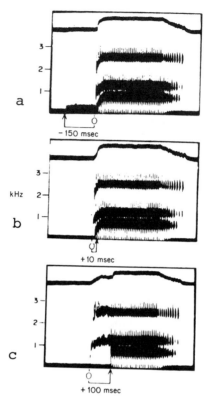

FIGURE 10.1 *Three conditions of VOT in synthetic labial stop consonants. From top to bottom, spectrograms of (a) voicing lead; (b) slight lag; and (c) long lag (after Abramson and Lisker, 1973).*

Figure 10.1a demonstrates the case in which there are 150 msec of voicing lead shown by the appearance of periodic excitation (indicative of glottal vibration) at F_1 150 msec prior to *onset* of acoustic energy at F_2 and F_3 (indicative of articulatory release). Note that there are quite noticeable voiced transitions at the levels of all three formants. These are indicated by a rise in frequency location of formants along the horizontal time coordinate. Figure 10.1b shows the case in which there are 10 msec of voicing lag. In other words, the onset of a periodic source at the level of F_1 one occurs 10 msec after the onset of energy at the levels of F_2 and F_3. Again there are noticeable formant transitions. Figure 10.1c shows the case in which there are 100 msec of voicing lag (i.e., a periodic source at F_1 begins 100 msec after the onset of energy at higher formants. In the case of voicing lag, F_2 and F_3 are excited by an aperiodic source during the interval of delay in onset of F_1 (representing aspiration in natural speech) and by a periodic source thereafter. This is most visible in Figure 10.1c.

In addition to VOT, three additional acoustic properties that vary in degree across part of the synthetic speech series can be observed by comparing Figures 10.1b and 10.1c. These variations are restricted to the voicing-lag region of the continuum (positive values of VOT):

1. The presence, absence or varying duration of aspiration or aperiodic energy in the interval between articulatory release and the onset of voicing. The presence of aspirated formants is an acoustic property that has been demonstrated to provide a positive cue for initial voicelessness to English listeners. (Winitz *et al.*, 1975).
2. The absence of periodic acoustic energy at the level of F_1, during aperiodic excitation of the vocal tract, referred to as "first formant cutback" (Liberman *et al.*, 1958). There is also evidence that the presence or absence of periodic energy in the region of F_1 provides a perceptual cue for an initial contrast in voicing for English listeners (Delattre *et al.*, 1955; Liberman *et al.*, 1958; Lisker, 1975).
3. Differences in the degree and temporal extent of formant transitions under conditions of periodic excitation of the vocal tract. There is some evidence that this acoustic variable may also provide a cue for initial voicing in English (Cooper *et al.*, 1952; Stevens and Klatt, 1974; Summerfield and Haggard, 1974).

There are additional acoustic properties in the natural speech versions of voiced and voiceless tokens in English and possibly also in Spanish that could provide acoustic cues for the voicing distinction. These will also be briefly described as knowledge of such potential cues in natural speech will help interpret some of the results being reported here.

One such property is the difference in fundamental-frequency change immediately following consonant release (Ewan and Krones, 1974; House and Fairbanks, 1953; Lea, 1973). This contrasting property has been demonstrated to serve as a perceptual cue for initial voicing for English listeners (Fujimura, 1971; Haggard *et al.*, 1970). A second potential cue might be provided by differences in the timing and spectral characteristics of stop consonant release bursts. Acoustic properties of the burst have been observed to differ systematically across initial voiced and voiceless stops in English and in Spanish (Halle *et al.*, 1957; Klatt, 1975; Williams, 1977b; Zue, 1976), although the perceptual significance of these differences has not been established.

Thus, as well as contrasts in VOT, there are several other potential cues for voicing present in natural contrasts of initial voicing as well as in a synthetic VOT continuum modeled after natural speech. A fundamental question in the present investigation was, how *necessary* or *sufficient* is the VOT cue to Spanish and English monolinguals? The answer to this question proves to be relevant to the interpretation of performance in the production and perception of the voicing distinction for both Spanish–English bilinguals and second-language learners.

Voice onset time, or VOT, has been established at least as a useful measure for characterizing cross-language differences in voicing production. VOT distinguishes voiced from voiceless stops within most languages studied, and provides a common basis for describing certain cross-language differences in the acoustic–phonetic realization of the voicing contrast (Caramazza et al., 1973; Dent, 1976; Lisker and Abramson, 1964; Streeter, 1976; Williams, 1974). There is also some evidence that VOT differences may provide the basis for the perceptual distinction between syllable-initial voiced and voiceless stops (Abramson and Lisker, 1970, 1972, 1973; Caramazza et al., 1973; Lisker and Abramson, 1970; Streeter, 1976; Williams, 1977a, 1977b, in press). When listeners from a single-language group label randomly presented synthetic CV syllables that vary along a VOT continuum, they typically divide the continuum into voiced and voiceless regions in a manner corresponding to their division of the VOT dimension in production. Furthermore, in a discrimination task, their detection of differences between pairs of such syllables is maximal at the crossover point between voiced and voiceless categories in the labeling task. Figures 10.2 and 10.3

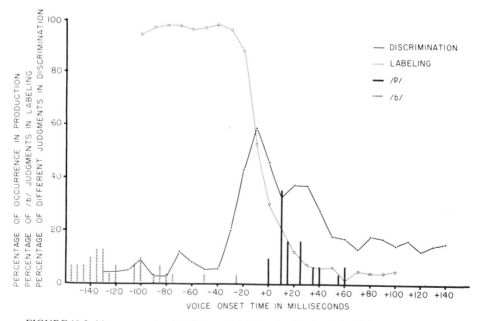

FIGURE 10.2 *Measurements of VOT in word-initial voiced and voiceless labial stop consonants and the results of labeling (– – –) and discrimination (———) of a synthetic series of speech stimuli varying in VOT by Spanish monolinguals. A 20 msec VOT step size was used in discrimination. /p/, solid vertical lines; /b/, broken vertical lines for production (Williams, 1977b).*

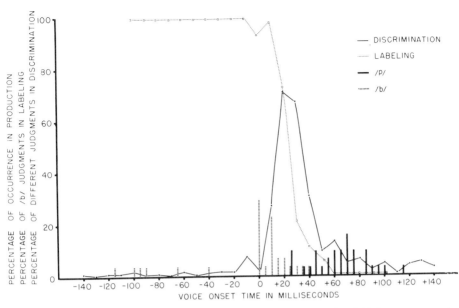

FIGURE 10.3 *Measurements of VOT in word-initial voiced and voiceless labial stop consonants and the results of labeling (– – –) and discrimination (——) of a synthetic series of speech stimuli varying in VOT by English monolinguals. A 20 ms VOT step size was used in discrimination. /p/, solid vertical lines; /b/ broken vertical lines, for production (Williams, 1977b).*

illustrate this correspondence between performance in perception and production of the voicing contrast in terms of VOT.

The data shown in these figures are taken from a study of eight Puerto Rican-Spanish and eight American-English monolinguals (Williams, 1977b). The average labeling function for each group, plotted as a percentage of /b/ judgments, crosses the 50% judgment point at a VOT location that lies between the distribution of [b] and [p] tokens in production for that language (since a forced-choice procedure was used, a function describing the percentage of /p/ judgments would be the complement of the functions shown in Figures 10.2 and 10.3). The discrimination of differences between pairs of stimuli drawn from the series, which always differed by 20 msec VOT, are plotted as the percentage of different judgments. The average peak in discrimination occured for each language group at the VOT locations where the average crossovers in labeling fall: − 4 msec VOT for Spanish monolinguals and + 25 msec VOT for English monolinguals.

The fact that performance within each language group showed sensitivity to comparable values of VOT in different perceptual tasks suggests that VOT may provide an important, if not primary, cue for word-initial stop voicing for Spanish and English monolinguals. The evidence is particularly strong when the labeling data of individual Spanish listeners is considered.

The majority of individual Spanish crossover locations in labeling fall within the voicing-lead region (negative values of VOT). Since voice timing is the only acoustic variable undergoing change in this region, these results suggest that VOT, or voicing lead of some duration, is a sufficient positive cue for voicedness (as opposed to voicelessness) for most of the Spanish listeners in this study. In fact, when one considers the duration of voicing-lead required to elicit voiced judgments 75% or more of the time from individual Spanish listeners, the evidence is even more compelling. These VOT values in msec are: -23, -20, -14, -13.5, -12, -3.5, -2, $+7$.

To further pin down the importance of VOT for one of the language groups being investigated, two additional experiments were carried out. In the first study, distributions of VOT values in voiced and voiceless initial stop consonants were compared across three Latin American-Spanish dialect groups to determine whether or not this property shows cross-dialect stability. Spanish minimal-pair words, beginning with either voiced or voiceless stops and sampling labial, dental, and velar place of articulation were produced by eight Spanish monolinguals, from each of three Spanish dialect groups: Venezuelan, Peruvian, and Guatemalan.[3] The sample was recorded as the subjects read the words that appeared on printed cards presented one at a time in different random orders: *baño, paño, boco, poca, dato, tato, dos, tos, gasa, casa, goma, coma*. Figure 10.4 shows the distributions of values of VOT time plotted according to dialect, voice category, and place of articulation with distribution means included. Results for labial stops from the Puerto Rican study were included for the purpose of comparison, although the data from this group are not comparable with the others in a strict sense as they did not sample the same range of phonetic environments. It is apparent from visual inspection of Figure 10.4 that distributions within voicing category and place of articulation are very similar across the four dialects. In fact, only differences across voice category ($p < .001$) and place ($p < .001$) were significant in an analysis that included the Venezuelan, Peruvian, and Guatemalan data.

---

[3] The Peruvian and Guatemalan monolinguals were recorded in their own countries, and the Venezuelan monolinguals were recorded in Boston, Massachusetts one week after they arrived in the United States to participate in English-language classes. All 24 speakers contributing to this sample were unable to comprehend or speak in any language but Spanish.

Wide-band spectrograms were made of the recorded words from which VOT was measured. Voicing lead was measured from the point at which the first visible periodic low-frequency energy appeared, indicating the onset of voicing, to the point at which there was a sudden spread in spectral energy, indicating articulatory release. This was frequently associated with a brief aperiodic burst of energy reflecting a turbulent noise source at the point of release. Voicing lag was measured from the same point of sudden spread in spectral energy to the point at which periodic low-frequency energy was visible, indicating onset of voicing.

The two low back vowels [o] and [a] were chosen as the vowels to follow initial stops, as prior evidence indicated that measures of VOT probably will not differ significantly within a low, back vowel environment (Klatt, 1975; Smith and Westbury, 1975).

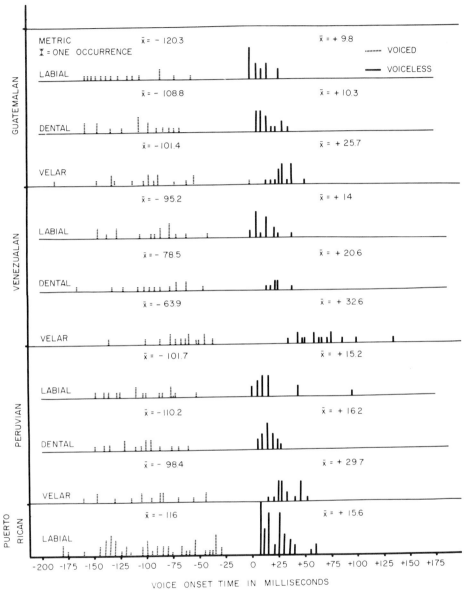

FIGURE 10.4 *VOT measurements from word-initial voiced (- - -) and voiceless (——) stops in four Latin American Spanish dialect groups with means for each dialect and voicing category (Williams 1977b).*

In summary, the results of this investigation provided no evidence for cross-dialect variation in terms of the realization of VOT in word-initial stops when these words were produced in citation form. Similar differences across voicing category and place of articulation exist in all three Spanish dialects studied. Furthermore, voicing lead was an extremely stable acoustic property in the initial voiced category in these data. Out of 144 words sampled, only one showed no evidence of voicing lead. The duration of voicing lead was characteristically quite long compared to the temporal extent of many other candidates for the status of an acoustic property cueing a phonetic contrast. The mean value of voicing lead in initial labial stops for all four dialect groups represented in Figure 10.4 was 100 msec with 180 msec being the largest value observed. It is known that, in the absence of coupling between oral and nasal passages, compensatory supraglottal and probably glottal gestures must operate to maintain glottal pulsing for such durations (Rothenberg, 1968).

A second study was undertaken to determine whether or not the results in the perception of a VOT continuum obtained with Puerto Rican mono-linguals could be replicated with another Spanish dialect group, providing further evidence for the sufficiency of voicing lead as a positive voicing cue in word-initial position in Spanish. Eight Peruvian monolinguals participated in a labeling task with a similar synthetic series of speech stimuli used with the Puerto Rican listeners. Labeling results from the Peruvian monolinguals did not differ significantly from the Puerto Rican labeling results. Figure 10.5 shows labeling functions for the two groups. Also included in the figure are 50% crossover locations for each individual and individual VOT values required for voiced judgments 75% or more of the time. The fact that all of the Peruvian listeners had individual crossover locations in the voicing-lead region, and the additional fact that six out of eight required 14 msec or more of voicing lead to be present to produce a voiced judgment 75% or more of the time, indicated that voicing lead was a sufficient positive cue for the voiced stop category for most Spanish listeners as this is the only acoustic variable undergoing change in that region of the synthetic continuum. Given that voicing lead is consistently present in Spanish word-initial voiced stops in the dialects studied with a characteristically long duration requiring com-pensatory articulatory adjustments, it is tempting to further hypothesize that voicing lead is produced by the Spanish speaker in word-initial stops to provide the Spanish listener with an important and perhaps necessary voicing cue.

In summary, the results of all of the experiments reported in this section indicated that the VOT measure is a good device to describe the cross-lan-guage differences in the perception and production of voicing by Spanish and English monolinguals. The results also suggested that VOT, at least voicing lead for Spanish listeners, is a sufficient cue for word-initial voicing.

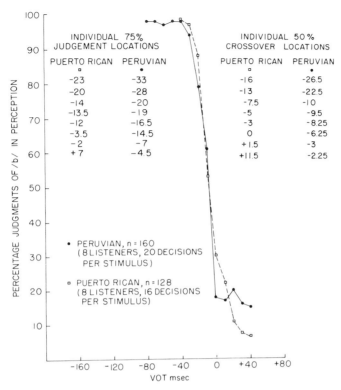

FIGURE 10.5 *Labeling functions for eight Peruvian and eight Puerto Rican Spanish mono-linguals using a synthetic series of speech stimuli varying in VOT. (●) Peruvian, n = 160 (eight listeners, 20 decisions per stimulus); (□) Puerto Rican, n = 128 (eight listeners, 16 decisions per stimulus) (Williams, 1977b).*

Bilingual Patterns in the Perception and Production of Voicing

The primary purpose of this experiment was to learn something about the perception and production of voiced and voiceless initial stops in a bilingual Spanish–English population, keeping in mind several possible outcomes of perceptual testing:

1. Bilinguals might have a *double standard* for perceiving speech that would show up as sensitivity to acoustic properties that provide perceptual cues for the voicing contrast in each language. This would appear as a non-monotonic function of the kind shown in Figure 10.6a. This function represents an increasing probability of labeling members of the continuum as /p/s as the stimuli move away from extreme voicing lead toward the region of VOT near the Spanish crossover location followed by a decreasing prob-

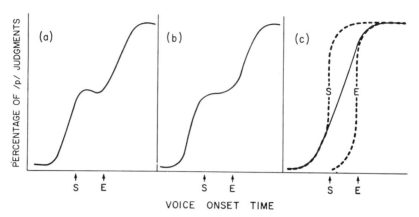

FIGURE 10.6 *Three theoretical functions describing percentage judgments of* /p/ *for bilinguals. The locations of 50% crossovers in labeling for monolingual Spanish and English groups are indicated on each graph by S and E, and idealized labeling functions for the two groups are plotted by dashed lines (Williams, 1977a).*

ability of /p/ judgments in the area of VOT approaching the English crossover location. A double standard in labeling performance might be considered to reflect bilingual perception. Accordingly, bilinguals would be expected to have four phonetic categories in terms of VOT, a Spanish /b/ and /p/ pair, and an English /b/ and /p/ pair, with two distinct boundaries dividing the members of each pair. The presence of two perceptual category boundaries might not be tapped in a single two-category forced-choice test. However, it might be demonstrated under the conditions of this experiment, in which there were two test conditions, one carried out in Spanish and one in English. This was done to tease out a perceptual set for each of the bilingual's languages. Combining the data from the two language-priming tests might result in a function of the type shown in Figure 10.6a.

2. Bilinguals might show *uncertainty* in labeling stimuli from the critical area between Spanish and English crossover locations. This could be reflected in a flattening of the function in the area lying between the Spanish and English crossover locations shown in Figure 10.6b. Uncertainty might also appear as a very gradual shift from the /b/ to the /p/ categories in labeling the VOT continuum. This is illustrated by Figure 10.6c. Uncertainty in labeling the stimuli in the critical area would presumably be the result of sensitivity to acoustic-phonetic information appropriate for a label of a Spanish /p/ as well as a label for an English /b/.

3. Bilinguals might employ a *single standard* in making a voicing judgment such that their labeling functions would be similar to those of monolingual speakers of either English or Spanish, illustrated in Figure 10.6c by the steep dashed-line functions. A single standard could also be reflected

by a steep labeling function lying somewhere between the monolingual Spanish and English functions.

Similar alternative results might be expected from a discrimination task with bilinguals, using the same set of VOT stimuli:

1. A double standard would be reflected in double peaks in discrimination over both Spanish and English crossover locations. Again, this might be considered the pattern of bilingual perception.
2. The results might also show broad discrimination peaks covering the area of Spanish and English labeling crossovers. Again, this could be interpreted as a pattern of bilingual perception.
3. A single standard could be shown as a sharp peak over either Spanish or English monolingual crossover locations or a peak lying somewhere between the two. If bilingual perception follows the course of monolingual perception, it would be predicted that for each bilingual, a peak in discrimination would correspond with the location of a labeling crossover.

In a similar fashion, there are several possible outcomes for results in production. The bilingual could keep his two languages clearly separate, preserving the acoustic–phonetic characteristics appropriate for the language he is speaking. Alternatively, there could be signs of interference, each language reflecting the phonetic characteristics of the other.

The experimental paradigm for investigating the realization of voicing in Spanish–English bilinguals was essentially the same as that employed in the study of Spanish and English monolingual speakers. Results of perception were obtained from labeling and discrimination tasks using the VOT series of synthetic speech stimuli already described. Measurements of VOT were derived from wide-band spectrograms of English and Spanish two-syllable, minimal-pair words contrasting in initial voicing. Spanish words were: *baño, paño, beso, peso, bulla, pulla, boca, poca.* English words were: *balmy, palmy, baying, paying, beaked, peaked, boaster, poster.*

The bilingual subjects were eight adults. English was the primary language, or language first learned, for three of the subjects (B.R., J.S., P.N.) and Spanish the primary language for five (N.L., F.M., D.D., R.M., E.G.). All but one subject (B.R.) acquired their second language either upon entering school in the primary grades or earlier. The subjects used both languages to varying degrees in their daily lives, but, typically, one language was spoken at home and the other in school or place of work. The bilingual subjects were between the ages of 17 and 30, and all came from well-educated backgrounds. Five were female (B.R., F.M., D.D., R.M., E.G.), and three were male (J.S., P.N., N.L.). A test of bilingualism was devised to provide for a measure of phonetic balance in Spanish and English as well as a criterion for entry into the subject pool[4]. Labeling and discrimination procedures were carried out under conditions designed to induce a perceptual set for Spanish in half of the trials and for English in the other half.[5]

As there were no significant differences in the locations of labeling crossovers or discrimination peaks as a function of language of presentation, the data for each task were collapsed across presentation language. The results of the perceptual tests are shown in Figure 10.7. Labeling functions are plotted as a cumulative percentage of /p/ responses and discrimination results appear as a percentage of different responses. With the exception of two subjects (F.M. and N.L.), the labeling functions for bilinguals are steep and monotonic, of the form predicted for performance using a single perceptual standard for making voicing judgments. Furthermore, the data from the eight bilinguals did not appear to be from a homogeneous population in terms of the location of 50% crossovers in dividing the continuum into voiced and voiceless categories. Three bilinguals performed more like Spanish monolinguals with crossover locations[6] at -15 (F.M.), -3 (N.L.), and $+3$ (B.R.), and five performed more like English monolinguals with crossovers at $+15$ (D.D.), $+16.5$ (J.S.), $+18$ (R.M.), $+20.5$ (P.N.), and $+22$

---

[4] All eight subjects answered five questions in single, complete sentences and read five prepared sentences that contained sounds known to bring out an accent in unskilled speakers of that language. Twenty such utterances, a set in English and a set in Spanish, produced by each of the bilinguals, contributed to a total of 80 Spanish utterances and 80 English utterances. To the English utterances were added a set of 10 utterances each from four monolingual speakers of English, all from the Boston area, and a set of 10 utterances each from four individuals recognized as speakers of English with Spanish accents. This made an additional 80 utterances that were added to the 80 English utterances produced by bilinguals. The grand total of 160 English utterances were spliced together in random order on a single tape with 12 sec between each utterance and 15 sec after each 10 utterances. A similar tape of 160 utterances in Spanish was prepared.

The test for bilingualism consisted of the judgments of teachers of English and Spanish who listened to the tapes and judged each utterance as being produced with or without an accent. The three teachers of English judged the English tape and three teachers of Spanish, the Spanish tape. The speech material was recorded using a Sony Model F-265 external cardioid microphone. Taped material was presented on a Tandberg 6000X tape deck with judges listening over matched Sharp Model 10 earphones. A bilingual subject met the criterion for entry into the experiment if at least 80% of his utterances were judged to be without an accent (i.e., at least 48 of the total 60 judgments of his utterances; 10 utterances $\times$ 3 judges $\times$ 2 languages). Eight of nine bilinguals interviewed passed the entry test. The results of this test were also used to order subjects in terms of their phonetic competence, reflected in their score in their test for each language.

[5] Each session was preceded by 10 min of conversation in the language of presentation with an experimenter who was a native speaker of the language. Instructions and experimental materials were also in that language, and brief conversations occurred while the stimulus tapes were being changed.

[6] All reported labeling results are based on data that was first converted by probit transformation (Finney, 1952). Crossover locations were then taken from best fitting straight line functions drawn to each bilingual's transformed data.

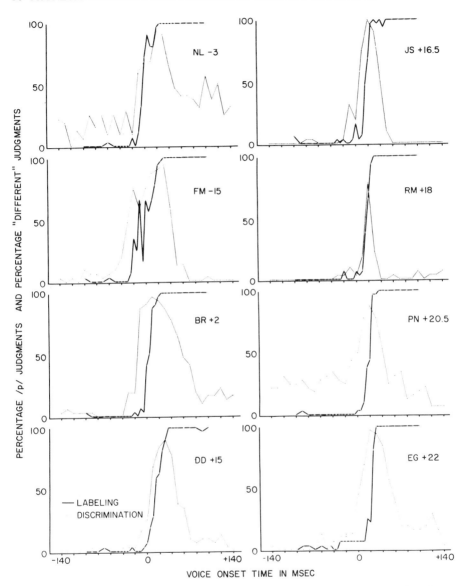

FIGURE 10.7 *Labeling and discrimination functions for eight bilinguals. Crossover locations, prior to probit transformation, are indicated on the graph for each bilingual; (Williams, 1977a).*

(E.G.). This difference in crossover locations between the Spanish-like and English-like subgroups was significant ($P < .01$).

Discrimination data for the bilinguals also divided into the same two subgroups. Subjects with Spanish-like crossovers (N.L., F.M., B.R.) had discrimination functions that were broad, covering the entire range of VOT from the monolingual Spanish location of -4 msec to the English location of $+25$ msec. This was a pattern predicted for listeners with a double standard in discrimination, or bilingual perception. The subjects with English-like crossovers (J.S., D.D., R.M., P.N., E.G.) had sharper discrimination functions, which fell closer to the English crossover location at $+25$ msec. Again, we see a split in the performance of bilinguals in a perceptual task: the same five with a pattern of perceptual discrimination more like that of English monolinguals and the same three with a pattern that might be described as more bilingual. Possible differences in the bilinguals' experience with each language (such as daily use of Spanish) that might predict the split in performance were examined, but no correlations between these factors and the results of the perceptual tests were found.

When production data from Spanish initial stops produced by bilinguals and Spanish monolinguals were compared, there was no significant difference in the values of VOT in Spanish words produced by the two groups. When VOT values in English initial stops produced by bilinguals were compared with similar data from English monolinguals, the bilinguals produced significantly ($p = .01$) more negative VOT values (voicing lead) for voiced stops than did monolinguals. In fact, bilinguals had an average VOT value for [b] in initial words that lay roughly between the mean values found for monolingual Spanish and English initial stops.

In summary, the perceptual data indicated that bilinguals do not have a double standard for judging the identity of speech stimuli employed in this experiment. The individual labeling functions did not conform to any of those predicted for perception by a bilingual using a double standard (see Figure 10.6). Instead, the functions were typically steep and monotonic, closely resembling the shape of pooled functions for monolinguals (see Figures 10.2 and 10.3). This suggests that bilinguals were dividing the voicing continuum into voiced and voiceless domains by utilizing changes in the acoustic variables that lay in a fairly restricted region of the speech-sound continuum. A similar conclusion can be made based on the results of discrimination for those individuals with English-like performance. Only the three bilinguals with broad peaks in discrimination showed any indication of sensitivity to acoustic–phonetic information present at both the English and Spanish crossover locations. Results of discrimination suggest the general principle that, for all of the bilinguals, differences between stimuli that were in the English crossover region of the VOT continuum could be discriminated. Only those bilinguals who demonstrated a Spanish-like pattern in dividing the continuum into voiced and voiceless domains in labeling could discriminate differences in stimuli in the Spanish crossover location.

The VOT measurements within each language made from words spoken by the eight Spanish–English bilinguals generally conformed to those results reported previously for Spanish and English monolinguals (Lisker and Abramson, 1964; Williams, 1977b; in press). The only significant difference in the distribution of VOT values between bilinguals and monolinguals was that reported for the production of English word-initial stops, that is, bilinguals, on the average, carry over into English the feature of voicing lead. This carry-over from Spanish to English in terms of VOT would presumably not interfere with the perceptual acceptability of the word-initial voiced stops spoken in English by bilinguals. Voicing lead in initial voiced stops has repeatedly appeared in studies of the English voicing contrast and is presumably an allophonic variant typical of some English speakers (Lisker and Abramson, 1964; Smith and Westbury, 1975; Zlatin, 1974). Producing an English initial voiced stop with voicing lead will, if anything, increase the acoustic–phonetic distance between voiced and voiceless phoneme categories, presumably accentuating their perceived contrast.

The results of this study appeared at first glance to present somewhat contradictory findings. In production, Spanish–English bilinguals preserve the characteristics of each language in which they are fluent. However, results in a perceptual labeling task showed that most bilinguals divide a VOT continuum into voiced and voiceless domains at a single compromise point lying close to either the Spanish or English monolingual dividing point. This would suggest that the bilingual cannot separate perceptually both Spanish and English voicing contrasts. The results of the discrimination task complement this by demonstrating that most bilinguals cannot discriminate stimuli in the two VOT ranges where maximum English and Spanish monolingual discriminations occur. However, it is premature to conclude that these fluent bilinguals were unable to distinguish a major phonemic class in each language. A reasonable explanation for the perceptual results of this study may come from consideration of the acoustic characteristics of the synthetic stimuli used in this study as well as the characteristics of the natural-speech analogs that were discussed in the previous section. This explanation will be carried out in detail in conjunction with the results of the final study of this series, which examined production and perception of the voicing contrast in second-language learning (i.e., during the process of becoming bilingual).

Patterns of the Perception and Production of Voicing in Second-Language Learners

The experiments described in the first section of this chapter established two different patterns of perception and production of initial stop consonant voicing for Spanish and English monolinguals. These patterns were described in terms of two different sets of values derived from measurements of VOT in word-initial voiced and voiceless stops. Within each language group, the perception of a VOT continuum, reflected in labeling and discrimination tasks, corresponded to the measurement of the VOT dimension in production. In summary, VOT was a good descriptive measure for the voicing distinction within and across the two languages studied.

In the experiments described in the second section of this chapter, we saw that two clear monolingual-like patterns of perception were *not* characteristic of a group of Spanish–English bilinguals as a whole or for individual bilinguals. Similarly, the measurement of VOT in bilingual production did not show as clear a separation between the two languages as was the case for monolinguals. In summary, in terms of VOT, the results of measurements of perception and production did not reflect two patterns of acoustic–phonetic competence in the bilingual subjects that could compare with patterns for monolingual speakers. Either such competence was not present in these bilinguals, or the VOT measure was not sensitive to bilingual performance within each language.

In this section, the perception and production of the voicing distinction by Spanish-speaking children learning English as a second language will be compared with the performance of Spanish and English monolinguals. The specific questions that this study addresses are the following:

1. Within the approximate compulsory school age range in the United States (8–16 years), will formerly monolingual Spanish children learn to perceive voiced and voiceless word-initial stop consonants in terms of VOT, with a pattern similar to that of native speakers of English?
2. If young second-language learners demonstrate acquisition of the voicing distinction in perception, will this learning also be manifested in their ability to produce these categories like a native speaker?
3. In the acquisition of new VOT values, characteristic of the English voicing contrast, will the age of the learner and the degree to which he has been exposed to English be systematically related to patterns of change?

The subjects in this experiment were 72 native speakers of Spanish who came from Puerto Rico to the mainland United States without prior speaking ability with or comprehension of English. All subjects were from small rural communities of Puerto Rico where little or no English is spoken and none had made return trips to the island since their arrival on the mainland. All children were enrolled in bilingual programs in schools of the Boston metropolitan area. However, they came from homes where only Spanish was spoken and lived in Spanish-speaking neighborhoods. The subjects were selected from three populations with differing amounts of exposure to English based on their length of stay on the mainland: 0–6 months, 1.5–2 years, and 3–3.5 years. Each exposure group was further divided into two age groups: 8–10-year-olds and 14–16-year-olds. Twelve subjects were in each of the six experimental groups. The materials and procedures used in this set of experiments were the same as those described for the experiments with adult monolingual and bilingual subjects, with the exception that a smaller number of responses was obtained from the children in the labeling and discrimination tasks (16 per stimulus or stimulus pair compared with 32 responses for adult subjects).

In Figures 10.8 and 10.9, raw labeling scores are plotted as a function of the percentage of /p/ judgments according to age and degree of exposure. Also shown are the mean crossover locations for each exposure group by age, after data conversion.[6] For both age groups, the location of 50% crossovers moved from a Spanish-like toward an English-like location with increasing exposure (p = .034) and evidence for change was found at the earliest period of exposure. This effect appeared to be greatest for younger subjects, although the effect of age was not significant. The shape of labeling functions for different groups is also informative. For the older subjects

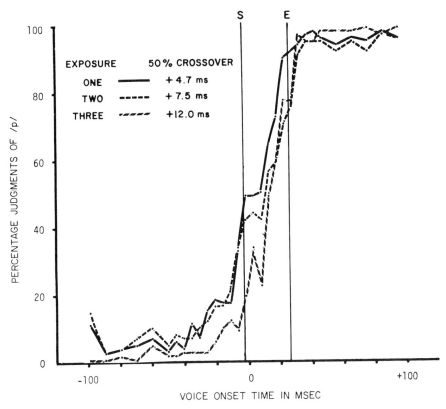

FIGURE 10.8 *Pooled labeling function. for native Spanish-speaking children 8–10 years old with three exposure groups according to time on the mainland United States: one (0–6 months); two (1.5–2 years); three (3–3.5 years),* n *= 192 per point. Monolingual Spanish and English labeling crossovers are indicated by* S *and* E.

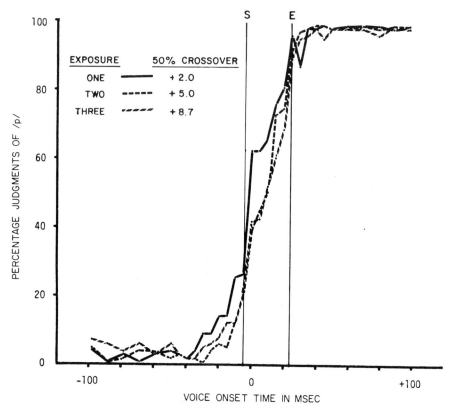

FIGURE 10.9 *Pooled labeling functions for native Spanish-speaking children 14–16 years old with three exposure groups according to time on the mainland United States: one (0–6 months), two (1.5–2 years); three (3–3.5 years), n = 192 per point. Monolingual Spanish and English labeling crossovers are indicated by S and E.*

(Figure 10.9), labeling functions are generally steep and monotonic, which is characteristic of results for adult monolingual groups. In the functions for the younger subjects (Figure 10.8), there are either plateaus or reversals in direction of the slopes between the monolingual Spanish and English cross-over locations. The question arises as to whether the three younger groups' labeling slopes take these forms simply as a result of averaging. Within each group, a portion of the subjects may have crossover locations closer to the Spanish monolingual location and another portion of the subjects may have locations closer to that of English monolinguals. In other words, the distribution of responses in each *group* may be bimodal. A cumulative function of averaged data of this kind could produce flattening or dipping of the slope in the area between the two true crossovers. However, *individual* subjects might be using a double, or bilingual standard in making judgments, the outcome being a cumulative function previously described as a putative bilingual function (see Figure 10.6). An inspection of data for individuals reveals that both factors may be operating to some degree. However, the data are not extensive enough to tease out a clear bimodal distribution for either individuals or groups.

In Figures 10.10 and 10.11, discrimination data are plotted according to age and exposure as a function of the percentage of "different" responses to pairs of stimuli. The outstanding characteristic of the discrimination data is the degree to which they "disagree with" the labeling data. Although none of the six groups had labeling crossovers near +20 msec VOT, all six had a major discrimination peak at +20 msec, which is just 5 msec away from the +25 msec value for English adult monolinguals. The functions for the three older groups also have secondary peaks falling near the average Spanish crossover location at −4 msec. For both age groups, there is, in addition, the suggestion of an ordering in the height of discrimination peaks as a function of exposure to English (i.e., the greater the amount of exposure, the higher the peak).

Voice onset time values in msec, derived from spectrograms of the production data in English and Spanish were compared with results obtained

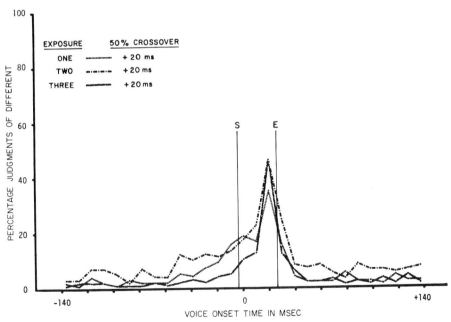

FIGURE 10.10 *Pooled discrimination functions for native Spanish-speaking children 8–10 years old with three exposure groups according to time on the mainland United States: one (0–6 months); two (1.5–2 years); three (3–3.5 years), n = 192 per point. Monolingual Spanish and English labeling crossovers are indicated by S and E.*

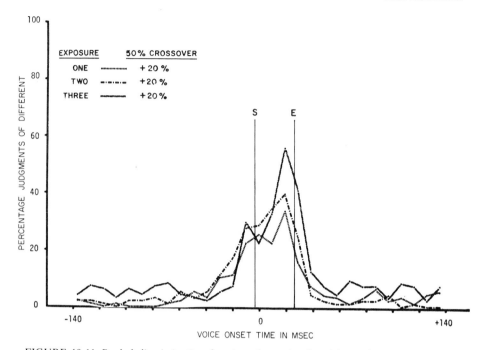

FIGURE 10.11 *Pooled discrimination functions for native Spanish-speaking children 14–16 years old with three exposure groups according to time on the mainland United States: one (0–6 months); two (1.5–2 years); three (3–3.5 years),* n = 192 *per point. Monolingual Spanish and English labeling crossovers are indicated by S and E.*

from the Spanish and English monolinguals. The following generalizations emerged from this analysis:

1. Both of the young second-language learner age groups used significantly less voicing lead in producing Spanish [b]s, and a greater amount of voicing lag in producing Spanish [p]s, than adult Spanish monolinguals ($p < .001$) and these differences were significantly greater for the younger groups, ($p < .001$).

2. Both second-language learner age groups used a significantly greater amount of voicing lead when producing English [b]s and significantly less voicing lag when producing English [p]s than did monolingual English speakers ($p < .001$), and the differences were greater for the older groups, ($p < .001$).

These two findings may be restated as an increase over time in English-like VOT characteristics when second-language learners were producing Spanish words and a decrease in Spanish-like VOT characteristics when they were producing English words. Both changes interact with age.

The results of the experiments reported here provided concrete evidence for perceptual learning at the phonetic level during second-language acquisition. This learning is manifested directly in the form of perceptual performance and indirectly as changes in speech-sound production, which presumably ensue from changes in the perception of acoustic–phonetic material. The fact that a modification from the standard Spanish monolingual performance was observed in both labeling and discrimination tasks, even for some groups with little exposure, suggests that very little experience may be required to activate this form of perceptual learning.

There was only slight evidence in individual or group data, in either labeling or discrimination results, to support the view that the children tested were retaining a Spanish-like standard while acquiring one that was more English-like. The only support for this position was the occurrence of plateaus and slope reversals in the labeling data for younger groups and the secondary peaks in discrimination over the Spanish voicing boundary for the older groups. Several possible explanations for these findings can be considered. The absence of strong evidence for the development of a bilingual pattern in perceptual performance suggests that a learner may choose some compromise value along an acoustic–phonetic dimension when his native and second language divide this dimension at different locations. If this were true, however, it would seem difficult for the learner to keep separate, in perception, the two sets of contrasting phonetic tokens that are characteristic of his two languages. For example, if an individual learner's crossover in labeling this series occurred at +10 msec VOT, voicing-lead stops (i.e., negative VOT) as well as short-lag stops (e.g., +5 msec VOT) would all fall into the voiced ([b]) category even though Spanish voiceless ([p]) stops are frequently produced with from 0 to +5 msec VOT. Thus, Spanish voiced and voiceless stops might be confused by this listener, if VOT constituted the only cue to initial-stop voicing.

Discussion

The major findings of this series of experiments can be summarized as follows:

1. Perceptual data from monolingual Spanish and English subjects revealed a clear separation in the manner in which they divided a bilabial VOT series. This perceptual performance matched the manner in which the subjects produced voiced and voiceless tokens in word-initial position.

2. Within the two monolingual language groups, the voicing characteristics of word-initial [b] tokens in production were not equally consistent. Whereas, in Spanish, voiced tokens were produced with voicing lead, in English voiced tokens were usually produced with little or no lag but could also be produced with voicing lead like their Spanish counterparts.

3. Data from bilingual Spanish–English subjects showed a considerable amount of individual variation in the manner in which the VOT series was divided in labeling and in discrimination. However, the data suggested a bimodal distribution in the location of labeling crossovers and discrimination peaks. Some subjects had a pattern approximating that of monolingual Spanish speakers but the majority had a pattern similar to that of monolingual English speakers.

4. In discrimination, all bilinguals distinguished stimuli lying in the vicinity of the monolingual English crossover, but only those subjects with Spanish-like labeling crossovers discriminated well the stimuli that lie in the vicinity of the monolingual Spanish labeling crossover.

5. The general tendency for all bilinguals was to have sharp monotonic labeling functions suggesting that each subject used a single criterion for dividing the VOT series. As noted earlier, there was some variability in the location of labeling crossovers. Similarly, discrimination peaks were generally unimodal and sharp with the exception of the peaks for those subjects with Spanish-like labeling crossovers.

6. In production, bilingual performance was similar to monolingual Spanish and English performance with the exception that bilinguals produced word-initial [b] tokens in English with more voicing lead than did monolingual English speakers.

7. Data from young native Spanish speaking subjects who were in the process of learning English showed a gradual shift from a Spanish-like pattern to an English-like pattern of labeling the VOT series, as a function of exposure to English. There was a tendency for this shift to occur faster for younger subjects, although the effect of age was not statistically significant.

8. The labeling data from young learners, coupled with data from bilinguals, suggested that the young learner will eventually acquire a compromise pattern of perceiving the VOT series somewhere between the monolingual Spanish and English patterns with a certain amount of individual variation in the exact form of this pattern.

9. The discrimination data from young learners departs sharply from their labeling data. There was no evidence of a gradual shift in discrimination peaks from a Spanish-like to an English-like location. Instead, all groups showed sharp major peaks lying over the vicinity of the English monolingual labeling crossover, although the three older groups also had minor peaks over the location of the monolingual Spanish labeling crossover.

10. The young learners also shifted, as a function of exposure, from a Spanish-like to an English-like manner in producing both English and Spanish word-initial voiced and voiceless tokens. This occurred more rapidly for the youngest group.

The tendency for the English voicing contrast to be readily *perceived* was illustrated in various ways in all three experiments: (*a*) by the existence in the monolingual Spanish data of a minor peak in discrimination over the area of VOT where the English voicing contrast is located; (b) by the fact that five out of eight bilinguals tested had labeling crossovers and discrimination peaks closer to the monolingual English than to the monolingual Spanish contrast location; (c) by the gradual shift with exposure toward the area of the English contrast in the labeling data from Spanish-speaking children learning English; and (d) by the fact that all discrimination peaks in the data from second-language learners were found close to the area of the English contrast. These regularities could be accounted for by three explanations: one sociolinguistic, one appealing to the nature of the acquisition process, and one psychoacoustic.

The Sociolinguistic Explanation

All bilingual subjects were residents of the United States. Pressures from their surrounding linguistic environment could force their pattern of *perceiving* speech to reflect the environmentally dominant language, even though, for five of these bilinguals, this would constitute a shift away from their native Spanish perceptual pattern.

In the case of the young second-language learners, this kind of explanation is even more reasonable. The prestige attached to English for this group of learners, primarily from socioeconomically disadvantaged origins, might well promote a shift in Spanish toward perceiving voicing characteristics appropriate for English, the higher prestige language. It is clear from the production data that second-language learners do shift their manner of *producing* word-initial labial stops toward an English pattern in both their primary and their secondary languages. The effect of a prestige dialect modifying the spoken phonetic characteristics of a former dialect has been shown by Labov (1966).

A related form of modification in the *production* of phonetic characteristics may be appearing in the monolingual and bilingual data of these experiments in the form of the occurrence of voicing lead of English [b] tokens. Lisker and Abramson (1964) have found similar instances of voicing lead in their monolingual English data but not in data from other language groups they sampled that share the phonetic characteristics of the English [b] (little or no voicing lag). It is also true that, among those languages, only in English does unbroken voicing fill the gap between [b] and a previously voiced segment in a sentence context (Lisker and Abramson, 1964). Voicing lead, that is voicing prior to the labial release of word-initial [b] in English, may be gradually emerging in American English as an instance of language in transition, a phenomenon that has also been described by Labov (1968).

The Acquisition-Process Explanation

Another possible explanation for the sensitivity of the second-language learners to the English voicing contrast, appeals to the process of acquisition itself. Perhaps, during the acquisition of another language, the learner becomes perceptually sensitized to acoustic properties of that language so that new phonetic distinctions are more salient than old ones.

There is also a tendency among the young second-language learners for voiced and voiceless tokens *produced* in English and Spanish to drift toward values appropriate to English as a function of exposure to English. This is not seen in the adult bilingual data in which Spanish-like values of VOT are maintained for both voiced and voiceless tokens. It could be the case that the Americanization of the Spanish voicing contrast in second-language learners is a temporary overcompensation that results from becoming sensitive to the voicing characteristics of the second language during the process of its acquisition. If this were the case, one would predict that, with the consolidation of the phonetic inventory of English, the pattern of production would eventually approach that found in the bilinguals who maintain voicing characteristics of Spanish.

The Psychoacoustic Explanation

A final and more plausible explanation than those already presented is provided when one considers what is known about the acoustic characteristics of naturally spoken voiced and voiceless stops in Spanish and English, which were discussed in some detail earlier in the chapter. In both languages, several acoustic properties differ systematically across an initial-stop voicing contrast in addition to VOT and its correlate properties; for example, differences in patterns of voice fundamental-frequency changes following release (Ewan and Krones, 1974; House and Fairbanks, 1953; Lea, 1973). Differences in postrelease fundamental-frequency changes have been shown to provide perceptual cues for the voicing contrast with English-speaking listeners (Fujimura, 1971; Haggard et al., 1970). In English, there are differences related to initial-stop voicing in the spectral characteristics of the brief burst of aperiodic noise associated with the articulatory release of the stop (Halle et al., 1957; Klatt, 1975; Zue, 1976). It also has been demonstrated that, when voicing lead is removed from voiced stops that initiate words spoken in Spanish, a relatively high-amplitude burst and the presence of low-frequency periodic energy following release favor voiced judgments by Spanish listeners (Williams, 1977b). A relatively high-amplitude burst and silence for 5–10 msec following release, however, favor voiceless judgments. These results suggest that information supplied by acoustic properties at the point of release, as well as voicing lead, may provide voicing cues for Spanish listeners.

Acoustic cues such as those just mentioned may be more perceptually salient than the relatively low-energy cues provided by differences in voicing lead. None of those potential cues were present in the synthetic continuum used in these studies. Perhaps the bilinguals and the second-language learners come to rely more heavily on additional cues such as these as they change from being Spanish monolinguals to Spanish–English bilinguals. If this is the case, the results obtained would be predicted (i.e., an absence of clear evidence for a developing bilingual pattern of perception using test materials lacking such potential cues.[7]

The evidence that acoustic–phonetic properties that discriminate the English voicing contrast are available to the young second-language learner with little exposure to English, suggests that this contrast may be a naturally distinctive one, perhaps because of psychoacoustic or auditory factors. A similar conclusion was expressed by Streeter and Landauer (1976) in the interpretation of their finding that Kikuyu children were able to discriminate VOT contrasts lying in the region of the English contrast (i.e., +10 versus +40 msec VOT) without experience with that acoustic–phonetic contrast. It is noteworthy that the strongest evidence for infant discrimination of synthetic stop consonants that contrast in VOT also occurs for contrasts that bracket the English phoneme boundary (Eilers et al., 1976; Eimas, 1975; Eimas et al., 1971; Trehub and Rabinovitch, 1972). Infant discrimination of degrees of voicing lead and of more extreme contrasts in voicing lag have been difficult to demonstrate (Eilers et al., 1979; Lasky et al., 1975; Streeter, 1976) even though phonetic contrasts do occur in these VOT regions in some languages. Evidence for discrimination of contrasts in the VOT vicinity of maximum English discrimination has also been obtained with the chinchilla (Kuhl, 1976), suggesting a nonlinguistic basis for this pattern of selective discrimination. Nonspeech stimuli, modeling the synthetic speech VOT continua have produced labeling and discrimination data with English listeners that look similar to the results obtained using the synthetic speech VOT series (Miller et al., 1976; Pisoni, 1977; Stevens and Klatt, 1974). These results again suggest that the basis for the perception of VOT with speechlike stimuli may be at least in part psychoacoustic in nature.

It may not even be necessary to search beyond an analysis of the acoustic characteristics of the voicing continuum used in this study to find an explanation for the apparent superiority of discrimination of VOT contrasts drawn from the +25 msec region. In the synthetic series used in the studies

---

[7] Elman, Diehl, and Buchwald (1977) found evidence that a language-triggered perceptual set can influence the location of a category boundary between voiced and voiceless syllable-initial stop consonants when Spanish–English bilinguals are tested. In their study, naturally produced voiced and voiceless stops in a CV context were embedded within strings of either Spanish or English filler words. The stop consonants varied in VOT values from −69 to +66 msec VOT. It is of interest that when Elman et al. tested Spanish–English bilinguals with the same paradigm, only replacing the naturally produced CV syllables with synthetic syllables of the kind used in the studies being reported here, they lost the effect of a language-specific perceptual set. One of the interpretations they placed on their finding is consistent with the explanation being presented here (i.e., that bilinguals and second-language learners may come to rely on a different set of acoustic–phonetic cues than do monolingual speakers of the representative languages). Some of these cues may not be present in the synthetic series.

of voicing perception that have been cited, a single property, VOT, varies in the voicing-lead region (negative VOT values). By contrast, a number of properties undergo parametric change in the VOT region bracketing approximately +25 msec VOT. These are also present in the naturally produced versions of these stimuli. Some such properties that were discussed in detail at the beginning of the chapter are the following:

1. The presence, absence, or varying duration of aspiration or aperiodic energy in the interval between articulatory release and the onset of voicing.
2. The absence of periodic acoustic energy at the level of F_1, during aperiodic excitation of the vocal tract.
3. Differences in the duration and amount of frequency change of transitions under conditions of periodic excitation of the vocal tract.

In a discrimination task, the young learner may have immediate access to this complex of contrasting properties providing for maximal discrimination of the relevant portion of the VOT continuum. The results of discrimination in this study support this conclusion. However, to use these potential voicing cues to organize phonetic distinctions into two separate systems appropriate for each language may require further experience with the second language. This notion is supported by the labeling results of the study with second-language learners that show gradual change with exposure.

The modification from Spanish to English-like performance, observed in the perception results, corresponds to a similar modification in production. This modification affects not only the production of the newly acquired language, but also the production of the native language, in terms of VOT characteristics. Thus, the young second-language learner gradually loses his Spanish-like manner of producing English words, while he develops interference from the second language on the primary language. The fact that these results were based on utterances that were repetitions of a model presented by a native speaker strengthens this finding. In repetition, one would expect speakers to attempt correct pronunciation, avoiding the encroachment of the phonetic effects of one language upon the other. Of course, it remains to be determined whether or not the observed degree of deviation from monolingual values of VOT constitute differences sufficient to be detected as a loss of Spanish accent in producing English, on the one hand, and an acquisition of an English accent in producing Spanish on the other.

Of further interest would be information about the patterns of an individual speaker's progress in modifying voicing characteristics in second-language learning. For example, is the pattern of change linear, or are there periods of acquisition interspersed with plateaus in progress? A definitive answer to the question relating to individual patterns of change in production would of course be best obtained from a longitudinal investigation of second-language learning. It would also be of interest to determine the exact relationship between changes in perception and production, again an issue best investigated by a longitudinal study of individual learners.

The apparent development of compromise VOT targets in both perception and production for bilinguals and second-language lerners may reflect a true convergence over time of the acoustic phonetic features of the two languages instead of the development of two separate phonetic systems. However, what we are suggesting here is rather a restructuring of the acoustic–phonetic space that encompasses both languages in the process of second–language acquisition. This restructuring may involve a developing sensitivity to supplemental acoustic cues that enable bilinguals to keep separate, in perception, the phonetic systems of their two languages. It may also entail, in production, a realignment of the total phonetic space of any single acoustic–phonetic dimension, such as VOT. Presumably, however, if a speaker is to become a fluent bilingual, without the phonetic encroachment of either language upon the other, such a change would not eliminate either the acoustic–phonetic distinction of contrasts within each language or the differences in the phonetic systems that exist across the two languages.

References

Abramson, A., and Lisker, L. (1970) "Discriminability along the Voicing Continuum: Cross-Language Tests," *Proceedings of the Sixth International Congress of Phonetic Sciences*, Prague 1967, Academia Publishing House of the Czechoslovak Academy of Sciences, pp. 569–573.

Abramson, A., and Lisker, L. (1972) "Voice-timing in Korean Stops," *Proceedings of the Seventh International Congress of Phonetic Sciences*, Mouton, Montreal, The Hague, pp. 439–446.

Abramson, A., and Lisker, L. (1973) "Voice-timing Perception in Spanish Word-initial Stops," *Journal of Phonetics*, 1, 1–8.

Bell-Berti, F. (1975) "Control of Pharyngeal Cavity Size for English Voiced and Voiceless Stops," *Journal of the Acoustical Society of America*, 57, 456–461.

Caramazza, A., Yeni-Komshian, G., Zurif, E., and Carbone, E. (1973) "The Acquisition of a New Phonological Contrast: The Case of Stop Consonants in French–English Bilinguals," *Journal of the Acoustical Society of America*, 54, 421–428.

Chomsky, N., and Halle, M. (1968) *The Sound Pattern of English*, Harper & Row, New York.

Cooper, F., Delattre, P., Liberman, A., Borst, J., and Gerstman, L. (1952) "Some Experiments on the Perception of Synthetic Speech Sounds," *Journal of the Acoustical Society of America*, 24, 597–606.

Delattre, P., Liberman, A., and Cooper, F. (1955) "Acoustic Loci and Transitional Cues for Consonants," *Journal of the Acoustical Society of America*, 27, 769–773.

Dent, L. (1976) "Voice Onset Time of Spontaneously Spoken Spanish Voiceless Stops, *Journal of the Acoustical Society of America*, 59, Supplement 1, S41.

Eilers, R., Gavin, W., and Wilson, W. (1979) "Linguistic Experience and Phonemic Perception in Infancy: A Cross-Linguistic Study," *Child Development*, 49, 14–18.

Eilers, R., Wilson, W., and Moore, J. (1976) "Discrimination of Synthetic Prevoiced Labial

Stops by Infants and Adults," *Journal of the Acoustical Society of America*, 60, Supplement, S91.

Eimas, P. (1975) "Speech Perception in Early Infancy," in L. Cohen and P. Salapateck, eds., *Infant Perception from Sensation to Cognition II*, Academic Press, New York, pp. 193–231.

Eimas, P., Siqueland, E., Jusczyk, P., and Vigorito, J. (1971) "Speech Perception in Infants, *Science*, 171, 303–306.

Elman, J., Diehl, R., and Buchwald, S. (1977) "Perceptual Switching in Bilinguals," *Journal of the Acoustical Society of America*, 62, 971–974.

Ewan, E., and Krones, R. (1974) "Measuring Larynx Movement Using the Thyroumbrometer," *Journal of Phonetics*, 2, 327–335.

Finney, D. (1952) *Probit Analysis: A Statistical Treatment of the Sigmoid Response Curve*, The University Press, Cambridge, England.

Fujimura, O. (1971) "Remarks on Stop Consonants: Synthesis Experiments and Acoustic Cues," in L. L. Hammerich, R. Jakobson, and E. Zwirner, eds., *Form and Substance: Phonetic and Linguistic Papers Presented to Eli Fischer-Jorgensen*. Akademisk Foilag, Denmark, pp. 221–232.

Haggard, M., Ambler, S., and Callow, M. (1970) "Pitch as Voicing Cue, *Journal of the Acoustical Society of America*, 47, 613–617.

Halle, M., Hughes, G., and Radley, J. (1957) "Acoustic Properties of Stop Consonants," *Journal of the Acoustical Society of America*, 29, 107–116.

Halle, M., and Stevens, K. N. (1971) "A Note on Laryngeal Features, *Research Laboratory of Electronics Quarterly Progress Report*, 101, MIT. Cambridge, Mass. pp. 198–213.

Heffner, R. (1969) *General Phonetics*, The University of Wisconsin Press, Madison.

Hockett, C. (1960) *A Course in Modern Linguistics*, MacMillan, New York.

House, A., and Fairbanks, G. (1953) "The Influence of Consonantal Environment upon the Secondary Acoustical Characteristics of Vowels," *Journal of the Acoustical Society of America*, 25, 105–113.

Klatt, D. (1975) "Voice Onset Time, Frication and Aspiration in Word-initial Consonant Clusters," *Journal of Speech and Hearing Research*, 18, 686–706.

Kuhl, P. (1976) "Speech Perception by the Chinchilla: Categorical Perception of Synthetic Alveolar Plosive Consonants," *Journal of the Acoustical Society of America*, 60, Supplement, S81.

Labov, W. (1966) "Hypercorrection by the Lower Middle Class as Factor in Linguistic Change," in W. Bright, ed., *Proceedings of the UCLA Sociolinguistics Conference*, Mouton, The Hague, pp. 84–113.

Labov, W. (1968) "On the Mechanism of Linguistic Change," *Georgetown University Round Table Selected Papers on Linguistics 1961–1965*, compiled by R. O'Brien, Georgetown University Press, Washington, D.C. pp. 260–282.

Lasky, R., Syrdal-Lasky, A., and Klein, R. (1975) "VOT Discrimination by Four to Six and a Half Month Old Infants from Spanish Environments," *Journal of Experimental Child Psychology*, 20, 215–225.

Lea, W. (1973) "Influences of Phonetic Sequences and Stress on Fundamental Frequency Contours of Isolated Words," *Journal of the Acoustical Society of America*, 53, 346.

Liberman, A., Delattre, P., and Cooper, F. (1958) "Some Cues for the Distinction between Voiced and Voiceless Stops in Initial Position," *Language and Speech*, 1, 153–167.

Lisker, L., and Abramson, A. (1964) "A Cross-language Study of Voicing in Initial Stops: Acoustical Measurements," *Word*, 20, 384–422.

Lisker, L., and Abramson, A. (1971) "Distinctive Features and Laryngeal Control," *Language*, 47, 767–785.

Lisker, L., Abramson, A., Cooper, F., and Schvey, M. (1967) "Transillumination of the Larynx in Running Speech," *Journal of the Acoustical Society of America*, 45, 1544–1546.

Miller, J., Wier, C., Pastore, R., Kelley, W., and Dooling, R. (1976) "Discrimination and

Labeling of Noise-buzz Sequences with Varying Noise-lead Times: An Example of Categorical Perception," *Journal of the Acoustical Society of America*, 60, 410–417.

Pisoni, D. (1977) "Identification and Discrimination of the Relative Onset Time of Two Component Tones: Implications for Voicing Perception in Stops, *Journal of the Acoustical Society of America*, 61, 1352–1361.

Rothenberg, M. (1968) *The Breath-Stream Dynamics of Simple-Released-Plosive Production*. Karger, Basel.

Sawashima, M., Abramson, A., Cooper, F., and Lisker, L. (1970) "Observing Laryngeal Adjustments During Running Speech by Use of a Fibroptics System, *Phonetics*, 22, 193–201.

Smith, B.L., and Westbury, J.R. (1975) "Temporal Control of Voicing during Occlusion of Plosives," *Journal of the Acoustical Society of America*, 57, Supplement 1, S71.

Stevens, K., and Klatt, D. (1974) "The Role of Formant Transitions in the Voiced–voiceless Distinction for Stops," *Journal of the Acoustical Society of America*, 55, 653–659.

Streeter, L. (1976) "Language Perception of 2-month-old Infants Shows Effects of Both Innate Mechanisms and Experience," *Nature*, 259, 39–41.

Streeter, L., and Landauer, T. (1976) "Effects of Learning English as a Second Language on the Acquisition of a New Phoneme Contrast," *Journal of the Acoustical Society of America*, 59, 448–451.

Summerfield, A., and Haggard, M. (1974) "Perceptual Processing of Multiple Cues and Contexts: Effects of Following Vowel upon Stop Consonant Voicing," *Journal of Phonetics*, 2, 279–295.

Trehub, S., and Rabinovitch, M. (1972) "Auditory–linguistic Sensitivity in Early Infancy, *Developmental Psychology*, 6, 74–77.

Williams, L. (1974) *Speech Perception and Production as a Function of Exposure to a Second Language*, Unpublished Doctoral Dissertation, Harvard University.

Williams, L. (1977) "The Perception of Stop Consonant Voicing by Spanish–English Bilinguals, *Perception & Psychophysics*, 21, 289–297. (a)

Williams, L. (1977) "The Voicing Contrast in Spanish," *Journal of Phonetics*, 5, 169–184. (b)

Williams, L. "The Modification of Speech Perception and Production in Second-Language Learning, *Perception & Psychophysics*, (in press).

Winitz, H., LaRiviere, C., and Herriman, E. (1975) "Variations in VOT for English Initial Stops, *Journal of Phonetics*, 3, 41–52.

Zlatin, M. (1974) "Voicing Contrast: Perceptual and Productive Voice Onset Time Characteristics of Adults," *Journal of the Acoustical Society of America*, 56, 981–994.

Zue, V. (1976) "Acoustic Characteristics of Stop Consonants: A Controlled Study," *Lincoln Laboratory Technical Report*, 523.

Chapter 11

RESEARCH IN CHILD PHONOLOGY: COMMENTS, CRITICISM, AND ADVICE

JAMES J. JENKINS

These volumes contain far too many chapters with too much to say to permit a concise summary. What I would like to do instead is stand back a little from the specific chapters and the particular issues involved and offer some observations about the research area as I see it from the outside. I am neither a developmental psychologist nor a child phonologist; I have never directly performed any research in the area; but I am very much interested in how the field is getting along. Sometimes a "near neighbor" or a "friend of the family" can see things that the family member is too involved to see.

Some Positive Comments

My first observation (which comes as no news) is that this is an exciting field. It is one of the most vigorous young fields that I have seen in some time. When one considers that the speech spectrographs is just about 35 years old, that even marginally acceptable synthetic speech is no more than 20 years old, that the first infant study with synthetic speech was performed only 10 years ago, then one realizes with a shock that the experimental aspects of the field are actually younger than the series of language confer-

CHILD PHONOLOGY
VOLUME 2: PERCEPTION

ences of which the conference on which these volumes are based is a member.

I did a quick count of the references in some of the chapters and discovered, probably to no one's surprise, that well over 90% of them are from the last decade and, even more remarkably, over 60% of these references are from the last 3–4 years. That is, this is a field that is fresh, young, and rapidly expanding. One consequence is that the field is exciting and stimulating. Another consequence is that the methodologies have moved so fast that what would have been an acceptable study only a few years ago might now be regarded as unacceptably crude.

This development puts a staggering burden on the investigators in the field, including, of course, those represented in this volume. In some sense, it would be reasonable to expect that an investigator who wanted to work experimentally in child phonology ought to have a grasp of voice science, audiology, acoustics, articulation, instrumentation, child development, behavior management techniques, linguistics, phonology, phonetics, psycholinguistics, speech synthesis, speech perception, psychometrics, and statistics. Obviously, this is an unrealistic expectation. Yet, the research that has been reported here suggests that many of you are meeting those demands in the course of your work. That is an important reason for optimism about the course of development of the field.

Invariants

It seems to me that the issues that have been raised here are the important and fundamental issues. From the very beginning, there has been a steady focus on the search for acoustic and articulatory invariants of linguistic units. If there is a key and crucial problem for all work in speech perception and production, it must be the search for invariants. Any research that sheds light on this problem, whether it is performed on adults or on children, will have a major effect on the entire field. It is vitally important that we know what is significant "out there" in the speech signal. We all want to know what it is that we are responding to. How can children know what it is that they are matching when they imitate? How can a child know that what is produced is acceptable when it is so acoustically different from the adult production in so many ways?

Acoustics–Phonetics Relations

As I reviewed the discussions of the relations between acoustics and phonetics, I realized that there is remarkable sophistication in this group of investigators in marked contrast to some of our simpler notions when Moffitt (1971) first undertook his infant research. Everyone is well aware of the fact that an acoustic cue is not identical to a phonetic contrast. For example,

VOT has been studied extensively, and there are many articles in which it is discussed but never so subtly and comprehensively as in this volume. There is a keen awareness that the particular acoustic manipulations of the Abramson and Lisker (1970) series are not in themselves voicing, even though they produce highly reliable perceptual phenomena.

Discrimination–Categorization

Another issue that has been raised here has to do with a fundamental problem in all perception, namely, the relation between discrimination and categorization. Suppose that we find that a subject can discriminate some values along an acoustic dimension when speech stimuli are presented in a psychophysical task. Does that mean that the subject will be able to classify (i.e., label) diverse instances of the stimuli when they differ along many continua simultaneously as members of a system? The immediate answer must be "No," of course. Such discrimination is no guarantee of categorization. But if that is the case, we must proceed slowly as we make inferences about what children perceive when we only have data from discrimination tasks. What does it mean when we find dishabituation of the sucking response as we move across the adult boundary of VOT? Does this mean that the child perceives *voicing* as a phonological feature, or does it merely mean that some basis is present on which perception of voicing will later be based? Discrimination of certain acoustic differences must be necessary, but it is not sufficient for the perception of appropriate categories in a phonological system.

Experience

I was pleased to read several discussions of the effects of experience on perception. Fortunately, this general topic is the subject of a book by Walk and Pick (1978). Two of the chapters in that book deal specifically with the effects of short-term and long-term experience on the perception of speech (Eimas and Miller, 1978; Strange and Jenkins, 1978). Several studies here illustrate ways to collect these data. One of the potent ideas that has been advanced has to do with extending this research into questions of perceptual constancy. I think this will prove to be an important way to extend this line of research. I will return to this topic later with a suggestion or two.

Skill Sequence

On the production side, there is much concern with the sequence of skill development in articulation. Many are looking for consistencies in the sequences that are observed in children's behavior over the course of development. Several have raised the question of the role of children's early vocal work, not just babbling, but also the vocables. Is it necessary for children to learn that language has some work to do? Do they have to begin inventing simple systems to begin to see the great system about them? There are many levels of consideration that must be entertained: Developmental progress of the most general sort concerning an understanding of the nature of language, progress in generating classes of sounds, progress in developing the specific oppositions and contrasts, and so on.

In terms of the relation between perception and production, I think considerable progress is being made. As the developmental picture on both sides is being filled in, the possibility of making substantive comments is increasing. At present, I think we can all agree that the greatest need is for more precise work to clarify the details of development. I will return to this theme a little further on.

Universals

In the 1950s, in most places in the United States, talk of universals would have been taken as evidence that one was not a serious linguist or investigator of language phenomena. The change in the last two decades is salutory. Such evidence may, indeed, be among the most important we can gather in unlocking the problems of the acquisition of spoken language.

Psychological Variables

Finally, as a traditional psychologist, I have been happy to see the recognition that there are variables other than the phonological system itself that must be considered in studying language acquisition. A whole set of hoary psychological variables are becoming visible. It is good to see that pragmatic variables such as frequency, and utility, or functional yield of an utterance, are again seen as important. I see this as parallel to the change in the research on the acquisition of syntax, where work in the last 5–6 years has turned from the syntactic system to the pragmatic variables that make syntax of some import for the developing child.

Some Critical Remarks

There are some instances in which data do not agree and several cases in which the same kinds of data are interpreted in different ways. Investigators have been very nice about this; perhaps too polite and a little too easy on one another. I confess that I am more comfortable in such an atmosphere, but some self-criticism is necessary. I hope that objective criticism can be added to the transactions without sacrificing the good will that already obtains.

As was mentioned earlier, this field is moving fast and becoming more demanding all the time. Very serious attention must now be given to increasing statistical standards and attending to some delicate control problems. Let me comment first on the statistical issue.

Statistical Issues

I have often gathered the impression that there is overly much reliance on "the law of large numbers." In general, of course, the acquisition of more and more data is to be applauded; but there are sharp limits on what increasing amounts of data can do for you.

Consider first the simplest case, collecting more and more data about a particular child. It is easy to see that increased data and more precise techniques lead to better and better description of that child. But no amount of data on *that* child permits generalization to other children; only increasing the *number of children* sampled can do that. Now, when stated in such blatant form, all of us would agree to the caution. But we are sometimes deceived by special cases. Suppose that all the world believes that all children develop in such-and-such a fashion. Then, one disconfirming case, studied carefully, is of enormous importance; it negates the supposed universal. Such case studies are scientifically crucial. But notice, that in denying the universal, the single case does not establish a new universal; it only says that the prior belief can no longer be held. It may *suggest* new generalities, but it cannot, in itself, establish them.

The second case is more subtle. It has to do with increasing the precision of poor measurements by making a lot of them. This is the law of large numbers at work in behalf of science. If a fair number of people measure the length of a box with a ruler, the average of their individual measures will ordinarily be a very accurate measure of the box. The same applies to estimating distances, determining how tall the average sixth grade boy is, and so on. The "catch" in relying on the law of large numbers is that it only applies to unbiased measurements. If the measurements themselves are biased, the only thing that happens with large numbers is that the bias is confirmed. Take a concrete instance in speech perception. Suppose that we wish to know at what age children begin to make a given distinction in perception. Suppose that the experimental procedure we are using requires a fair amount of attention, memory, or verbal response skill, all of which are known to increase with age. Now you can see that it will be easy to get false negatives (that is, failures of discrimination) from the younger children, even though they might really be able to make the discrimination. Increasing the number of children measured will not correct this problem because the bias affects all the measurements that we make. We will simply pile up instances of the same kind of error. The only cure for this problem is to achieve precise measurement of the individual case. Rather painfully, this means that we must have a sufficient number of measures of each child when we can show that the child is paying attention, has the proper memory span, and has sufficient response skill. This means, ideally, that we must map something that the child can do and something that the child cannot do in the same situation (with the same task demands) before we can conclude that the child fails the discrimination for the "right" reason.

I might also say something about the "sufficient number of measures." Even after we have controlled the questions of extraneous variables, we must still pay attention to statistics. In a two-choice situation, the child has a fair chance of being correct (or incorrect) by chance alone. By expanding the ordinary binomial, we can see that a child must be correct on 9 *out of 10* trials before we can say, with the usual levels of confidence, that the child is not guessing. When the individual child is the unit we are counting, we must make enough measures to determine what each child can really do.

I do not think that we must be depressed by these considerations. We simply must appreciate when they work for us and when they work against us. An instance in which the law of large numbers worked for the research is found in Templin's (1957) articulation norms for children. You will recall that Templin used an imitation task and judged successful articulation of the target sounds by the child. The imitation task appears to be one that children understand. It puts minimal demands on memory. The investigator can tell when the child is "out of the situation," or not paying attention. All children were successful on at least some of the productions, and so on. It is likely that some children were not given credit for sounds that they could produce correctly some of the time, and some children were given credit for sounds that they only occasionally produced correctly. It also seems plausible that such errors tended to balance. In general, the data appear to be very stable and seem to stand the test of time. Thus, it appears to be a positive instance where sizable numbers contributed to accuracy. For the reasons given, however, I do not think such factors apply to most perceptual measures.

Improved Designs

Increased precision in the measurement of the individual is also called for by the kinds of questions many are now raising. For instance, investigators are no longer just asking whether a child detects the difference between a voiced and an unvoiced stop consonant. They are beginning to ask whether the child's boundary is in the same place as the adult boundary on some dimension, or whether the identification boundaries are as steep for children as they are for adults. Such studies obviously call for far more sensitive experimental techniques and for serious attention to the reliability of measures.

As has been pointed out, the same kinds of pressures are going to require change in some experimental designs. When research in the area was initiated, it was exciting to discover that infants could perceive the differences between radically different speech sounds. As research has progressed, however, it has become apparent that the infant can do much more than that. How much more? If the infant can do all tasks we set before it, we are back where we started; being able to do everything gives us no more information about the emergence of speech perception than being able to do nothing.

Clearly, this calls for more subtle and sensitive experimental designs. The more careful selection of subjects and of materials, the invention of experimental procedures, and, especially, the development of sensitive control conditions are demanded. Controls must be employed to test whether or not the children are adequately under experimental control. Controls must show where the boundaries of the phenomena are located. Controls must be developed to help us define the nature of the concepts the child is forming in both the productive and perceptive domains. I believe that this is going to tax the ingenuity of experimenters and theorists, but I already see evidence of movement in these directions.

There is evidence, too, that experiments are going to change in other ways. The early studies tended to be studies of one item, one acoustical dimension, or one distinction. Several are now moving to multiple-variable experiments. What sensitivities go together? What distinctions are related? Are richer signals (more redundant signals) handled differently from simpler signals? Many are working with both natural and synthetic speech as experimental materials. This is a very important development.

Converging Experiments

Accompanying this enrichment of materials and variables, I see an increasing appreciation that one experiment cannot be expected to solve all problems of interpretation at a single stroke. There is greater appreciation of the fact that many different kinds of experiments are required to develop understanding of an area. One does not conduct one perfect experiment; one conducts many experiments that are interrelated in such a fashion as to make possible increasingly accurate interpretations. The current jargon for this in experimental psychology is "converging operations." Acceptance of this view argues for diversity of measures and situations on the route to fuller understanding. It accepts the fact that all experiments and all measures are prone to artifacts; there is no single, correct way to do research. This is a sign of growing maturity in this area.

Optimal–Ordinary Performance

Finally, I urge the explicit recognition of an implied distinction. One must distinguish between what children *can do* and what they *do do*. Usually we want to know both what the child can do when driven to the limit in optimal conditions and what the child does do under the ordinary circumstances of daily life. There is typically a considerable gap between these performances. If we confuse the two kinds of information, we can have apparent disagreement where none really exists.

At the extremes, we can see that these are very different kinds of procedures. The diary study, for example, is a record of what the child *did do* under some ordinary set of circumstances. It is interpreted by skilled observers and fitted into a pattern of development. At the other extreme, we might find the psychophysical experiment with a trained, highly motivated, and knowledgeable observer working under superb conditions in a soundproofed laboratory on noise-free stimuli. We will not be surprised if these procedures give us different data or even a different pattern of development. In intermediate cases, we may have more difficulty sorting our studies into types, but the distinction may be useful nonetheless.

Some Advice

When I was a little boy, I learned a riddle that went like this: "What is it that everybody asks for, everybody gives, and yet, no one ever takes?" The answer, of course, is "Advice." Even at the risk that no one will heed it, I cannot resist this opportunity to offer some advice.

The Analogy of Visual Development

If I were working in this field, I would try to think seriously about the analogy with research in visual development. I know that many investigators are flirting with the idea, and I want to encourage them. The researchers who have been studying infant vision have been having a field day. Their area is racing ahead in great excitement. Of course, the experimental work of the visual researchers has been facilitated by the simple fact that the experimenter can tell where the infant is looking. Work in audition struggles with the handicap that we cannot tell what, if anything, the infant is listening to. By watching what infants look at in some clever experimental situations, important advances have been made.

In a study by Cohen *et al.* (1971), infants were habituated to a *red circle*. Then they were tested for preferences for four targets: a *red circle*, a *green circle*, a *red triangle*, and a *green triangle*. The infants preferred to look at green rather than red and at triangles rather than circles. In addition, the preferences were additive; they preferred the green triangles over all other stimuli.

Recently, with a similar technique, Bornstein *et al.* (1976) showed that infants 4 months of age showed dishabituation across adult color-category boundaries. It appears that infants have the ability to discover and respond to invariance during the first year of life. With their experiments, many investigators are now asking just which invariants the child is responding to. Cohen (1977) sketched a hierarchy (at present only suggested by a small number of studies) that develops from simple to complex concepts in the course of the first year. Supporting studies are encouraging. Multiple instances of a class must be presented to achieve the conceptual result. For example, many different variants of the concept must be presented to achieve habituation to new instances of the concept; One example presented for a long time will not achieve the result. In addition, habituation with a three-dimensional object transfers to colored pictures of the object and to black and white pictures. All of this suggests that the infant is categorizing and ordering its visual world. It is progressively moving to higher and higher perceptual–cognitive categories in what appears to be an orderly development.

I must suppose that some parallel process is going on in the auditory domain. If we can develop some experimental paradigms that will measure more than the presence or absence of a single discrimination, we may be able to study such developments. The work that has been discussed in this volume concerning perceptual constancies is most closely related to this direction of research. Such studies may provide the means of asking about the auditory concepts that the child is developing.

One vast difference between the visual and the speech-perception areas of research is in respect to the perception–production question. The visual researchers do not really know how to ask that question. In speech, the term production means the production of some sort of acoustic parallel to what the child perceives. In the visual area, the parallel must be something like the child's producing some representation of space that we can only infer from the skill the child displays in moving through space and handling spatial problems. One general tendency, however, is to suppose that, at some point, the child's perception is excellent and that only his motor control is poor. Thus, we may easily believe that the child perceives the visual world completely but is prevented from showing his perception because of his immature motor control. (There is some tendency to apply such thought to the speech area too. I believe that some researchers would argue that the child perceives perfectly from the start, but that his motor control is poor, so his production of language lags behind.)

I think this line of thought must be held in check until data are brought out to support it. One of the reasons I am reluctant to assume perfect perception (thus, pushing all development onto the production side) is the visual case itself. When one wants to train an adult to draw, one begins by "training the eye." That is, artists believe that adult nonartists, far from having perfect perception, have uneducated and undeveloped perceptions. Art teachers have a host of exercises devoted to training people to look at the world in such a way that they see those aspects of things that the artist believes to be important. In another example, there is evidence that the perceptions of chess experts are not at all like the perceptions of novices (Chase and Simon, 1972; de Groot, 1965). The point is that we do not yet know the extent to which motor behaviors and systems of organized knowledge influence our perceptions of the world. It is surely far too early to conclude that perception and production are independent in the development of the child's phonological system.

Experiments of Nature

Second, if I were working in the field, I would be on the lookout for "experiments of nature." Many people are moving from one nation to another, and children of all ages are being thrust into new language settings and encouraged to learn new languages. Consider a case in point. We know that adult Japanese do not perceive the difference between the English /r/ and /l/ (Miyawaki, et al., 1975). We have every reason to suppose that infants can discriminate that distinction (Eimas, 1975). Many Japanese families with small children are moving into English-speaking countries. It is possible to find many children of varying ages who are being exposed to the English /r/ and /l/ for the first time. We can readily study the course of acquisition of the distinction by Japanese speakers of all ages who are now functioning in English-speaking settings. Williams (1974), of course, has performed this kind of study on Spanish speakers acquiring the English voicing distinction with very interesting results.

Motor Control

Third, if I had any idea how to do it, I would work very hard on a key problem that has been mentioned here: the flexibility of control of the motor system. If anyone has any ideas about how the motor system develops and where it gets its fantastic capacity to adapt itself and function adequately in some situation in which it has never been before, they should certainly pursue them. This is a fascinating puzzle. It has wide ramifications in many other parts of psychology. If perception and action can be linked together, the perception and production of speech just might be the best area in which to examine and test hypotheses.

Technical Meetings

Finally, I have some practical suggestions. It seems to me that two kinds of meetings are definitely called for. First, I think a series of technical group meetings should be planned. These would probably best be organized by specialty. For example, I think the phonologists all ought to get together.

They should read each other's work, criticize one another's ideas, try to evaluate their contributions to the field, and so on. The people in perceptual experimentation should get together and talk about their experimental paradigms, about problems of measurement, about designs, about statistical refinements, and the like. The field is about ready for some experimentation that is aimed at solving some of the questions about the paradigms themselves and their comparabilities; such research could be designed. The same thing should be done by the researchers working on production and articulation.

I urge the funding agencies to support just such small work groups. We must try to make the field better by solving some of the technical problems that now stand in the way. A meeting for a week, once a year or once every two years would provide an enormous stimulus to the progress of the field. It might push the field ahead by another quantum jump.

Interdisciplinary Groups

The other practical suggestion is to give serious thought to integrating the direction of the research. The working groups that guide research in universities from week to week ought to be teams of investigators made up of the various specialties. Working groups in all disciplines need team members from the other areas we have mentioned. One thing that has been made clear is that all of the disciplines can make active contributions to the total endeavor. The team approach will result in better research, better interpretation of findings, and better dissemination of the results. In the long run, the team approach may be the only way to cope with the extraordinary technical requirements of this area.

In summary, a very exciting and rapidly maturing field of research is making great progress against unusual difficulties and demands. As a result of the progress, the field is now confronting new demands for sophistication in methodologies, statistics, experimental design, and theoretical conception. A major contribution to the further progress can be made by refining efforts within specialties through a series of technical conferences. Broadened research teams including the various specializations are called for.

References

Abramson, A.S., and Lisker, L. (1970) "Discriminability along the Voicing Continuum: Cross-language Tests," in *Proceedings of the Sixth International Congress of Phonetic Science*, Academia, Prague, pp. 569–573.

Bornstein, M.H., Kessen, W., and Weiskopf, S. (1976) "Color Vision and Hue Categorization in Young Human Infants," *Journal of Experimental Psychology: Human Perception and Performance*, 2, 115–119.

Chase, W.G., and Simon, H.A. (1973) "Perception in Chess," *Cognitive Psychology*, 4, 55–81.

Cohen, L.B. (1977) "Concept Acquisition in the Human Infant," Paper presented at the Society for Research in Child Development Meeting, New Orleans.

Cohen, L.B., Gelber, E.R., and Lazar, M.A. (1971) "Infant Habituation and Generalization to Differing Degrees of Stimulus Novelty," *Journal of Experimental Child Psychology*, 11, 379–389.

de Groot, A.D. (1975) *Thought and Choice in Chess*, Mouton, The Hague.

Eimas, P.D. (1975) "Auditory and Phonetic Coding of the Cues for Speech: Discrimination of the [r–l] Distinction by Young Infants," *Perception & Psychophysics*, 18, 341–347.

Eimas, P.D., and Miller, J.L. (1978) "Effects of Selective Adaptation on the Perception of Speech and Visual Patterns: Evidence for Feature Detectors," in R.D. Walk and H.L. Pick Jr., eds., *Perception and Experience*, Plenum, New York, pp. 307–345.

Miyawaki, K., Strange, W., Verbrugge, R.R., Liberman, A.M., Jenkins, J.J., and Fujimura, O. (1975) "An Effect of Linguistic Experience: The Discrimination of [r] and [l] by Native Speakers of Japanese and English," *Perception & Psychophysics*, 18, 331–340.

Moffitt, A.R. (1971) "Consonant Cue Perception by Twenty- to Twenty-four-week-old Infants," *Child Development*, 42, 717–731.

Strange, W., and Jenkins, J.J. (1978) "Role of Linguistic Experience in the Perception of Speech," in R.D. Walk and H.L. Pick Jr., eds., *Perception and Experience*, Plenum, New York, pp. 125–169.

Templin, M. (1957) "Certain Language Skills in Children: Their Development and Interrelationships," *Institute of Child Welfare Monograph 26*. University of Minnesota Press, Minneapolis.

Walk, R.D., and Pick, H.L. Jr., eds., (1978) *Perception and Experience*. Plenum, New York.

Williams, L. (1974) "Speech Perception and Production as a Function of Exposure to a Second Language," Unpublished Doctoral Dissertation, Harvard University, Cambridge, Mass.

GLOSSARY

KAY ATKINSON-KING

Acoustic—Refers to the physical properties of a sound (cf. auditory).

Affricate—A consonant sound beginning as a stop but ending as a fricative with approximately the same place of articulation (e.g., /tʃ/ as in *church*, which begins with /t/ as in *tie* and is followed by /ʃ/ as in *shy*). It may be specified as a stop with delayed release.

Allophone—A nondistinctive or noncontrastive phonetic realization of a phoneme in a given language (e.g., the aspirated and unaspirated versions of the bilabial voiceless stop in *pot* [pʰ] and *spot* [p] in English are classified as allophones of the phoneme [p]; cf. phoneme).

Alveolar—A consonant sound articulated with the tip or blade of the tongue against the alveolar ridge (e.g., /d/).

Alveolar ridge—The bony ridge located behind the upper teeth.

Alveo–palatal—A consonant sound articulated with the blade of the tongue against the alveolar ridge and the main body of the tongue raised toward the palate (e.g., /ʃ/ in *ship*).

Amplitude—The magnitude of maximum displacement of air molecules in response to a vibratory force. In speech production, amplitude may be considered a function of the energy with which the vocal cords vibrate (cf. loudness, intensity).

Analysis-by-synthesis—A theory of speech perception in which the

CHILD PHONOLOGY
VOLUME 2: PERCEPTION

hearer internally generates speech signals to find the best match to an incoming signal.

Antiformants—Resonant qualities of the nasal cavity that obscure formants (cf. formants).

Aphasia—A language disorder resulting from brain injury or disease in the areas of the brain associated with linguistic ability.

Assimilation—A phonetic process in which one sound affects another sound in such a way that the sounds become more like each other. Children acquiring language may simplify through the process of assimilation (e.g., /gəgi/ for *doggy*, /næm/ for *lamb*).

Audiometry—The systematic measurement of auditory acuity by means of a calibrated instrument known as an audiometer.

Auditory—Refers to the perception of a sound (cf. acoustic).

Autonomous phonemic level—A type of analysis used by structuralists in which phonology is entirely independent of syntax and morphology (cf. systematic phonemic level).

Behaviorism—A theoretical inductivist view that attempts to explain behavior only by reference to directly observable events rather than to underlying mental processes (cf. mentalism).

Bilabial—A consonant sound articulated with a combined movement of both lips (e.g., /p,b,m/).

Blade of tongue—Part of the narrow extremity of the tongue that is immediately behind the tongue tip and in front of the middle of the tongue.

Canonical form—The most basic or simplest form of a word or morpheme.

Categorical perception—Refers to the inability of listeners to hear the acoustic differences among sounds that they identify as belonging to the same phonemic category and their ability to discriminate among stimuli that fall at phoneme category boundaries. Thus, categorical perception occurs when there is a close relationship between identification and discrimination (cf. continuous perception).

Cinefluorography—See cineradiography.

Cineradiography—X-ray motion picutres. In speech research they are used to study the movements of the articulatory organs during speech activity (syn.: cinefluorography).

Coarticulation—An overlap in the production of gestures in successive and in some cases nonsuccessive segments of a speech utterance. The effects of coarticulation may be anticipatory or perseveratory.

Communicative competence—The ideal speaker–hearer's tacit knowledge underlying communicative behavior, including not only the language itself, but the rules for using it appropriately in the social world (cf. competence, performance).

Competence—The ideal speaker–hearer's tacit knowledge of his or her native language (he/she grammar) that allows the production and comprehension of an infinite number of grammatical sentences, among other things (cf. communicative competence, performance).

Consonant—A speech sound produced with partial or complete constriction of the vocal tract at one or more points.

Content words; contentive—A noun, verb, adjective, or adverb that carries lexical meaning (cf. function words).

Continuant—A speech sound produced with incomplete closure of the vocal tract, allowing the airflow from the lungs to continue to pass through the mouth relatively unimpeded. All speech sounds are classified as continuants except stops, where the airstream from the oral cavity is completely obstructed (cf. stops).

Continuous perception—Refers to the ability of listeners, when presented with continuously varied acoustic stimuli, to make fine discriminations among stimuli of the same or of different categories while they are unable reliably to identify stimuli as belonging to a small set of categories. Thus, there is no one-to-one relationship between discrimination and identification (cf. categorical perception).

Cross-sectional study—A method of investigation in which a number of individuals are tested and/or observed for a short period of time (cf. longitudinal study).

Decibel—A unit representing 10 times the logarithm of the ratio of the intensity of the given sound to the intensity of a referent sound.

Deep structure—In the standard theory of transformational grammar, the abstract underlying form of a sentence generated by the phrase-structure rules. The deep structures interpreted by the semantic rules provide the meanings of sentences. Transformational rules apply to deep structures to produce the surface structures (cf. surface structure).

Degemination—The process of depriving a sound of its geminated (doubled or lengthened) quality (i.e., shortening of contact; cf. gemination).

Dental—A consonant sound articulated with the tip of the tongue against the upper teeth (e.g., /θ/ in *thin*).

Diachronic—Refers to the changes in a language occuring over time (i.e., historical change; cf. synchronic).

Dichotic listening tests—A task in which two different auditory signals of equal intensity and duration are simultaneously presented to a listener, one to each ear. The subject is asked to report on what is heard in one or both ears.

Diphthong—A vowel sound whose quality changes from its beginning to its end within one syllable. Phonetically, it is analyzed and transcribed as a sequence of two vowels, or vowel plus glide within one syllable combining to form a single unit (e.g., [aɪ] (or [ay]) in *kite*; [aʊ] (or [aw]) in *cow*; and [ɔɪ] (or [ɔy]) in *coy*).

Distinctive feature—A phonetic feature or property of a language that distinguishes one phonological segment from another (e.g., /p/ and /b/ are distinguished by a different value of the voicing feature with /p/ being [− voice] and /b/ being [+ voice], or both may be distinguished from /m/ by the value [− nasal] from [+ nasal]. Distinctive feature theory postulates that there is a finite set of phonetic features from which all languages draw their phonological oppositions. Although as yet there is no universally accepted set of features, the most commonly used today is the binary system suggested by Chomsky and Halle (1968). Ladefoged (1971) has proposed an n-ary set of features that is also used.

Dorsum—The upper surface of the back portion of the tongue. It lies below the palate and the velum.

Electromyography (EMG)—A technique for measuring electrical voltages produced by muscles as they contract. It is used in speech-production research to study the action of speech muscles.

Empiricist theory of language acquisition—A theory that language is learned through experience by such factors as reinforcement and generalization of verbal behavior (syn.: learning theory; cf. nativist theory).

Feature detector—A hypothesized genetically determined perceptual mechanism that functions to discover and analyze just those acoustic cues serving as distinctive features. Whether the perception is at a peripheral acoustic (auditory) level or higher phonetic level is an open question.

Flap—A sound resulting from an articulator, most commonly the tip or blade of the tongue, making rapid contact with the articulating region, usually with the alveolar ridge, and then immediately releasing; the approach and release together are made by one ballistic movement. In American English, alveolar stops are generally produced as flaps (or taps) when they occur intervocally after stressed vowels (e.g., *writer–rider, latter–ladder*).

Formant—A frequency region for vowels and resonant consonants in which a relatively high degree of acoustic energy is concentrated. Formants are characterized by dark horizontal bands on a spectrogram. Three formants (F_1, F_2, and F_3) are generally considered of primary importance in the analysis (and perception) of speech sounds.

Fourier analysis—The analysis of a complex wave as the sum of a number of simple sine waves of different amplitudes, frequencies, and phases. This was first done by the French mathematician Joseph Fourier.

Free variation—Different versions of a sound that can occur in the same environment without changing meaning (e.g., the final consonant in *hat* may optionally be released with or without aspiration, the allophones [tʰ] and [t] in free variation. Also the phonemes /Θ/ and /ð/ in *with* vary freely with some speakers; (cf. phoneme, allophone).

Fricative—A consonant produced with partial closure in the vocal tract such as to cause audible friction as the air is expelled from the lungs (e.g., /f/ as in *fig*; syn.: spirant).

Function words; functors—A small, closed class or morphemes or words expressing grammatical or syntactic relationships and having little or no lexical meaning. This class includes pronouns, prepositions, conjunctions, articles, and modal and auxiliary verbs (cf. content word).

Fundamental frequency (F₀)—The lowest frequency component and principal component of a sound wave that generates a series of harmonics. Auditorily, it corresponds to the pitch of a speaker's voice and thus to the intonation of an utterance. The fundamental frequency is produced by vibrations of the voice cords; the faster the rate of vibration, the higher the pitch.

Gemination—Doubling that is often indicated in written form by a doubled consonant or vowel letter, and in speech by lengthening of a sound or of the period of closure before a stop consonant is released (cf. degemination).

Generative phonology—The theory of phonology related to transformational grammar. It is best exemplified by the model proposed in Chomsky and Halle (1968). The "standard theory" has been modified and revised in the last few years (see, e.g., Anderson, 1974).

Generative Syntax—A theory of syntax, usually used to refer to transformational (generative) grammar. "Generative" refers to the requirement that the theory be explicit and automatically account for all and only the well-formed sentences and syntactic structures of a language.

Glide—A speech sound characterized primarily by the shifting of the vocal organs from the articulation of one sound to another. Glides also are sometimes called semivowels, as they may function like vowels or like consonants (e.g., /y/ in *yellow* and /w/ in *win* precede vowels occurring in syllable-initial position like consonants). In many languages, vowels become glides intervocalically, or glides may become vowels. In distinctive feature terms, glides are specified as [−syllabic, −consonantal] differing only in one feature value from vowels that are [+syllabic, −consonantal].

Glottal—Pertaining to the glottis (see glottis).

Glottal stop—A sound produced by the vocal cords closing tightly, creating a complete closure of the airstream at the glottis (e.g., a glottal stop occurs between the two vowels in the negative expression *uh uh*).

Glottis—The space between the vocal cords.

Grammatical morpheme—A morpheme that expresses a grammatical relationship or a category (e.g., plurality, possession, verb tense, negation; cf. morpheme, function words).

Harmony—In language, phonetic constraints on the types of vowels (or consonants) that may cooccur within a word (e.g., only front vowels or only back vowels may occur together, or vowels within a word must be all [+round] or [−round].

Hertz (Hz)—The number of cycles completed in 1 second (formerly cps), the rate of oscillation of a periodic sound wave. Hz is a measure of frequency.

Historical linguistics—The branch of linguistics that studies how and why languages change over time (cf. diachronic).

Homophone; homonym—A word that is pronounced the same as another word but has a different meaning (and sometimes a different spelling) (e.g., *bear*—"to give birth to" or "to tolerate;" and *pair–pear*).

Homorganic consonants—Consonants with the same place of articulation, but differing in one or more features (e.g., /p,b,m/ are all bilabial but differ with respect to voicing and/or nasality).

Innateness hypothesis—See nativist theory.

Intensity—In the measurement of sound, the flow of energy or power, transmitted along the wave. The level of sound intensity is usually measured in decibels (cf. loudness, amplitude).

Intonation—The linguistic pitch pattern of the voice, rising and falling, over the sentence or phrase. In many languages, the intonation pattern may be grammatically distinctive. For example, in English "He's here" produced with a falling pitch reflects neutral, declarative status, whereas when it is produced with a rising intonation ("He's here?") it is interpreted as a question (cf. suprasegmental; pitch).

Labio–dental—A consonant sound articulated with the upper teeth against the lower lip (e.g., /f/).

Larynx—The cartilaginous structure located below the hyoid bone and tongue roots and at the top of the trachea. It houses the vocal cords and is the primary organ of phonation.

Lateral—A consonant sound produced with the tip of the tongue touching the alveolar ridge and one or both sides of the tongue down so that the airstream passes laterally around it.

Laws of irreversible solidarity—One of the fundamental factors governing Jakobson's (1941) postulated universal order of acquisition of phonemic feature contrasts by children. Such laws state that there are universal asymmetries in the phonemic systems of all languages, which Jakobson claims affect the order of acquisition (e.g., no language has back consonants without also having front consonants, though the converse is not true; therefore, front consonants are acquired first).

Lax vowels—See tense vowels.

Liquid—A frictionless sonorant sound produced with only partial obstruction of the airstream in the mouth (e.g., English /l/ and /r/). Like vowels, liquids have formant structure. They are distinguished from vowels in distinctive feature terms by being [+ consonantal, + vocalic] with vowels being [− consonantal].

Long vowels—Vowels in some languages are distinguished solely by length or duration (e.g., /a/ versus /aa/). In other languages, vowel length is completely predictable from the phonetic environment or from other feature specifications (e.g., in many languages, like English, tense vowels are longer than lax vowels; cf. tense vowels).

Longitudinal study—A study in which the same individual or individuals are observed and/or tested over a period of time, generally to assess development (cf. cross-sectional study).

Loudness—The subjective counterpart to the intensity of sound. An attribute of auditory sensation that enables a listener to order sound on a perceptual continuum from soft to loud. The unit of loudness is the sone.

Mean length of utterance (MLU)—The average number of morphemes in a child's utterance, computed by dividing the total number of morphemes in a speech sample by the total number of utterances in that sample. It is frequently used to indicate the stage of a child's linguistic development.

Mentalism—The theoretical point of view that postulates underlying mental processes and internalized cognitive systems (cf. behaviorism).

Metathesis—Transpositions of the order of sounds in a word or between two words (e.g., some dialects of English pronounce *ask* as /æks/.

Minimal pair—Two words that have the same set of phonemes in the same sequence with the exception of one phoneme (e.g., /plt/ versus /blt/ are minimal pairs, whereas /plt/ versus /tlp/ and /plt/ versus /pad/ are not).

Morpheme—The smallest meaningful unit of language (e.g., the word *writer* consists of two morphemes, *write* and *er*).

Morpheme structure rules (or conditions)—See redundancy rules.

Morphology—The study of the structure of words (i.e., the rules for the combination of morphemes; cf. morpheme).

Morphophoneme—The unit by means of which morphemes are phonologically represented. In structural linguistics, the morphophonemic representation of a morpheme differed from the phonemic representation. This distinction no longer holds in the standard theory of generative phonology.

Morphophonological level—See morphophoneme.

Motor theory of speech perception—A model of speech perception in which segmental phonemes are mainly perceived by reference to their articulation or production.

Myographic analysis—See electromyography.

Narrow band—See spectrograph.

Nasal—A consonant sound produced with the velum lowered to permit the airstream to pass through the nasal cavity.

Nativist theory of language acquisition—Refers to the proposal that there exists an innate language acquisition device or system (LAD or LAS) that biologically predisposes a child to acquire language as natural maturation proceeds. Experience serves to trigger the innate mechanism rather than to account directly for language learning (syn.: rationalist theory; Cf. empiricist theory).

Natural class—A set of sounds grouped together by virtue of their sharing one or more phonetic features or properties (e.g., sounds specified as [+nasal] [m, n, ŋ] form a natural class of "nasals"). Such classes are frequently referred to in the phonological rules of the world's languages).

Neutralization—The suspension of the opposition between the values of a distinctive feature, or of the opposition between phonemes in specific environments. For example, the [+voice] / [−voice] distinction is "neutralized" in syllable-final position in German, as all voiced obstruents are "devoiced" in that position.

Obligatory environment—A linguistic context in which a given linguistic form or segment is required by the rules of that language (e.g., in English, the third person singular present tense verb form requires an −s: "He sings;" also, a voiceless stop consonant is aspirated in word-initial position; such as /p/ in *pig*, [pʰIg]).

Obstruent—A sound in which the airstream is obstructed before it is released (e.g., fricatives, affricates, nonasal stops; syn.: nonsonorant; cf. sonorant).

Oral stereognosis—The ability to use lip and tongue sensations to discriminate and identify different types of objects and their locations.

Oscillograph—An instrument that registers oscillations of electric current and records the variations. In phonetic research, it is used to convert sound waves into electric impulses that can be registered and recorded to permit the analysis of peak amplitude of waves and differences between pure and complex tones.

Output constraint—A term used in generative grammar for a set of constraints or conditions on the surface structure of sentences. These constraints reject sentences generated by the grammar that do not meet these conditions.

Palatal—A consonant sound articulated with the front portion of the tongue against or near the hard palate (e.g., *ich* in German).

Palate—The roof of the mouth; the long anterior portion is referred to as the "hard palate," whereas the posterior portion is called the "soft palate" or "velum."

Paralinguistic features—Features that are not part of the formal linguistic system but may carry information about the speaker's emotional state, sex, size, etc. (e.g., variations in loudness, pitch, duration, and facial gestures).

Performance—The actual production or comprehension of speech. It may be affected by grammatically irrelevant factors such as fatigue, memory limitations, nervousness, etc. (cf. competence).

Pharynx—A tube composed of muscle and mucous membrane situated behind the larynx, mouth, and nose. It acts as a resonating chamber for the voicing produced by the vocal cords in the larynx; it also provides a passageway for air into the larynx.

Phone—A single phonetic segment or speech sound, specified by the phonetic properties, articulatory or acoustic, that distinguish it from all other phonetic units.

Phoneme—An abstract contrastive phonological unit in a language; two sounds are separate phonemes when the phonetic difference between them contrasts meaning (e.g., in English /f/ versus /v/ distinguishes *fan* and *van*; cf. allophone, phone, distinctive feature).

Phonetics—The study, analysis, and cassification of the production and perception of speech sounds (see the table of phonetic symbols; cf. phonology).

Phonological rules—In generative phonology, rules operating on the underlying representation of words (systematic phonemic level) to yield the pronunciation (systematic phonetic level; cf. redundancy rules, realization rules).

Phonology—That part of a grammar accounting for speakers' knowledge of the sounds and sound patterns of their language. Also refers to the study or science of sound systems (cf. phonetics, phonological rules).

Phonotactics—Limitations on the phonological sequences and structure of words or syllables occurring within a given language (e.g., in English, nonlow lax vowels, like /ɛ/ in *bet*, never occur word finally; also initial clusters like /bn/ do not occur; (cf. redundancy rule).

Pitch—The subjective counterpart to the frequency of sound. An attribute of auditory sensation that enables a listener to order sound on a perceptual continuum from low to high. Pitch is related to the acoustic property known as the fundamental frequency of that sound (cf. fundamental frequency).

Plosive—See stop.

Pragmatics—The study of the rules underlying an individual's functional use of language in its social context, an ability that is part of that speaker's communicative competence.

Prosody; prosodic features—See suprasegmental features.

Psychoacoustics—A branch of psychophysics dealing with the relationship between acoustic stimuli and accompanying psychological sensations. The concern of psychoacoustics is the quantification of behavioral responses to a variety of auditory stimulus configurations.

Psychological reality—The goal set for linguistic theory by those concerned that models of grammar reflect the actual (though idealized) competence of native speakers. What constitutes a test of psychological reality is under discussion and is being debated widely by linguists and psycholinguists.

Psychophysics—The study of the relation between stimulus and response, wherein the measurement and specification of the stimulus are encompased by the science of physics, and the measurement and specification of the response are encompassed by the field of psychology.

Quantity—In phonology, quantity refers to length or duration. Speech sounds are labeled "long" or "short" when their relative duration is phonologically important in a language.

TABLE
Phonetic Symbols

Consonants						
Stops			**Affricates**			
p	pig	[pɪg]		tʃ (tš, č)	choke	[tʃ ok]
b	big	[bɪg]		dʒ (dž, ǰ)	joke	[dʒ ok]
t	tip	[tɪp]				
d	dip	[dɪp]				
k	cap	[kæp]				
g	gap	[gæp]				
Nasals			**Liquids**			
m	sum	[sʌm]		l	led	[lɛd]
n	sun	[sʌn]		r	red	[rɛd]
ŋ	sung	[sʌŋ]				
Fricatives			**Glides**			
f	fan	[fæn]		w	wet	[wɛt]
v	van	[væn]		y (j)	yet	[yɛt]
θ	thigh	[θaɪ]				
ð	thy	[ðaɪ]				
s	sip	[sɪp]				
z	zip	[zɪp]				
ʃ (š)	shun	[ʃʌn]				
ʒ (ž)	vision	[vɪʒən]				
h	hat	[hæt]				

Vowels						
Front			**Central**			
i	beet	[bit]		ə	above	[ˌəˈbʌv]
ɪ	bit	[bɪt]		ʌ	but	[bʌt]
e	bait	[bet]				
ɛ	bet	[bɛt]				
æ	bat	[bæt]				
Back			**Diphthong**			
u	boot	[but]		aɪ (ay)	bite	[baɪt]
ʊ	put	[pʊt]		aʊ (aw)	bout	[baʊt]
o	boat	[bot]		ɔɪ (ɔy)	boy	[bɔɪ]
ɔ	bought	[bɔt]				
a	pot	[pat]				

Various phonetic markings

: indicates preceding sound is lengthened (e.g., [e:])

h indicates preceding sound is aspirated (e.g., [tʰ])

~ indicates a nasalized vowel (e.g., [æ̃])

ʔ indicates a glottal stop (e.g., *oh oh!* [oʔo])

ˈ indicates the following syllable has primary stress (e.g., the first syllable of *eggplant* [ˈɛgˌplænt])

ˌ indicates the following syllable has secondary stress (e.g., the second syllable of eggplant [ˈɛgˌplænt])

Rationalist theory—See nativist theory.

Realization rules—In phonology, rules that convert abstract, underlying phonological forms of a grammar into actual phonetic form are called realization rules (e.g., one such rule may specify that an underlying bilabial stop is pronounced as voiced in word-initial position and voiceless in word-final position; cf. phonological rules).

Redundancy rules—In phonology, language-specific rules accounting for the predictable, general, nonidiosyncratic phonemic representations of words in that language. Redundancy rules (also called morpheme structure rules or conditions) may be segmental or sequential (e.g., in English, the rule that all nasal phonemes are voiced is a segmental redundancy rule; the rule that the first segment of a word-initial obstruent cluster must be /s/ is a sequential redundancy rule). Phonological redundancy rules distinguish "accidental gaps" (e.g., in English /bllk/ is permissible although not in the lexicon) from "Systematic gaps" (e.g., in English /bnlk/ cannot occur) by defining admissible sequences (cf. phonological rules).

Reduplication—Either the repetition of syllables in a word (e.g., in the English *mama*), or a rule or process in a language using this kind of repetition to derive morphologically complex words.

Retroflex—Sounds that are produced by curling the tip of the tongue back behind the alveolar ridge (e.g., English /r/).

Rewrite rules—In generative grammar, a formal mathematical rule in which an arrow acts as an instruction to replace the symbol on the left of the arrow with the symbol or string of symbols on its right (e.g., $X \rightarrow Y + Z$; noun phrase $\rightarrow$ article + noun). Rewrite rules are used formally to express linguistic operations such as deletion (e.g., deletion of a final nasal would be shown by the rule /n/ $\rightarrow \emptyset$ / #, where $\emptyset$ indicates deletion, / indicates "in the environment of," and # indicates final position).

Sandhi—Adaptive changes in speech sounds occurring at the boundaries of words as the result of their mutual influence on each other.

Semantic features—A set of general elements or components of meaning that are used to analyze word meaning (e.g., *man* is analyzed as having such features as "human," "animate," "male," and "adult").

Semivowel—See glide.

Sensorimotor—Piaget's first stage in the development of intelligence in which the form of knowledge is linked with the content of specific sensory input or motor actions.

Short vowel—See long vowel.

Sibilant—A hissing fricative sound like [s], [z], [ʃ], and [ʒ]; or the affricates [tʃ] and [dʒ].

Sociolinguistics—The study of language in society, variations and dialect differences existing between social classes, groups or regions. These differences may be phonological, syntactic, semantic, or pragmatic.

Sonorant—A sound produced with a relatively unobstructed airstream.

Sounds in this category are vowels, liquids, glides, and nasals. Although there is an obstruction in the oral cavity with nasals, the open nasal passage permits the air to resonate (cf. obstruents).

Sonority—One of the two classes of inherent features defined by Jakobson and Halle (1956). Sonority features deal with the amount and concentration of energy in the spectrum and in time (e.g., consonantal versus nonconsonantal are sonority features that acoustically show low, as opposed to high, total energy).

Spectrogram—The visual representation of an acoustic speech signal produced by a spectrograph.

Spectrograph—An instrument used to analyze sound signals and to produce a visual display of frequency and intensity as a function of time. The spectrograms produced may be the result of analysis with a narrow band filter (usually at 45 Hz) or a wide band filter (usually at 300 Hz).

Spectrum—A graph or diagram displaying the relative amplitudes of the frequency components of a complex acoustic signal.

Spirant—See fricative.

Steady state—The relatively nonchanging portion of a speech sound (e.g., time midsection of a vowel with onset and offset transitions not included.

Stop—A consonant sound produced with complete closure of the articulators in the mouth, thus totally blocking the airstream (e.g., /p,g/; syn.: plosive).

Stress—Emphasis or accent on a syllable that is produced by increased duration, pitch, and/or intensity on some syllables as compared with others (cf. suprasegmental).

Structuralism—A theoretical approach in the social sciences that is usually associated, in linguistics, with De Saussure and his followers. It views "facts" or data in terms of their functions in a system, and sharply separates historical (diachronic) phonomena from the linguistic system at any one point in time (synchronic). Units in the system are viewed both paradigmatically (e.g., the phonemes /t/ and /d/, which, when substituted for each other, change meaning, as in *tip* and *dip*) and syntagmatically, (e.g., the phonemes /t/, /I/, /p/ concatenate to form a larger unit, the morpheme *tip*).

Subglottal—The parts of the speech mechanism that are below the glottal opening between the vocal cords (i.e., the lungs, trachae, etc.).

Supraglottal—The parts of the vocal tract that are above the glottal opening between the vocal cords (i.e., oral, pharyngeal, nasal, and buccal cavities).

Suprasegmental—Nonsegmental, prosodic features of speech that may be superimposed over one or more speech segments (i.e., over consonants and vowels) and that function linguistically. These nonsegmentals may include stress, tone, rhythm, intonation, and duration.

Surface structure—The phrase marker (or tree structure) of a sentence that is derived from its underlying deep structure by the application of transformational rules. Phonological rules apply to surface structures to produce the systematic phonetic representations of sentences (cf. deep structure).

Synchronic—Refers to language at a specific point in time, or at a given stage of linguistic development, divorced from the historical developments that produced that system (cf. diachronic).

Systematic phonemic level—The lexical (phonological) representation of formatives and sentences prior to the application of phonological rules (cf. autonomous phonemic level; morphophoneme).

Systematic phonetic level—A level of representation used in generative phonology, that is the surface-structure phonetic output of the phonological component.

Taxonomic—Refers to categorization and classification. In linguistics it is the approach transformational grammarians attribute to American structuralists such as Bloomfield.

Tense vowels—A class of vowels distinguished from those specified as "lax." For example, in English, /i, u, e, and o/ are in some descriptions specified as [+tense] whereas their counterparts /I, ʊ, ɛ, ʌ/ are marked as [−tense]. The tense vowels in English are longer in duration, diphthongized, and sometimes produced with a slightly higher tongue position and a narrower glottis.

Token—An instance of a general type or category (e.g., when one repeats a word five times, each production is a token of the word; cf. type).

Tonality—One of the two classes of inherent features defined by Jakobson and Halle (1956). Acoustically, tonality features deal with the ends of the frequency spectrum (e.g., grave versus acute are tonality features that acoustically show a concentration of energy in the lower, versus upper, frequencies of the spectrum; cf. sonority).

Tone language—A language in which relative pitch is used to distinguish lexical units.

Transcription—The written symbolic representation of utterances. "Broad" or "phonemic" transcription is enclosed within slashes (e.g., /plt/); "narrow," "fine," or "phonetic" transcription is indicated by brackets (e.g., [pʰlt].

Trill—One articulator (e.g., tongue tip or uvula) vibrating against another, such as the roof of the mouth or the velum.

Triphthong—A sequence of three adjacent vowels or glides within a single syllable (e.g., /auər/ in *hour*; /faɪər/ in *fire*. Note the *r*s may be syllabic in these words.)

Type—Refers to a general category (e.g., all the vowel segments in *bee*, *neat*, and *eel* are tokens of the vowel type /i/; cf. token).

Underlying form—Usually refers to the lexical representation of morphemes. Thus, two words that differ phonetically but contain the same morphemes may be represented by the same underlying form of the morpheme (e.g., *telegraph, telegraph-ic, telegraph-y*).

Uvula—The small cone-shaped appendage that hangs down at the end of the velum.

Uvular—A consonant sound articulated by raising the back portion of the tongue near the uvula.

Velar—A consonant sound articulated with the back portion of the tongue against or near the soft palate (e.g., /k/).

Velum—The soft palate (cf. palate).

Vocal folds—Folds of ligaments located on each side of the larynx and extending from the arytenoid cartilages at the back of the larynx to the Adam's apple at the front (syn.: vocal cords). There is a superior pair referred to as the ventricular or false folds and the inferior pair called the true vocal folds.

Vocal fry—A series of low-frequency oscillations of the vocal cords in which the closed phase is longer than the open phase, creating a series of relatively sharp acoustic impulses and a "crackling" type of phonation (syns.: laryngealization; glottal fry; "fry" register; pulsated voice).

Voice onset time (VOT)—The interval between the release of closure (burst) and the onset of vibration of the vocal cords in the production of stop consonants. It is used as an acoustic measure to distinguish voiced and voiceless stops in most languages (cf. voicing lag, voicing lead).

Voiced—A sound produced with vibrating vocal cords (cf. voiceless).

Voiceless—A sound produced with the glottis open, as in breathing, without any vibration of the vocal cords (cf. voiced).

Voicing lag—A category of voice onset time in which the onset of glottal vibration (voicing) follows the burst release. The onset of voicing may coincide with or immediately follow the consonantal burst (short lag), or it may be somewhat delayed (long lag; cf. voice onset time).

Voicing lead—A category of voice onset time in which the onset of glottal vibration (voicing) precedes the burst release (cf. voice onset time).

Volume—In speech, the loudness of a sound, determined by frequency and intensity (cf. frequency; intensity).

Vowel—A speech sound produced by the unobstructed passage of air through the oral cavity; the most prominent portion of a syllable.

Vowel nucleus—The portion of a vowel cluster (e.g., dipthong) that is loudest and most resonant.

Vowel quality—The characteristic that distinguishes one vowel from another, determined mainly by the resonance of the vocal tract in production.

Vowel shift rules—Phonological rules that account for modern English vowel alternations reflecting the phonological changes of the middle-English vowel system (e.g., the pronunciation of the second vowel in *serene–serenity*).

Vowel space—When the vowel frequencies of Formants 1 and 2 are plotted against each other, the resulting diagram provides a picture of how the vowels relate to each other in what is called the "vowel space." In perception experiments using multidimensional scaling methods, it is also common to refer to the results as representing perceptual vowel space.

Wave form—A visual representation of a sound wave displaying its amplitude as a function of time; time analysis of an acoustic signal (syn.: wave shape).

Wide band—See spectrograph.

References

Anderson, S. (1974) *The Organization of Phonology*, Academic Press, New York.
Chomsky, N., and Halle, M. (1968) *The Sound Pattern of English*, Harper & Row, New York.
Jakobson, R., and Halle, M. (1956) *Fundamentals of Language*, Mouton, The Hague.
Ladefoged, P. (1971) *Preliminaries to Linguistic Phonetics*, The University of Chicago Press, Chicago.

SUBJECT INDEX

A

Acoustics, phonetics, relationship, 218–219
Adult, *see also* Speech, adult–adult; Speech, mother–child
  discrimination
    bilabial stop consonant, 83F, 84F
    tone onset time, 82F
  labeling data, 93
  labeling function
    consonant stop, 72F
    tone onset time, 82F
  messages, to child, 176
  perceptual categories, phonologically distinctive, 71
Affricate, 229, *see also* Consonant stop; Fricative
AHAS, *see* Paradigm
Allophone, 229
Alveolar ridge, 229
Amplitude, 229
Analysis
  Fourier, 232
  spectrographic, 130
    schematized, 133F
Antiformant, 230
Aphasia, 230

B

Behaviorism, 230
Bilabial, 230
Bilabial stop, discrimination, 26–27
Bilingual
  discrimination, 197, 199F
  double standard, speech perception, 195–196, 200
  labeling function, 199F, 208

Articulation, *see also* Speech production
  alveolar, 12–13
  development, rule-governed system, 118
  identification, relationship, 141
  labial, 12–13
  norm, for child, 222
  place, 31–32
    discrimination, 30
  skill development, sequence, 219–220
  velar, 12–13
Assimilation, 230
Attenuation, discriminability, 87
Auditory, mammalian, constraint, 82
Auditory Discrimination Test, 102–103
Auditory system, human, specialization, 88

G

Glide, 233
Glottal stop, 233
Glottis, 233

H

Harmony, 233
HAS, *see* Paradigm
Haskins Laboratories, 2, 9, 137
Head-turn technique, *see* Paradigm, visually reinforced
Hertz, 233
Homophone, 234
HR, *see* Paradigm

I

Infant, *see also* Child; Newborn
   abilities, origin, 23
   acoustic change, detection, 148
   contrast, discrimination, 120
   discrimination
      fricative, 29
      modified staircase procedure, 90
      nonspeech stimuli, 3
      of phonetic categories, 43
      of phonetic contrasts, 80
      place-of-articulation distinction, 19
      voicing contrasts, 81
   English-learning, 29, 33
      discriminate French vowel, 34
   fricative, perception, 32, 85
   Guatemalan, 27
   invariance response, first year, 225
   Japanese, postnatal environment, 86
   Kikuyu, 27
   labeling data, 93
   labeling task, analog, 92
   perceptual constancy, pitch, 35
   perceptual mechanisms, innately determined, 68
   predisposition, toward sound recognition, 63

prelinguistic
   environment, 68
   process speech sounds, 69
response validity, difficulty, 1
selectivity, in visual attention, 45
Spanish-learning, 33
speech
   discrimination, 1
   discrimination measurement, 89
speech perception
   configurational aspect, 63
   experience, 28
   phonetic similarity, 44
   study methodology, 23–25
   voice onset time perception, hemispheric cortical activity, 30
   voicing category, relevance, 70
   voicing perception, 4
Information
   formant-transition, 31
   invariant, developmental phenomenon, 45
Innateness, reexamined, 62–63
Intensity, 234
Intonation, 234
Invariant
   acoustic, 11, 218
   articulatory, 218

L

Label, phonetic, 46
Labio-dental, 234
Language
   acquisition, psychological variables, 220
   learning, child, 68
   natural, phonology, 68
Larynx, 234
Lateral, 234
Law, of large numbers, 221–222
Learning
   perceptual, theory, 150–151
   second-language, critical period, 186
Linguistic experience
   early, role, 84
   perception, phonetic element, 34
Linguistics, historical, 234
Liquid, 43, 234
   discrimination, infant, 86

In preparation

FRANCIS J. PIROZZOLO and MERLIN C. WITTROCK (Eds.). Neuropsychological and Cognitive Processes in Reading

JASON W. BROWN (Ed.). Jargonaphasia